Contents

Søren Brier, Dirk Baecker and Ole Thyssen
Foreword: Luhmann Applied—For What?. 5

Lars Qvortrup
Luhmann Applied to the Knowledge Society:
Religion as Fourth-Order Knowledge 11

Søren Brier
Applying Luhmann's System Theory as Part of a Transdisciplinary Frame
For Communication Science. 29

Rudi Laermans
Theorizing Culture, or Reading Luhmann Against Luhmann 67

Ole Thyssen
Luhmann and Globalization: The Interplay Between Nation, State
and World Society 85

Morten Knudsen
Structural Couplings Between Organizations and Function Systems:
Looking at Standards in Health Care. 111

Werner Schirmer and Claus Hadamek
Steering as Paradox: The Ambiguous Role of the Political System
in Modern Society 133

Niels Thyge Thygesen
Steering Technologies as Observation 151

Eva Buchinger
Applying Luhmann to Conceptualize Public Governance of
Autopoietic Organizations 173

Column

Ranulph Glanville
A (Cybernetic) Musing: Ashby and the Black Box 189

ASC Pages

Ray Ison
Epistemological Awareness: A Systemic Inquiry 197

Subscription Form 201

The artist for this issue is Stafford Beer

CYBERNETICS & HUMAN KNOWING
A Journal of Second-Order Cybernetics, Autopoiesis & Cyber-Semiotics

Cybernetics and Human Knowing is a quarterly international multi- and transdisciplinary journal focusing on second-order cybernetics and cybersemiotic approaches.

The journal is devoted to the new understandings of the self-organizing processes of information in human knowing that have arisen through the cybernetics of cybernetics, or second order cybernetics its relation and relevance to other interdisciplinary approaches such as C.S. Peirce's semiotics. This new development within the area of knowledge-directed processes is a non-disciplinary approach. Through the concept of self-reference it explores: cognition, communication and languaging in all of its manifestations; our understanding of organization and information in human, artificial and natural systems; and our understanding of understanding within the natural and social sciences, humanities, information and library science, and in social practices like design, education, organization, teaching, therapy, art, management and politics.

Because of the interdisciplinary character articles are written in such a way that people from other domains can understand them. Articles from practitioners will be accepted in a special section. All articles are peer-reviewed.

Subscription Information

Price: Individual $93 / £49. Institutional: $199 / £105. 50% discount on full set of back volumes. Payment by check in $US or £UK, made payable to Imprint Academic to PO Box 200, Exeter EX5 5HY, UK, or Visa/Mastercard/Amex). Contact sandra@imprint.co.uk

Editor in Chief: Søren Brier, Copenhagen Business School, Management, Politics and Philosophy, Porcelænshaven 18A, DK-2000 Frederiksberg, Denmark. sbr.lpf@cbs.dk

Associate editor: Jeanette Bopry, Instructional Sciences, National Institute of Education, 1 Nanyang Walk, Singapore 637616. bopry@nie.edu.sg

Associate editor: Dr. Paul Cobley, Reader in Communications, London Metropolitan University, 31 Jewry Street, London EC3N 2EY. p.cobley@londonmet.ac.uk

Managing editor: Phillip Guddemi, The Union Institute and University, Sacramento CA, USA. pguddemi@well.com

Art editor and ASC-column editor: Pille Bunnell, Royal Roads University, Victoria BC, Canada. pille@interchange.ubc.ca

Journal homepage: www.chkjournal.org
Full text: www.ingenta.com/journals/browse/imp

Copyright: It is a condition of acceptance by the editor of a typescript for publication that the publisher automatically acquires the English language copyright of the typescript throughout the world, and that translations explicitly mention *Cybernetics & Human Knowing* as original source.

Book Reviews: Publishers are invited to submit books for review to the Editor.

Instructions to Authors: To facilitate editorial work and to enhance the uniformity of presentation, authors are requested to send a file of the paper to the Editor on e-mail. If the paper is accepted after refereeing then to prepare the contribution in accordance with the stylesheet information at www.chkjournal.org

Manuscripts will not be returned except for editorial reasons. The language of publication is English. The following information should be provided on the first page: the title, the author's name and full address, a title not exceeding 40 characters including spaces and a summary/abstract in English not exceeding 200 words. Please use italics for emphasis, quotations, etc. Email to: sbr.lpf@cbs.dk

Drawings. Drawings, graphs, figures and tables must be reproducible originals. They should be presented on separate sheets. Authors will be charged if illustrations have to be re-drawn.

Style. CHK has selected the style of the APA (*Publication Manual of the American Psychological Association*, 5th edition) because this style is commonly used by social scientists, cognitive scientists, and educators. The APA website contains information about the correct citation of electronic sources. The APA Publication Manual is available from booksellers. The Editors reserve the right to correct, or to have corrected, non-native English prose, but the authors should not expect this service. The journal has adopted U.S.English usage as its norm (this does not apply to other native users of English). For full APA style informations see: apastyle.apa.org

Accepted WP systems:
MS Word and rtf.

Beer, S. (n.d.). *Computer Volvox*.

Cybernetics And Human Knowing. Vol. 14, nos. 2-3, pp. 5-10

Foreword: Luhmann Applied—For What?

Søren Brier, Dirk Baecker and Ole Thyssen

For some years Luhmann's work has been under discussion in the Sociocybernetic group in the International Sociological Association in a way that is symptomatic for the institutions also in the home countries Germany and Denmark of the present editors. Luhmann's theory is rather counter-intuitive, complicated and in its coolness difficult for many researchers and teachers to understand and accept. Naturally they then ask: Is it really worth the trouble to learn? What can it do in practice? We do not see many apply it successfully? Who has done anything worth mentioning with it? Show us and then we will consider if we find it worth bothering with this complicated and far fetched construction of system theory, second-order cybernetics, autopoiesis theory, phenomenology, and information theory.

At that time Søren Brier had been working at the Department of Management, Politics and Philosophy side by side with Ole Thyssen for a couple of years and interacting with the so called "political group" headed by Niels Åkerstrøm Andersen at the department. This group has developed the application of Luhmann on organization and management problems in a unique way. In connection with the International Sociology Associations world conference in Durban 2006, Brier, as a member of the board of the Sociocybernetic group by invitation of the president Bernd R. Hornung, decided to set up a panel on the question and invited all the "Luhmannians" we knew to send in abstracts and try to find travel money. We managed to get it approved by the ISA and with the help of Ole Thyssen's use of what was left of capital in his Centre for Corporate Communication, we managed to finance the trip to South Africa.

Several people came, some who would have come had to cancel, and other that did come could not find the time to write. Those present at the conference that contribute here are Lars Qvortrup, Ole Thyssen, Morten Knudsen, Eva Buchinger, and Søren Brier. Others then contributed later. All these contributions make up this special double issue on the application of Niklas Luhmann's theories to various questions and some of them in a very critical way. We want to underline that this special issue is not necessarily pro-Luhmann. It is an open critical investigation of how to apply Luhmann's work in various areas.

To have an outside expert referee and editor, the Luhmann expert professor Dirk Baecker was asked to take on the task of second editor and kindly said yes. As it later became difficult to get further expertise that could do a swift and thorough job refereeing all the various aspect of Luhmann's work that were presented in the articles, Ole Thyssen was asked to be the second referee and third editor to work on the papers already screened and selected by Brier and refereed by Baecker. Thyssen and Brier's paper was then refereed with the help of extra referees supplementing Baecker's evaluation.

As to the content of this volume, many of the articles discuss Luhmann's peculiar twist of familiar concepts like knowledge, communication, consciousness, and culture and the productive capability of using these concepts in analyzing social phenomena. Qvortrup and Brier's articles both work with Luhmann's concepts of knowing and how it leads to a reformulation of the ultimate understanding of knowledge, experience and faith in existential, mythological and religious frames of "knowing about non-knowing." For the past decade Lars Qvortrup has been writing about the knowledge society understood through a system-theoretical view of learning levels and hypercomplexity, as for instance in *The Hypercomplex Society* and *Knowledge, Education and Learning - E-learning in the Knowledge Society*. On the basis of this work, Qvortrup in his article, "Luhmann Applied to the Knowledge Society: Religion as Fourth Order Knowledge," claims that though we are in a "knowledge society" we do not have an adequate concept of knowledge for a theory of the social and communicative (which for Luhmann is nearly the same). Qvortrup's basic question is whether Luhmann's theory of society – his "operational constructivism" – can help us solve this problem. Is it possible to construct a concept of knowledge informed by operational constructivism, which is adequate for a theory of the so-called knowledge society? Qvortrup presents a sociological operative definition of knowledge, divided or specified into four level categories inspired by Gregory Bateson's hierarchy of learning levels. Radically new, he is suggesting that "fourth-order knowledge stands for that kind of knowledge that has traditionally been represented by the concept of religion." His penetrating analysis here goes back especially to the church father St. Augustine's analysis of the Trinitarian concept of God that has played such a crucial role in the development of the Christian idea of the relation between faith and knowledge. But now a new understanding is conceived by understanding the problem through system theory viewing "Christ" as a doppleganger concept.

In "Applying Luhmann's system theory as part of a transdisciplinary frame for communication science" Søren Brier is taking a critical look at the concept of the psychic system in Luhmann's theory. Luhmann sees that cybernetics and system theory based on thermodynamical complexity views of the world do not have a first person consciousness concept or a theory of qualia. He then attempts to save this missing foundation of consciousness by integrating Husserl's phenomenology into his system theory the way he has integrated Bateson's theory of eco-mental systems, second order cybernetics and autopoiesis theory. The article investigates if this important transdisciplinary project succeeds. It is well-known that Maturana does not like the way Luhmann has generalized his concept of autopoiesis by adding to the original biological concept a psychic and a socio-communicative aspect. Already here Luhmann is stretching somebody else's theory in order to make it solve basic problems in his framework and integrate it with it.

There seem to be the same problem with the way he uses Husserl's concepts. But he is not alive and therefore unable to protest. Luhmann's concept of the psychic (autopoietic) system does not include a Kantian or Husserlian transcendental ego; nor does it use Heidegger's *Dasein* as a model for psyche as an autopoietic system.

Luhmann's concept of person is a social one. It is a constructed "mask" and does not refer to subjectivity or even the psychic system. Thus there seem to be no *locus observantis* in spite of the fact that observation and distinction are fundamental concepts in Luhmann's paradigm of operational constructivism. Then where is the observer in the theoretical framework of system theory and where is the power of free will and action in the human? Although there is an inspiration from Hegel's objective idealism in Luhmann's theory he has not accepted his full metaphysical frame. Instead he relies on Spencer-Brown's philosophy in *Laws of Form* that all knowing start by making a distinction, which ties nicely with Bateson concept of information and Peirce's concept of semiosis. But what or where is the mind that observes and freely decides to make distinctions? The article compares Spencer-Brown's strategies with C. S. Peirce's, the latter of whom built an alternative transdisciplinary theory of signification and communication based on a Panentheistic theory of knowing. By digging into other writings of Spencer-Brown under the name of James Keys— especially *It Takes Two to Play This Game*—a common ground is found between him and Peirce that changes the received view of Luhmann's philosophical foundation.

The problem of the basis of meaning is taken up from another angle in the next article. Rudi Laermans analyzes another problematic concept in Luhmann's theory, namely culture. In the article "Theorizing Culture, or reading Luhmann against Luhmann" Laermans tries to counter Niklas Luhmann's outspoken theoretical skepticism about the notion of culture. It is argued that Luhmann's concepts of memory, semantics or semantic structures, and knowledge are all conceptualizing various aspects of culture and the interrelationships between them is analyzed. What seems to be at stake is the double process of condensation and confirmation of meaning in the phenomenological sense. It is the production of *meaning kernels* in the form of symbolic generalizations, schemes or identities that seems unavoidable even in system theory when constructing a communication theory. Culture must be considered as a medium of meaning that ensures "the structural coupling between social and psychic systems. Social systems therefore presuppose that condensed forms, or cultural elements, are always already known by all participating psychic systems." Laermans then proposes the notion of operative fiction as a necessary concept to make a system theoretical theory of culture working.

Ole Thyssen discusses the relation between Luhmann's concept of society and *the nation*. The article is called: "Luhmann and Globalization: The Interplay Between Nation, State and World Society." Thyssen argues that the way Luhmann defines social systems as borderless communication, then society becomes first of all a world society seen as the system of all communication. It is on this general level that society is differentiated in functional subsystems such as art, love, economy, politics, and science the dynamics of which makes globalization a basic concept in Luhmann's theory of social systems. It is therefore of consequence that Luhmann considers nationalistic semantics to be outdated and unable to describe modern society and its temporal global evolution. Still, Luhmann does recognize the political functional significance of the nation in the form of its political representative, the state as the self-description of the political system. But to be consistent his theory design should only deal with a global political system. As Thyssen points out then there still is no effective world state and no global political self-description. Thus Thyssen sets out to show that for system theory "the dilemma between the global and the national perspective is not a real one. Functional subsystems, organizations and states are structurally coupled and together account for the dynamics of world society." Still he also emphasizes that it is not possible to harmonize the problems arising from the anarchic interplay of the three systems. Thus he is skeptical whether second-order super nations such as the EU would solve these types of problems, or only rearrange them.

From these philosophical and global perspectives we move into the more practical realm of the organization and functional system with Morten Knudsen's article: "Structural Couplings Between Organizations and Function Systems: Looking at Standards in Health Care." It is concerned with the relationship between organization and society. He reinterprets Luhmann's "conceptualization of the relation between decision-making organisational systems and code-based function systems in order to enable the theory to observe (historical and current) changes." Organizations make themselves irritable to functional systems through deparadoxisation strategies. The example analyzed is standards in health care and how they form structural couplings between decisions in health care organizations and function systems. They can do this because they deparadoxify decisions and in this way make themselves irritable from a multiplicity of functional systems.

This leads us to the problem of steering systems, which is a major point in Luhmann's theory. Werner Schirmer and Claus Hadame write on "Steering as Paradox: The Ambiguous Role of the Political System in Modern Society." They address the fact that social problems such as unemployment, demographic aging, and uncontrolled immigration cannot be easily and effectively met by counter steering by the state, in spite of the common belief. The authors take up the inherent paradox in the approach to steering society that Luhmann saw so clearly: Steering is necessary because it is impossible. Modern functionally specialized society no longer has a central place from which the symbolic generalized media can be controlled. Modern societies no longer have a well-defined centre or top. Still the vacuum must be filled semantically and that is what the political system is forced to do. Neither science nor economy is able to do what it takes to work through the mass media and manage: to bind a collectivity, and at the same time to be made responsible for it. But it is also this double role that makes it impossible for politics to get full steering control over the nation state or conglomerates of nation states, and the reason why there continue to so much attention on leadership and steering technologies on all levels of society.

Niels Thyge Thygesen writes about "Steering Technologies as Observation" and illustrates how technology can be observed as observation. Thygesen shows how steering technology works by providing public management with specific forms of observation. Luhmann's systems theory provides us with three different concepts of analysis here: technology, steering, and management through which we can attempt to observe, construct and influence the whole form within by focussing on selected courses as a construction of causality. In other words, the technology opens up for the observation of management as a function of a person, which is shaped by expectations about the mastership of causality, writes Thygesen. He then focuses on goal management in the Danish public sector, as a steering technology that focuses on time, not in the form of sequences as in the case of scientific management, but through the observation of the organization as a future desired state.

Eva Buchinger continues this investigation into steering or governmental problems viewed from a system theoretical perspective in the article "Applying Luhmann to Conceptualize Public Governance of Autopoietic Organization." She concentrates on the question on how it is possible to govern operationally an interrelated ensemble of autopoietic systems, which according to the theory are closed entities? Although Luhmann himself was a steering-pessimist Buchinger uses his theory to develop ideas about governing. In the article she shows how the conceptualization of the governance of autopoietic systems is possible by using concepts like resonance, openness to the environment, and media of steering on public governance of organizational systems.

As such this double issue leaves us with the impression that Luhmann can be applied in fruitful ways even though there are "holes" here and there in this theories that need to be filled out with new material or new-made connections. The road from theory to practice is never an easy and straightforward one. Application is a craft in itself and it feeds back on theory and shows lacks in it or new areas to develop. But that insight came from the boldness of developing a theory in the first place! Yet, we may also take account of the fact that Luhmann indeed did already "apply" his theory when working on it in the first place. For Luhmann there is no possible distinction between developing a theory, on one hand, and applying it on the other. How are we meant to be able to prove a theory's worth when developing, or prototyping, it if we don't look, while developing it, at its possible scope with respect to phenomena of all kinds, drawing on a comparison here and the observation of already fruitful notions there? Luhmann's theory indeed is applied research in that he proposed descriptions of the society and its functional systems, and of organization and of interaction, which aimed at being read within the society he was describing and so to take part, even if only marginally or peripherally so, in the communication operationally reproducing that society. He knew that collecting dust on the shelves of libraries might be the ultimate destiny of his theory, not to mention that of his teacher Parsons. But of which books would collect dust, and why, he could not have been sure. Would it be for their insistence on difficult notions like self-reference and complexity, and on notions of differentiation and evolution, or for the application of these notions to the empirical phenomena of society? Is it the theory which somehow makes its readers look for more accessible models to work with? Or does our image of modern society demand too much sociological coolheadedness with its emotional and moral distance from the suffering of human beings? Luhmann would have hesitated to bet on the one or the other.

In his column "A (Cybernetic) Musing: Ashby and the Black Box," Ranulph Glanville analyzes one of the basic epistemological and methodological concepts of cybernetics, be it of first or second order. It is the idea of the black box, which he presents as such a powerful device, that it is time to explore it seriously, in its own right; for it allows us that most magical of tricks, a way of acting confidently with/ from the unknown/unknowable. This allows us something that is basic to the function of science as such; namely the possibility to build descriptions of the world that, ultimately, are based not in presumed knowledge but in ignorance. This ability to handle ignorance in a productive way is also what Qvortrup talks about in his fourth-order knowledge.

Ray Ison writes the ASC Column: "Epistemological awareness: A systemic inquiry." He has turned it into an extended invitation to readers to contribute to a systemic inquiry into epistemological awareness through the auspices of this journal, and when it becomes available, the new ASC website. This is also what we in CHK attempt with our new website, which can be found at www.chkjournal.org. The site is designed and maintained by the Department of Product and Systems Design Engineering of the University of the Aegean in Syros, Greece and its primary role is to provide better and more usable access to the content of the journal, to better disseminate the content among scholars as well as researchers in other scientific disciplines, and to link to relevant journals and pages. Additionally, an electronic forum of discussions related to journal articles will be offered as well as an asynchronous system to optimize the peer-review process for articles and enhance the communication between the reviewers and the editors.

The artist for this issue is the late system scientist, Stafford Beer. He was a multifaceted person, who did more than contribute to management cybernetics! I refer to his essay "On Strength" in this journal Vol. 9, no. 3-4. His work was lent to CHK by Allenna Leonard, to whom we are grateful for this contribution.

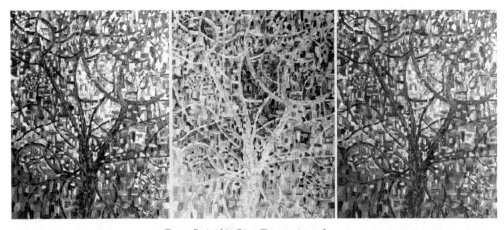

Beer, S. (n.d.). *Pine Tree at Arcachon.*

Cybernetics And Human Knowing. Vol. 14, nos. 2-3, pp. 11-27

Luhmann Applied to the Knowledge Society
Religion as Fourth-Order Knowledge[1]

Lars Qvortrup[2]

This article demonstrates that current theories of society—even if the theory is called "knowledge society"—do not have an adequate sociological concept of knowledge. Thus, a sociologically-operative definition of knowledge is offered; It is categorized into four levels of knowledge based on self-reflection. Finally, it is suggested that fourth-order knowledge stands for that kind of knowledge that has traditionally been represented by the concept of religion.
Keywords: Operative constructivism; Knowledge; Knowledge Society; Religion.

Introduction

We are in a paradoxical situation. On the one hand it is widely assumed that knowledge is a basic phenomenon of and an adequate basic concept for our current so-called knowledge society. On the other hand we do not seem to know how knowledge should be defined within the context of a theory of society. Most of the current theories of knowledge society do not suggest an explicit concept of knowledge, and even if they do, generally speaking the concept is a narrow one, restricting knowledge to certified knowledge.

My basic question is whether Luhmann's theory of society – his "operative constructivism" – can help us in solving this problem. Is it possible to construct a concept of knowledge informed by operative constructivism which is adequate for a theory of the so-called knowledge society?

In this article I will first demonstrate that current theories of society, even if they call it "knowledge society," do not have an adequate sociological concept of knowledge. Then I will present a sociological operative definition of knowledge, followed by a categorization of knowledge into four categories. Finally, I will suggest that fourth order knowledge stands for that kind of knowledge that has traditionally been represented by the concept of religion. Here, I am particularly referring to St. Augustine's analysis of the Trinitarian God (Augustinus, 2001).

What Is the Basic Distinction of the *Knowledge Society*?

It seems to be generally assumed that present-day society is rapidly moving away from being an industrial society, the basic function of which was to develop

---

1. An earlier version of this article was presented at the XVI ISA World Congress, Durban 2006, RC51, session 4. Parts of the article are based on my book *Knowledge, Education and Learning – E-Learning in the Knowledge Society* (Qvortrup, 2006). Thanks to referees for valuable comments on an earlier version of the article.
2. School of Education, University of Aarhus, Denmark. Email: lq@dpu.dk

mechanical systems of production and organization that could transform nature into industrial products, towards a knowledge society, the basic function of which is to handle complexity with the aid of knowledge, no matter whether this knowledge exists as a resource in the individual worker or as knowledge systems in companies and organizations. Avoiding an ontologicalization of society one might say that the self-description of society is moving from a notion of *industrialism* or *capitalism* via a notion of *post-industrialism* to *knowledgeism*. This raises the question of how adequately to observe society as *knowledge society*.

150 years ago Karl Marx confronted a similar challenge: capitalist society developing into its industrial phase. His answer to this challenge and to his aim of understanding the functional mechanisms of capitalism was to identify and to analyze the basic atom of that society: the commodity.

The fundamental challenge of creating a theory of society is to choose an adequate starting point, or—in a post-ontological jargon—to make an adequate, initial distinction. For Karl Marx this starting point was the commodity as the atom of capitalist society. Based on a post-ontological understanding and thus replacing identity (atoms) with differences (distinctions) one might call it the marked state of the initial distinction. The commodity is the marked state of capitalist society. However, Marx also added a normative value to his distinction. Thus, he created a normative distinction between a commoditized society versus a (utopian) non-commoditized society, implying that the crossing of the border would liberate society from the commodity as its value form.

In comparison, in *Soziale Systeme* (Luhmann, 1984), Luhmann chose *system* as his initial distinction with *communication* as his basic atom of analysis. His theoretical experiment was to investigate whether systems defined through the concept of autopoiesis would be an appropriate starting point for developing a self-restricting system of concepts through which society could be observed. What would society look like if seen through this set of theoretical lenses? Marx developed one set of restrictions for the observation of society, Luhmann developed another set. For both, the consequence was that some parts of reality could be better observed than others. Developing a theoretical paradigm, some phenomena will have light cast upon them, while others will be less clearly seen.

Similarly, in order to observe society as a knowledge society and to understand the functional mechanisms of an emerging knowledge society—or, as I would prefer: a knowing society (see Qvortrup, 2004)—one should focus on the marked state of this self-observation of society: knowledge, thus implying that knowledge/non-knowledge is an adequate basic distinction.

But in order to test whether this initial distinction is adequate and to investigate what it implies for the observation of society, the concept must be taken seriously. It must be defined in such a way that it is robust as the basis for further conceptual determinations. What is knowledge? Which knowledge categories can be identified?

The Missing Concept of Knowledge

In most theories of the knowledge society, any explicit, sociologically relevant, definition of *knowledge* is absent. As early as 1959, the English economist and organization analyst Edith Penrose emphasized the growing importance of knowledge in economy, but in addition she admitted that the whole subject of knowledge is so "slippery" that it is impossible to get a firm grip of it (Penrose, 1959, p. 77). In 1969 Peter Drucker announced that knowledge has become the central capital, cost centre and basic resource of the economy (Drucker, 1969, p. ix). Still however he did not suggest how to appropriately define this basic resource. Moreover, he didn't realize that changing a basic conceptual distinction also implies that other concepts—indeed, the very architecture of concepts—must be changed. One cannot just replace capital by knowledge, letting other things remain equal. Approximately thirty years later, Luhmann correctly summarized: "What is knowledge? If one starts in the theory of society and even if one categorizes modern society as "knowledge society," one does not find any adequate concept of knowledge" (Luhmann, 2002, p. 97, my translation).

However, in some of the theories subscribing to the knowledge society idea, definitions of knowledge have been suggested. Still, to my mind these definitions are not adequate.

Sometimes, often in relation to information and communication technologies (ICTs), knowledge is defined as an essence or substance, as in, for instance, the OECD report from 2004, *Innovation in the Knowledge Economy,* which focuses on implications for education and learning. Here, it is emphasized that it is important to have a clear idea of "what it is that is passing through the electronic pipelines: knowledge, information or data?" (OECD, 2004, p. 18). However, the challenges of education and learning (Why doesn't teaching automatically lead to adequate learning, if teaching is only a matter of transporting knowledge?) and of knowledge sharing (Why is knowledge sharing actually most often *not* happening automatically?) cannot be answered if it is assumed that knowledge is a substance that can easily be transported from one person to the other. It is well known that this is *not* what happens in the classroom or in the knowledge-sharing organization. Knowledge about something is a representation of something according to interpretation standards, which may change from person to person and from teacher to pupil. My knowledge is not equal to your knowledge, and it cannot be transported from me to you.

In other contexts, knowledge has been defined in a restricted way as certified knowledge. In his classical book about the post-industrial society Daniel Bell defined knowledge as "a set of organized statements of facts or ideas, presenting a reasoned judgment or an experimental result, which is transmitted to others through some communication medium in some systematic form" (Bell, 1973, p. 175). In his book about the network society, Manuel Castells has, as he says, "no compelling reason to improve on" this definition (Castells, 1996, p. 17). But certified knowledge is only one aspect of knowledge, as for instance Michael Polanyi has convincingly argued (see Polanyi, 1983). Also, tacit knowledge – the knowledge of how, for example, to ride a bike – is knowledge, although it cannot be written down or "proved" and certified in any traditionally scientific way.

In the 2004 OECD report this is reflected upon by making a distinction between on the one hand certified (tested) and practical (uncertified) knowledge, or in French: between *savoir* and *connaissance*, and on the other hand between codified and tacit knowledge (OECD, 2004, p. 18ff), and although no systematic categorization of knowledge forms is provided, at least it is made clear that the question of knowledge is complex.

Yet another systematization has been suggested by Bengt-Aake Lundvall in the OECD 2000 report *Knowledge Management in the Learning Society*. Here he suggests a categorization into four forms of knowledge:

- Know-what that refers to knowledge about facts;
- know-why that refers to knowledge about principles and laws governing facts;
- know-how that refers to skills, i.e. abilities to do something with one's factual knowledge;
- know-who that refers to the ability to trace knowledge providers across disciplines and specializations (OECD, 2000, p. 14f).

While I agree to some of these categories, I think the fourth knowledge form, know-who falls outside the paradigm hidden behind the categories. While know-what, know-why and know-how may refer to different levels of knowledge abstraction, know-who refers to a certain type of knowledge, knowledge of the person or persons that have provided some factual knowledge. In this sense, however, know-who is just a subset of know-what.

A different theory of knowledge and knowledge categories has been developed by Max H. Boisot (1995, 1998). In a way that can be compared with the one that I am proposing in this article, Boisot conceptualizes knowledge as "a set of probability distributions held by an agent and orienting his or her actions" (Boisot, 1998, p. 12). This definition seems to be inspired by Shannon's definition of information, that the more probable a state is, the less information it represents. However, it is hard to see that knowledge is directly related to probability. If I know that a bridge is always down, I can drive my car according to this knowledge. Thus, even though it is valuable to know, there is not much information in saying that a bridge, which is always down, is down.

Boisot suggests a typology of knowledge depending on whether it is diffused/ undiffused and codified/uncodified. This leads into four categories of knowledge: personal knowledge (undiffused and uncodified), common-sense knowledge (diffused and uncodified), proprietary knowledge (undiffused and codified), and public knowledge (diffused and codified) (Boisot, 1995, pp. 145-149). Based on these categories and adding a third dimension (abstraction), Boisot has suggested a description of the use and distribution of knowledge in organizations within the so-called Information-Space or just I-Space. In particular, a social learning cycle can be identified as a movement of knowledge, or information, within the I-Space (Boisot, 1995, 184ff).

Taking a different tack, Claus Otto Scharmer has suggested that within knowledge management theories, in addition to talking about explicit knowledge which equals certified knowledge, one should include two additional categories: *processual* knowledge and *emerging* knowledge (Scharmer, 2001). Again, I am inspired by this approach which refers to different levels of knowledge abstraction. However, building categories of knowledge doesn't answer the question concerning a definition of knowledge, and I agree with the French philosopher Michel Serres who has argued that it is not sufficient just to develop a categorization of knowledge dimensions. On the contrary, the very nature of knowledge should be reconsidered. Knowledge cannot be understood as a fixed, centripetal field, such as is assumed in the encyclopedic tradition, in which one aimed at creating a finite, universal and all-inclusive file of knowledge. No, knowledge has to be understood as an unlimited, growing and dynamic polycentric system (cf. Serres, 1997).

In a paper from 2004, Max Boisot and Augustí Canals suggest a definition of data, information and knowledge along the following lines: data can be treated as originating in discernible differences in physical states-of-the-world. Information can be defined as data observed by an agent: information sets up a relation between in-coming data and a given agent. Finally, knowledge is a set of expectations held by agents and modified by the "arrival" of information (Boisot & Canals, 2004, p. 8). This implies that data generates thermodynamic entropy, information generates symbolic entropy, while knowledge generates cognitive entropy (Boisot & Canals, p. 29).[3]

On the one hand this reminds one of the famous definition suggested by Gregory Bateson, that information is a difference which makes a difference. On the other hand the definitions suggested by Boisot and Canals imply a very specific ontology with a physical world, human agents and a cognitive apparatus creating expectations. This imposes a number of epistemological problems. What is the basis of the ontological differences of the world? How or by whom are they created, and what about Kant's *Ding an sich*? What is the difference between information and knowledge. My question is, what or who sets up the relation between data and the (observing or acting) agent, if not expectations produced by this agent?

My conclusion on this brief review of existing sociological knowledge theories is that we must leave the model of knowledge as an essence, which can be transported from place from place, that is, from the research laboratory to the enterprise. Similarly, we must give up the idea that knowledge as suggested by Bell and Castells can be defined only as certified knowledge, or that knowledge can be categorized

---

3. The distinction of data, information, and knowledge (sometimes, even wisdom is included) is quite old and well-known. Traditionally, it has been based on an ontological categorization of e.g. data as atoms, information as cells and knowledge as organic structures. In 1979, Daniel Bell presented a scheme that can be compared to the one suggested by Boisot and Canals. According to Bell, data is basic distinctions, information is patterns of data, and knowledge is organized and reasoned sets of propositions of facts and ideas (see Bell, 1979).

according to what is known: facts, persons, abilities or laws. In comparison, as I will argue in the following section, I prefer to define information in more abstract terms as the outcome of observation as an abstract operation, or as the outcome of the operation making a distinction between distinction and designation; and knowledge as the outcome of condensed observations.

Knowledge: A Definition

Knowledge: Condensed observations
What is knowledge? The question sounds simple, but as I have exemplified, providing an answer is difficult. It has occupied people's minds ever since the first philosophical questions were formulated. Right now, I am looking out of the window at the snow melting and at the fir trees with their dripping branches. But how do I know that what I am looking at are trees, and that what covers the ground is snow? If one asks the snow, it does not know that it is snow, and the tree hardly has sufficient self-awareness to observe itself as something with a name. It does not stretch up tall, even though I am sitting inside here praising its tree-ness. The knowledge we have of the world is thus a knowledge that we have created.

For me, a very simple, yet practical and applicable sociological definition of knowledge is that knowledge is confirmed or condensed observations. Observations may be confirmed over time or in society. When I observe something and then repeat my observation with the same result, it becomes a confirmed observation and thus personal knowledge. Similarly, when I observe something and another person can confirm this observation, it becomes social knowledge.

Knowledge: A Quality of Observing the World
This implies that knowledge is not a quality of the world, but a quality of observing the world. Knowledge isn't something that we find "out there," but something that is created by observing the world and by comparing world observations over time and/or among different observers, bearing in mind, of course, that the observer is part of the observed world (von Foerster, 1984). This implies that knowledge isn't created and re-created from moment to moment, but is always a matter of confirmation of observations through repeated self-observations and through communication of others' observations. Thus, knowledge systems are always relatively stable, yet dynamic, and different mechanisms have been created to establish such stable, but dynamic systems.

Consequently, although knowledge is always stabilized in systems of confirmed information, it may change over time or between social systems: knowledge of one society or organization may be different from the knowledge of another society or organization. Thus, knowledge is contextual, which explains why knowledge sharing is not just a question of transmitting facts, but is also a question about the negotiation of a shared knowledge context.

Summing up, knowledge is a concept for confirmed observations. If I say, that I know that the plant outside my window is a fir tree, this implies that it has been confirmed through earlier observations or through communication with others that the denotation of the thing outside the window that has precisely that shape and those colors is a fir tree. Similarly, I can say that I know that hotplates can indeed be hot, and that doors are hard if one does not open them before passing through. I know that my neighbor buys breakfast rolls at the baker's every day at 7 am. Those who believe know that God created the world. Well, maybe they have not made that observation themselves, but they trust others who say that that is the way it is. A workman knows how to use an electric screwdriver and a saw. In the 15th century, people knew that the earth was the center of the universe. And my bank adviser knows how to stretch money.

Knowledge, observation and information
Based on the above, I would define knowledge as *observations that have been condensed over time*. But what is the outcome of observation? For me it is information, defining observation "extremely abstract and independently from the material substance" as "distinction and indication" (Luhmann, 1997, p. 69, my translation). Similarly, to inform is to put in form, that is to clove a space and indicate one of the sides of the distinction. Thus, information is the result of observation.

Consequently, knowledge can be defined as condensation of information, that is, as condensation of observations. Actually, a similar definition can be found in Niklas Luhmann's *Die Wissenschaft der Gesellschaft*. Here he defines knowledge "as condensation of observations" (Luhmann, 1990, p. 123, my translation). A similar definition is found later in the same volume: "Knowledge is ... in an extremely general (and not culturally specific) sense condensated observation" (Luhmann, p. 145, my translation).

According to Spencer Brown (1971, p. 12) the form of condensation is:

This means that knowledge and true knowledge represent two different phenomena. True knowledge is a special case of knowledge. The general concept of knowledge "includes first and foremost everyday life behavior, which is not observed in relation to science, yes even not in relation to true and not-true" (Luhmann, 1990, p. 138, my translation). Consequently, "even object knowledge is knowledge" (Luhmann, p. 124, my translation).

On the other hand, knowledge—including object knowledge—is always, whether it is known to the observer or not, reflective knowledge. Thus, even object knowledge is based on a distinction which could have been different. For instance, even though she has no idea of this distinction, my three year-old granddaughter's knowledge of the tree outside the window being a fir tree is based on the distinction of trees into coniferous and deciduous tree.

This implies that knowledge is always not just knowledge in reference to something, but also knowledge in reference to its own boundaries of knowledge. Thus, condensation of observations into knowledge does not just happen one way or the other, but in reference to a specific distinction, opening up the space for different kinds of knowledge. Consequently, knowledge is also a way of dealing with, or to manage, non-knowledge, and to coming around with the fact that knowing something implies that this "something" is known in a specific way, and that it could as well have been known in a different—and unknown—way. To know something is to ignore something else, and to know something reflectively is to know that something else is ignored. In this sense a knowledge society is a society of ignorance, whether this is reflectively known or not.[4]

Observations of observations, knowledge of knowledge
How does knowledge emerge? According to Luhmann, knowledge is the result of structural irritations of meaning-based systems, that is, of psychic and social systems. "Knowledge emerges through the reaction of the system on irritations. It activates the available resources recursively in order to give the problem the form of 'knowledge'" (Luhmann, 1990, p. 165, my translation). Luhmann refers directly and explicitly to Piaget's psychological concept of *accommodation*. According to Piaget, in order to learn, a psychic system has to accommodate to an external irritation. For me it is obvious that Luhmann generalizes this idea to meaning-based systems as such. However, with the concept of accommodation Piaget only refers to one type of learning and knowledge. If I know the name of six Danish kings and then add a seventh name to my list, this learning process cannot be characterized as a process of accommodation, but rather as a cumulative process. One piece of knowledge is added to what I already knew, but my cognitive framing is not affected. Still, however, the seventh name is also part of my knowledge resources and the result of learning. This implies that other categories of knowledge must be added to the one emerging from accommodative learning.

Forms of Knowledge

Domains of knowledge
One of the results of the development of a modern society is that various forms of knowledge have developed, forms of which each is connected to a specific function system. Scientific knowledge has developed into *cognitively* stylized meaning with very highly formalized demands concerning the condensation of observations, that is, into knowledge of the relation between true and non-true knowledge, while legal knowledge is the result of *normatively* stylized knowledge of the relation between

---

4. Thanks to Dirk Baecker for suggesting that I address this point (personal communication).

right and wrong (Luhmann, 1990, p. 138). In comparison, religious knowledge can be defined as theologically stylized and highly ritualized knowledge of the relation between immanence and transcendence.

This implies that in a functionally differentiated society second-order observation of knowledge is a common operation. Here, knowledge exists in different styles, depending on the ways in which knowledge is stylized in the different functional systems. In one system, the scientific system, observations are condensed into knowledge according to highly formalized truth criteria. In another system, the religious system, observations are condensed into knowledge according to formalized belief criteria and/or religious dogma. In a third system, the system of mass media, knowledge is equal to common knowledge. We know what we know because observations are condensed by the media. I can refer to the newspaper I read, when discussing politics with my friends. What I have read constitutes my condensed observations of world politics. Our known reality is equal to the reality of the mass media. In a fourth system – the art system – a work of art provides knowledge, if it is, for example, beautiful or sublime, while a less challenging work of art is said to contain no new knowledge. This implies that in the art system observations are condensed into knowledge according to aesthetic criteria.

Take, for instance, the case of global warming. How do we know of global warming, and how do we know that it is an important issue – how is global warming an instance of common knowledge? As a scientist, one knows that global warming is the effect of human behavior, in so far as this is the outcome of highly formalized observations and equally formalized condensations of such observations. As a religious believer, one's knowledge of global warming results from the condensation of observation through the lenses of the distinction between immanence and transcendence. Here, global warming is given transcendental meaning. Consequently, the knowledge of global warming is a knowledge of global knowledge as the sign of something else, for instance God or the anger of God. Global warming is equal to transcendentally based global warning. As a user of mass media, one knows that global warming is an issue, because for example, Al Gore, in a dramaturgically convincing way, has argued that this is the case, or because one has seen it in numerous television programmes. Here, global warming is an instance of our common knowledge. Finally, as a life-world actor one simply observes that seasons have changed compared with what one believes they used to be. Thus, one knows that global warming is a fact, it is part of so-called *object knowledge*.

However, one functional system can observe the knowledge of other functional systems, and it can use the irritations from other functional systems as a resource for its own knowledge constructions. Al Gore refers to scientific knowledge, if it fits into his message, and scientific knowledge constructions are always also influenced by what is appropriate according to common knowledge.

Consequently, in a functionally differentiated society it is realized that there are different domains of knowledge or *knowledge regimes*, and that as a result one must make a distinction between object knowledge and knowledge of knowledge.

Particularly, it is widely recognized that so-called object knowledge is always already reflective knowledge. This implies that in a functionally differentiated society it is obvious that a distinction should be made between different categories of knowledge, based on their level of observation.

Reflective knowledge: Knowledge of knowledge
We have already seen that knowledge can be defined as condensation of observations, and that knowledge emerges as the way in which meaning-based systems manage irritations.

But now we can add that in order to separate, for instance, legal knowledge from scientific knowledge – and, again, to separate both legal and scientific knowledge from everyday life knowledge – one has to make second-order observations. "If one wants to check whether … knowledge is true knowledge, one has to observe it at a distance, that is, with the use of the distinction true/non-true" (Luhmann, 1990, p. 169, my translation). But if one aims at deciding, whether a legal decision is correct (*correctness* being the correlation to truth in the knowledge of the legal system), one must refer to the formalized history of the legal system, its precedents.

Thus, based on Luhmann's concept of knowledge a distinction can be made between first and second-order knowledge – knowledge as such and knowledge of knowledge – adding, as already emphasized, that "knowledge as such" is always also based on reflective knowledge, and, vice versa, that second-order knowledge is always also first-order knowledge, the difference being that in the latter case the object of knowledge is knowledge.

This leads to the conclusion that we can make a distinction between true and non-true knowledge, and between knowledge and non-knowledge. Particularly, this implies that knowledge is different from true knowledge, and non-true knowledge is different from non-knowledge.

Finally, although one can make a distinction between knowledge and true knowledge, which means that the concept of knowledge is broader than the concept of true knowledge or formally certified knowledge, these two definitions are often mixed together. Luhmann expresses this fact in the way that only "for the immediate observer knowledge is always true knowledge, or otherwise it isn't knowledge at all. He only knows one kind of knowledge. For him (and only for him) the expressions "x is" and "it is true that x is" are logically equivalent, that is redundant. (Luhmann, 1990, p. 169) Thus, Luhmann implies that although knowledge is always reflective knowledge, this is not always known to be the case.

Categories of knowledge
Based on this definition of knowledge, knowledge can be categorized into different categories or levels of knowledge, depending on the level of reflectivity. I suggest, based on empirical observations, that four categories can be defined: 1st, 2nd, 3rd and 4th-order knowledge.[5] First-order knowledge is simple knowledge: knowledge about something. This is what Luhmann calls object knowledge. Second-order knowledge is

knowledge about knowledge, or reflective knowledge. One reflects, what is already known, for instance in relation to a situation or to a problem to be solved. Thus, it may also be called situative knowledge or competence. This category corresponds to Gilbert Ryle's concept of "knowing-how" (Ryle, 1949). Third-order knowledge is knowledge about knowledge about knowledge, that is, knowledge about the preconditions for reflective knowledge. It may also be called creative knowledge, because it is knowledge about the way in which knowledge comes about. Compared with Gilbert Ryle's category *knowing-how*, this might be called *knowing-why*. Finally, one can identify a fourth category of knowledge, which represents the social evolution of knowledge, that is, the collective and perhaps unconscious knowledge process and the total knowledge potential. This is closely related to what Edmund Husserl called the meaning horizon of society. It represents all that may be known in contrast to what cannot be known.

Each of these knowledge categories can be analyzed within a knowledge-sociological context.

1. Knowledge of the world: the search for object—sometimes mistaken for "objective"—knowledge. The core example here is the development of rational knowledge that started in the 17th and 18th century, culminating in logical positivism at the beginning of the 20th century.
2. Knowledge of knowledge, or *competencies*: The attempt to describe and document so-called practical or applied knowledge. These attempts have roots stretching back to the portfolios of the Renaissance (where artists, architects, and others documented their competencies), but culminate in the competence descriptions and accounts of current years.
3. Knowledge of the criteria for knowledge: Here the focus lies on efforts to develop a theory of art and philosophy as a medium for revealing (the normally self-evidenced) criteria for world-knowledge. In this connection, one also speaks of "true" creativity, that is, the ability to rethink our normal knowledge.
4. Knowledge of the boundaries of possible knowledge: Here the focus lies on an analysis of religion as a medium for the revealing of non-knowledge and of God as the concept of the non-accessible knowledge of the boundary between knowledge and non-knowledge. Special emphasis is placed on the development and discussion of the Trinitarian formula, which took place in the first centuries AD and culminated in St. Augustine (Augustinus, 2001, pp. 399-419).

Categories of Knowledge – a Distinction Theoretical Approach

In the introduction to his *Tractatus Logico-Philosophicus* from 1921, Ludwig Wittgenstein stated that to be able to create an image of what our human knowledge comprises, it must be possible to raise oneself above this knowledge. In other words,

---

5. This is inspired by Gregory Bateson's article "The Logical Categories of Learning and Communication," which was written during several phases: in 1964, 1968, and 1971, (cf. Bateson, 2000, pp. 279-308.)

one must be able to see its boundaries. Wittgenstein's goal was to draw up boundaries for knowledge: what do we know, and what do we not know? The point, however, is that in order to be able to see where the boundary for possible knowledge goes, one must be able to imagine this boundary both from the inside and from the outside. "In order to draw a boundary to thinking, one should be able to think both sides of this boundary" – "Um den Denken eine Grenze zu ziehen, müßten wir beide Seiten dieser Grenze denken können" (Wittgenstein, 1969, p. 7).

To be able to talk about what we know, it is, then, necessary to imagine that there is something beyond what we know. That alongside or over and above our knowledge there is non-knowledge – and not just non-knowledge as what we still-do-not-know, but non-knowledge as absolute non-knowledge – as that which we can-not-know.

But what do we know about what we cannot know? And what can we know? Nothing, says Wittgenstein. About what we cannot speak, we must remain silent, Wittgenstein states in the famous final paragraph of *Tractatus*. But the fact is, of course, that the converse holds good: What we can-not-know is that about which we incessantly attempt to speak.

Instead of remaining silent about what we cannot speak, because the distinction between knowledge and non-knowledge cannot or should not be crossed, another possibility is to re-enter the distinction of knowledge and non-knowledge into itself.

I have already said that one of the facts about knowledge is that it can be applied to itself. If one tries to translate it into the language of cybernetics, one would talk about the re-entry of the output as input in the same system. In the language of distinction theory one would talk about the re-entry of the form in the form. Here, first-order knowledge is indicated knowledge, second-order knowledge is indicated knowledge observed in relation to non-knowledge, that is, as what is not yet known. Third-order knowledge is knowledge concerning the distinction between knowledge and non-knowledge, that is, as the knowledge that knowledge could be constructed differently, that is according to another distinction. Finally, fourth-order knowledge is knowledge of the system of knowledge, non-knowledge and knowledge distinctions pointing towards a *knowledge space* in which knowledge universes can be built.

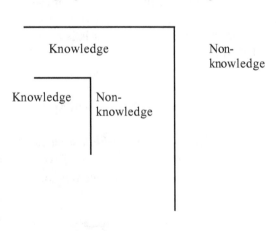

4th-Order Knowledge

Finally, I will provide a perspective of the theory of knowledge by adding a bit on what I call fourth-order knowledge or religious knowledge.

This last section is influenced by Jean Clam, who on the last page of his book *Was heißt, sich an Differenz statt an Identität orientieren?* refers to Ricarda Pfeiffer, who says that while art answers the world problem with an "incitement to observe," religion confronts "the unobservable as such" (Clam, 2002, p. 110). Inspired by Clam, I will particularly focus on 4th-order knowledge and discuss whether 4th-order knowledge can inform our understanding of religion. In order to do so it is appropriate to compare St. Augustine's classical Trinitarian formula with the category of 4th-order knowledge (Augustinus, 2001).

According to Niklas Luhmann, the religious code of observation and communication can be characterized as the one that is based on the relation between immanence and transcendence. His definition is as follows: "a communication is always religious, when it observes the immanent under the point of observation of transcendence" (Luhmann, 2000, p. 77).

This relation between immanence and transcendence has always been a characteristic of religious observation and communication, unlike other forms of observation and communication. At the same time, though, it has also represented a problem in terms of observation, communication and epistemology. For how does one make the non-observable observable? How does one communicate about the non-communicable? How can one know anything about what one can know nothing about?

The classic answer is that one reintroduces the distinction between immanence and transcendence into the immanent. In that way, one pulls the abstract—even the inaccessible—down into the sphere of the concrete and accessible. This can be done by introducing God, or whatever transcendental powers one happens to deal in, into the immanent sphere. God is transformed from being absolute non-knowledge into being an ontological creator and communicator.

Unless one applauds an ontological conception of God (i.e. claims that God is a person with an address), one thereby commits an error. For was God not precisely characterized by being unobservable? One cannot simply solve the problem of transcendence by making the transcendent tangible.

How, then, is the problem to be solved? My assertion—one that I have busied myself with for some time, but which I was encouraged and assisted in formulating more precisely by a Ph.D. thesis written by Kirsten Lundager Knudsen on Trinitarian communication (see Lundager Knudsen, 2005)—is that the trinitarian formula represents an interesting proposal for solving religion's problem of observation and communication.

> There is … one good, which alone is simple and for that reason alone unchangeable, namely God. From this good all good things have been created, but they are not simple, and therefore they are changeable. … The two we call Father and Son, and both these with their Spirit are one God. This

Spirit of the Father and Son is called, with a special meaning of the word, the Holy Spirit. (Augustinus, 2002, p. 488)

We believe and maintain and faithfully declare that the Father bore the Son, … that one father bore one Son, an eternal and correspondingly eternal, a supremely good and equally good; that the Holy Spirit is at one and the same time the Spirit of both the Father and the Son and itself is consubstantial with and eternally as those two; and that this unity is both a Trinity on the basis of the individuality of the persons and one God on the basis of the indivisible deity. (Augustinus, 2002, p. 501)

What is this? Medieval mysticism taken from Umberto Eco's novels? One of the coded documents from the Da Vinci mystery? Hocus pocus and abracadabra? No, the quotation, written by St. Augustine in 426 AD, is in my opinion a tremendously advanced proposition for solving a fundamental, epistemological problem (Augustinus, 2002). How does one make a transcendental God visible?

The solution proposed by Christianity is incarnation. A person is created who is both God and man, namely Jesus Christ. This double figure solves the paradox problem of religion by itself being a paradoxical figure: both man and the Son of God. Jesus Christ is the example *par excellence* of what Spencer Brown calls *re-entry*, that a distinction is inserted into its own inside. The relation between world and God is one between immanence and transcendence. How does one go beyond the distinction that this relationship involves? How does one get from world to God? This is done by inserting the relation between immanence and transcendence, between the world and God, into a person that belongs to the immanent world, that is, into a human. This human is Jesus, who therefore becomes a Doppelgänger: Jesus Christ, and who therefore is admittedly born of the Virgin Mary, but conceived by the Holy Spirit. Jesus Christ is the re-entry Proto-figure of Christian civilization.

Even so, there is still a problem: According to this solution God is unambiguously transcendent. He is what we are not. We are evil, he is good. If we are humans, he is non-human. This is difficult to reconcile with the idea of incarnation, which claims that God is both human and non-human. The problem we would like to overcome is, then, that God is both on the one side and the other side of the distinction.

This brings us to the point of departure: The apparently mystic and inaccessible text of St. Augustine. The solution—and here we are dealing, as mentioned, with a solution that is epistemologically particularly advanced and sophisticated—is to move God out of the binarity of the distinction, that is, out of either/or and into a both/and position. This brings us to the Trinitarian proposal: Instead of operating in a binary fashion with the world/God and with Jesus Christ as the one that transcends the distinction, we must operate with a solution where we move God out into a fourth position, as the presupposed space which, to use Spencer Brown's previously mentioned formulation, is severed and becomes a universe when a distinction is made: "A universe comes into being when a space is severed or taken apart" (Spencer Brown, 1971, p. v). The solution, in other words, is to insert the Son in the position of the immanent, the Father in that of the transcendent, the Holy Spirit in that of the distinction, and make God the presupposed space. This is precisely why the emphasize, preceding St. Augustine, were forced as they were to emphasize that the persons of the Father, Son and Holy Spirit are on the one hand different (for they occupy different aspects of the distinction) but that their divinity, as it says, is, on the other hand, one and the same. God as the presupposed and inaccessible space becomes accessible as the totality or as the universe of Son (immanence), Father (transcendence) and Holy Spirit (the distinction or the blind spot between immanence and transcendence).

At the same time, it must naturally be maintained that Jesus is a Doppelgänger: That he, by virtue of his paradoxical uniting of Son and Father, can cross the distinction by, in Spencer Brown's formulation, being the result of a re-entry of the distinction on the distinction's immanent side.

In conclusion, at least we know that beyond the horizon of knowledge there is something, which can be called non-knowledge. Thus, at least we know that there is a knowledge beyond socially possible knowledge, a knowledge that can only be accessed negatively, that is, in a knowledge of its inaccessibility. We know, *what* we know, and we know *that* we know. But we also know that we don't know what we don't know. This knowledge of not knowing what we don't know, can be named: 4th-order knowledge. The only thing that we know about this non-knowledge is that it presupposes a knowing instance or space which exists beyond all possible knowledge. This instance has been given different names and characteristics: It is the non-observable observer. It is that which forms without having been formed. The non-created creator, or, in the words of Nikolaus Cusanus: "Non aliud non aliud est quam non aliud" or "One cannot add further qualities to the non-otherness than that it is beyond otherness" (quoted in Kirkeby, 2005, p. 111).

This was, I assume, what Wittgenstein sensed as he finished his *Tractatus*. On that, which we cannot speak about, we must be silent. "What lies beyond the boundary, will simply be senseless" (Wittgenstein, 1969, p. 7, my translation). This is the reason why the book is finished by the famous and tragic sentence: "Wovon man nicht sprechen kann, darüber muss man schweigen" (Wittgenstein, 1969, p. 115), translated as: "On what one cannot speak, on that one must be silent." That it is tragic is explained by Wittgenstein himself: Consequently he adds, against his own epistemological programme: "However, the unutterable exists. This becomes visible, it is the mystical." (Wittgenstein, p. 115, my translation).

This was what Kurt Gödel proved negatively in 1931: That somebody or something can observe that which human beings cannot observe themselves. He expressed in a formal language that not everything in or of the world can be observed from a position within the world. Ontology must be replaced by autology (cf. Luhmann, 1997). Thus, there must be something beyond the border of possible knowledge.

But this was also what St. Augustine tried to express, although in a different language, but still more explicit and detailed, at the end of the 4th century A.D. He articulated in a way, which is very close to the system of knowledge categories, that we know, that we don't know what we don't know, and that there must be a knowledge instance, which exists beyond all possible knowledge. That which St. Augustine called

God as the totality of Son, Father and the Holy Spirit; that which we call space as the presupposed totality of immanence, transcendence and the blind spot of distinction; that is what I call fourth-order knowledge.

Conclusion

Two conclusions can be made, one concerning religion as fourth order knowledge, and another concerning knowledge in general.

Concerning religion as fourth order knowledge I have demonstrated that contrary to what has been the "motto" of enlightenment the relation between reason and belief is not a zero-sum game. It is not true that more reason, that is, more scientifically based knowledge, creates less belief, and that finally religion will fade away as a result of enlightenment. No, scientifically based knowledge and religious knowledge represent two different regimes of knowledge.

Also, in my analysis of religion as a knowledge category I have focused particularly on Christian religion, because it particularly unfolds the categorization of God into the Trinitarian formula. Here, God is not a transcendent actor, he is not an ontological instance who has crossed the boundary between immanence and transcendence. Here, God is rather that space which is turned into a universe by being cloven by the marked/unmarked distinction Son/Father, with the Holy Spirit as the blind spot of the distinction, that is, as the unobservable observer of this distinction.

Concerning knowledge as a sociologically operative concept I have suggested defining knowledge as condensed observations and to categorize knowledge into two dimensions. First, we have a list of knowledge regimes, the number of which can only be decided empirically, with each their own stylization of knowledge, for example, science's true knowledge, mass media's common knowledge, and so forth. Second, we have four knowledge orders, based on the different levels of knowledge reflection. First-order knowledge is object knowledge. Second-order knowledge is knowledge concerning the relation between what is known and what is not yet known; this is normally called competence, that is, the knowledge of applying one's knowledge to something, for instance to itself. Third-order knowledge is knowledge concerning the distinction of knowledge/non-knowledge, that is, knowledge of the unspoken and invisible distinction on which our knowledge is based. This is often called creativity, because knowledge of the blind spot of knowledge makes it possible to know something differently. Finally, fourth-order knowledge is the designation of that space, which constitutes the precondition for knowledge: that which we know that we don't know.

References

Augustinus, A. (2001). *De trinitate*. Lateinisch – Deutsch (J. Kreuzer, Trans.) Hamburg: Felix Meiner Verlag.(Written between 399 and 419 A.D.)

Augustinus, A. (2002). *Guds Stad*. Aarhus: Aarhus Universitetsforlag. (Danish translation of *De Ciuitate Dei*, which was written between 413 and 426 A.D.)

Bateson, G. (2000). The logical categories of learning and communication. In *Steps to an ecology of mind* (pp. 279-308). Chicago: The University of Chicago Press.

Bell, D. (1973). *The coming of post-industrial society*. New York: Basic Books.

Bell, D. (1979). "Information and Telecommunication in the Post-Industrial Society." In M. L. Dertouzos & J. Moses (Eds.), The computer age: A twenty years view. Cambridge, MA: The MIT Press.

Boisot, M. H. (1995). *Information space: A framework for learning in organizations, institutions and culture*. London: Routledge.

Boisot, M. H. (1998). *Knowledge assets: Securing competitive advantage in the information economy*. Oxford: Oxford University Press.

Boisot, M., & Canals, A. (2004). Data, information and knowledge: Have we got it right? Working Paper Series WP04-002, Internet Interdisciplinary Institute, UOC, Catalonia, Spain.

Castells, M. (1996). *The rise of the network society*. Malden, MA: Blackwell Publishers.

Clam, J. (2002). *Was heißt, sich an Differenz statt an Identität orientieren?* Konstanz: UVK.

Drucker, P. F. (1969). *The age of discontinuity: Guidelines to our changing society*. London: Heinemann.

Foerster, H. von (1984). *Observing systems*. Seaside, CA: Intersystem Publications.

Kirkeby, O. F. (2005). *Eventun Tantum: Begivenhedens Ethos*. Copenhagen: Samfundslitteratur.

Lundager Knudsen, K. (2005). *Trinitarisk kommunikation. Folkekirke og teologi i mediesamfundet systemteoretisk belyst*. Unpublished Ph.D. thesis, The Faculty of Theology, University of Aarhus.

Luhmann, N. (1984). *Soziale Systeme*. Frankfurt: Suhrkamp Verlag.

Luhmann, N. (1990). *Die Wissenschaft der Gesellschaft*. Frankfurt: Suhrkamp Verlag.

Luhmann, N. (1997). *Die Gesellschaft der Gesellschaft*. Frankfurt: Suhrkamp Verlag.

Luhmann, N. (2002). *Das Erziehungssystem der Gesellschaft*. Frankfurt: Suhrkamp Verlag.

Marx, K. (1973). *Das Kapital. Kritik der politischen Ökonomie, Vol. 1*. Berlin: Dietz Verlag.(Originally published in 1867).

OECD. (2000). *Knowledge management in the learning society*. Paris: OECD.

OECD. (2004). *Innovations in the knowledge economy*. Paris: OECD.

Penrose, E. (1959). *The theory of the growth of the firm*. Oxford: Oxford University Press.

Polanyi, M. (1983). *The tacit dimension*. Gloucester, MA: Peter Smith.

Qvortrup, L. (2003). *The hypercomplex society*. New York: Peter Lang Publishers.

Qvortrup, L. (2004). *Det vidende samfund* [The knowing society]. Copenhagen: Unge Pædagoger,.

Qvortrup, L. (2006). *Knowledge, education and learning: E-learning in the knowledge society*. Copenhagen: Samfundslitteratur.

Ryle, G. (1949). *The concept of mind*. London: Hutchinson.

Scharmer, C. O. (2001). Self-transcending Knowledge: Organizing around Emerging Realities. In I. Nonaka & D. Teece (Eds.): *Managing industrial knowledge: Creation, transfer and utilization*. London: Sage Publications.

Serres, M. (1997). *The troubadour of knowledge*. Ann Arbor, MI: The University of Michigan Press. (Originally published in 1991.)

Spencer Brown, G. (1971). *Laws of form*. London: George Allen and Unwin.

Wittgenstein, L. (1969). *Tractatus logico-philosophicus*. Frankfurt: Suhrkamp Verlag. (Originally published in 1921)

Beer, S. (n.d.). *Travelling* (detail).

Beer, S. (n.d.). *Thoth*.

Cybernetics And Human Knowing. Vol. 14, nos. 2-3, pp. 29-65

Applying Luhmann's System Theory as Part of a Transdisciplinary Frame For Communication Science[1]

Søren Brier[2]

Luhmanian sociocybernetics is an observation of socio-communicative systems with a specific difference. It is a second order observation of observations understanding society as being "functionally differentiated" into autonomous autopoietic subsystems or *meaning worlds* in the symbolic generalized media such as money, power, truth, love, art and faith. Only communication communicates and the social is communication. The social system creates products of meaning which do not represent an aggregation of the content of individuals' minds. The bio- and psychological autopoietic systems only establish boundary conditions for the socio-communicative systems; they do not control the socio-communicative system in any way. Somehow the socio-communicative systems seem to develop on their own (by will?) although they have no body and no subject. The psychic system in Luhmann's theory is thus not a Kantian or Husserlian transcendental ego in spite of Luhmann's use of aspects of Husserl's phenomenology (while at the same time destroying its philosophical frame). On the other hand, Luhmann works with an open ontology, combined with Spencer-Brown's philosophy that making distinctions is what creates the difference between system and environment. Thus observation is basic to the theory—but where is the observer in the theoretical framework of system theory? The inspiration from Hegel is hidden here, where distinction, creation and evolution merge. Also, Hegel has been taken out of his metaphysical frame while Luhmann never took the time to finish his own. On the other hand, the father of the pragmatic triadic semiotic C. S. Peirce—also inspired by Hegel—explicitly confronted some of these problems. Like Bataille, Peirce sees a continuity between mind and matter and his Firstness contains *pure feeling*, meaning that there is also an inner experience aspect of matter. The article compares Luhmann's and Spencer-Brown's strategies with Peirce's, the latter of whom built an alternative transdisciplinary theory of signification and communication based on a Panentheistic theory of knowing. Surprisingly it fits well with Spencer-Brown's metaphysics, which makes it possible to establish a consistent foundation for system theory.

The Luhmannian System World and the Role of the Subject

In general it seems that any kind of natural, psychological, linguistic, and social (nomothetic) science, in its immanent aim towards universal knowledge of regularities or laws determining the behavior of its objects, systems and "subjects," will tend to either eliminate or at least minimize the causal influence of individual conscious choice and subjective free will (Brier, 1993). Thus Luhmann's attack on the

---

1. This article is developed from a talk given to the round table *Luhmann Applied*, arranged by RC51 (Sociocybernetic Group) at the XVI ISA World Congress of Sociology July 2006 in Durban and published in a short form in the proceedings in CD-ROM form as *The Missing Bodily Situated Subject*.
2. Centre for Language, Cognition and Mentality, Department of International Culture and communication, Copenhagen Business School, Dalgas Have 15, DK-2000 Frederiksberg, Denmark.

transcendental subject for the sake of building a social science from a system theoretical foundation is no surprise.

To analyze the individual, the subjective, and the unique is something entirely different from both social and natural science and has therefore been called ideographic "science." The problem has also been conceptualized as the difference between objective and subjective approaches and between quantitative and qualitative approaches and between research aimed at descriptive modelling and research aiming at understanding (hermeneutic). Since the second world war there have been a growing number of transdisciplinary[3] research programs (as Lakatos defines them), especially in the area of information, cognition, signification and communication science, that try to overcome this incommensurability.

The problematic analyzed in this article is Luhmann's triple autopoietic and second-order cybernetic version of system theory. If it gives a new fruitful synthesis that in its transdisciplinarity solves some of these deep problems in social science— among them the problematic relation between the qualitative social construction of knowledge, understanding of human action and communication and more realistic quantitative scientific approaches in methods and analysis—then does it still leave room for voluntarism, first person experience, and understanding in a social science of communication?

The foundational theories within the area, such as Bertalanffy's general system theory and Wiener's cybernetics, already aimed at making a transdisciplinary framework for science and the humanities in their original version, but as I have shown (Brier, 2002/2003, 2005a, 2005b), these theories—since they are based on systemic part-whole concepts, information and circulatory causality through circulating differences—have great problems in including human voluntary agency and a theory of consciousness, qualia, emotions, and signification (Brier, 2007) in their purview. What seems to be missing is a theory of first person consciousness, signification, and subjectivity that is connected to both society, meaning and nature, which—as (Sheriff 1994) argues—is the center of C. S. Peirce's semiotic philosophy, which is why I will compare Luhmann's work with his. On the other hand the social communication aspect, which is Luhmann's strength, is not well developed in Peirce's semiotic philosophy.

Luhmann's theoretical strategy, of taking Maturana and Varela's bio-cybernetic concept of autopoiesis and generalizing it to also cover the psychological and the social and further forming a model of an independent psychic system, is new in systems and cybernetics. It can be viewed as an interesting attempt to solve the problem that systems, cybernetics, and informatics/information science have with

---

3.   Since the task of these paradigms is not to make interdisciplinary connections between subject areas as they are
     already defined by the present research programs in the area, but to attempt through a redefining of the whole
     subject area of several and often very different smaller subject areas to make a new framework and synthesis, I
     call them transdisciplinary (Brier, 2006). Cybernetics, systems, Peirce's semiotics, information science,
     complexity science and cognitive science are examples of such attempt of transdisciplinary frames in the area of
     information, cognition and communication, as well as my own Cybersemiotics (Brier, 2007).

subjectivity, embodied meaning and therefore the social (Brier, 2006, 2007), the latter of which, to Luhmann, is communication based on differences in a field of meaning. He assumes that every experience of meaning is a difference between what is given and what is possible, a horizon of possibilities from which to select again, thus introducing time and evolution in as important elements of the theory. Meaning emerges from this theory as the unity of the difference between actuality and a never exhausted horizon of possibilities (Luhmann, 1995)[4]. In my opinion Luhmann's is the only system science and cybernetics version that gets close to C. S. Peirce's transdisciplinary attempt from the phenomenological and semiotic side.[5] That is what makes him so interesting from my point of view.[6]

Further Luhmann's idea of drawing on Husserl's phenomenology as a foundation for the psyche and a concept of meaning, is new in systems and cybernetics which, in general, have had problems in this area of mind and signification (Brier, 1992). Making a theory of mind functioning within their framework, be it Bertalanffy's organismic theory of emergence or Norbert Wiener's negentropic concept of cybernetics and information, has been the deep problem in systemic, cybernetic[7] approaches leading into cognitive science's information processing paradigm and its problem in establishing artificial intelligence and linguistic machine communication and translation. In general, there are ongoing discussions of what it is that a theory of mind built on an informational world view can deliver, even in the ecological and anthropological settings of Gregory Bateson (Brier, 1992, 2007; Brier, in press), the cybernetician that has worked in the most determined fashion on this problem.

If the concept of mind created in cybernetics as *circulating differences* works for computers, animals, humans, and inanimate nature as well (Bateson 1973, 1980; Bateson & Bateson, 2005), one wonders if it can distinguish between them and if it really includes feeling, motivation, free will, signification, and meaning. Both Bateson and Luhmann refer to these aspects of human experience and social interaction. But my concern is whether these concepts are defined within their paradigms or whether

---

4. See also Laermans' article in the present publication, which goes deeper in describing this and further connects system theory with Saussurian semiology, seeing the sign as the unity of the difference between a signifier and a signified, to which it seems to fit much better than Peirce's triadic semiotics. But in contrast to Saussure, Husserl, and Luhmann, Peirce dares to develop a transdisciplinary (metaphysical) theory of meaning – how the field of meaning that the differences and selections are made in comes into existence.

5. As I have had to keep the length of this article reasonable I have chosen not to use much space to document Peirce's views. They have been taken for granted and only referred to. I have then referenced earlier work where I have made interpretations of Peirce's work, as well as interpretations of Bateson and von Foerster. I also refer to the recognized works of Brent, Sheriff, and Raposa, and Peirce's own writings in original in the reference list.

6. I want to underline that this is the perspective, from which I am observing Luhmann' and that this might not have been Luhmann's view and is certainly not the view of most of those sociologists and social philosophers that use Luhmann's theories in social analysis. I have realized that for the most part my approach may irritate their autopoiesis and they do not feel obliged to make structural couplings or even interpenetration. But it is nevertheless in Luhmann's spirit that I chose the difference from which I want to observe, knowing well that many other choices were possible.

7. I am aware that in the present it is fashionable to forget about cybernetics, which seems to many to have run out of steam; many instead refer now to the new "paradigm" of *complexity science* or of *complex adaptive systems* (CAS), which seems to be more readily accepted to fit the received view of science. But one should know the actual historical roots (Heims,1991; Hayles, 1999).

they just refer to common sense understandings of them and take them as theoretically given in this theoretical inconsistent way. The conclusions of my analysis are that it cannot (Brier, 2007; Brier, in press). It is a major problem of systems and cybernetics even in Bateson's version. This—and Luhmann's great influence on socio-cybernetics—is why Luhmann's attempt to solve this problem is so interesting, if solving this problem was one of his aims. Because, although Luhmann touches on a lot of epistemological and ontological problems, he is not a philosopher by training and—in contrast with Peirce—he does not really care to complete the philosophical work on his own system theory's foundations.[8] Thus I am aware that the results of this exercise will in one way be negative, but as a result of Luhmann's greatness it will also be interesting.

Another aspect of Luhmann's theory that bothers me as a fellow transdisciplinarian, is that it consists of components from so many different sources without a thorough investigation of the compatibility of the frameworks or paradigms that give the source theories and their concepts scientific or scholarly meaning. For instance: Both Shannon and Wiener use the concept of information, but their conceptions are fundamentally different. Thus there are very many ways to use the concepts of information, meaning and communication (as, for example, analyzed by Qvortrup, 1993). In contrast, Peirce builds up a system from his own foundational work (see e.g., Peirce, 1992). Therefore I want to contrast Luhmann's solutions with Peirce who, on the other hand, did not really develop the fruitful idea of self-organizing systems, autopoiesis, and socio-communicative systems and seems to miss that potential in his theory. Further, there is an interesting meeting between Peirce and Luhmann in the understanding of the subject as a dialogical process and a system with a limited horizon. Neither of them embraces the traditional transcendental subject. My concern here is whether the difference in the paradigmatic background on which this vital concept is established can be overcome. My aim is thus not to dispatch Luhmann but to further develop my cybersemiotic framework of which his theory is a part (Brier, 2007).

The cybernetic mind problem Luhmann inherited from Bateson

It seems to be a general feature of cybernetics and the system theory versions, which integrate cybernetics as a part of them, that you do not need have to be a conscious embodied individual with emotions and qualia in order to be an observer! In his book *Steps to an Ecology of Mind* Bateson defines a cybernetics mind as follows:

---

8. As Thyssen (2006), who is a philosopher, writes: "Luhmann is not a philosopher. And yet we are able to trace a philosophical dimension in his works since he is no naïve empiricist but extraordinarily attentive to his method. With his ambition to develop a new paradigm for the observation of social systems he is forced to study the conditions of observing. ... However, although he makes frequent reference to philosophers, he is unfamiliar with the philosophical tradition and also does not respect it ... As a sociologist, he focuses on the unfolding of social systems and considers philosophical qualms irrelevant. As a consequence of this philosophical blindness, he entangles himself in a series of philosophical inconsistencies." (Thyssen, 2006, abstract).

1. The system shall operate with and upon differences.
2. The system shall consist of closed loops or networks of pathways along which differences and transforms of differences shall be transmitted. (What is transmitted on a neuron is not an impulse; it is news of a difference).
3. Many events within the system shall be energized by the responding part rather than by impact from the triggering part.
4. The system shall show self-correctiveness in the direction of homeostasis and/or in the direction of runaway. Self-correctiveness implies trial and error. (Bateson, 1973, p. 458)

This is developed further in his later book *Mind and Nature*:

1. A mind is an aggregate of interacting parts or components.
2. The interaction between parts of mind is triggered by difference, and difference is a non-substantial phenomenon not located in space or time; difference is related to neg-entropy and entropy rather than to energy.
3. Mental processes require collateral energy.
4. Mental processes require circular (or more complex) chains of determination.
5. In mental processes, the effects of difference are to be regarded as transforms (i.e., coded versions) of events preceding them. The rules of such transformation must be comparatively stable (i.e., more stable than the content) but are themselves subject to transformation.
6. The description and classification of these processes of transformation disclose a hierarchy of logical types immanent in the phenomena.(Bateson, 1980, p. 102)[9]

Although the concept of information is not mentioned here, we know that Bateson defined information as a difference that makes a difference and it is those differences that are central to his definition of mind. Thus, the definitions here amount to a refined version of the *information-processing paradigm*. This transdisciplinary framework is based on the assumption that it is the software and not the hardware (or wetware) that is the basis for intelligence and mind. It is the system of information processing independently of the material substrate. This is the basic assumption that the whole idea of AI and cognitive science rests upon (Brier, 2007).

Bateson further develops the idea of the biosphere as the ultimate cybernetic mind and others (e.g., Chaitin, 2005) widen the computational concept beyond the Turing computer and image the whole world as a computational system and most processes in nature, mind, culture and machine as being computational.[10] We can call this *pan-computational philosophy*.

In accordance with that tradition, Luhmann allows social systems to "observe" each other and to communicate. But, on the other hand, he differentiates his theory from both the information-processing paradigm and pan-computational philosophy, because in his system theory the embodied psychic system is the indispensable environment for this socio-communicative system to function. It is the vital environment for communicative systems. As such, his theory is not only meta-biological but also meta-psychological. Because, as the individual mind is somewhat constrained by the biology of the body, society is constrained by the capability of

---

9. These ideas were later reiterated in Bateson & Bateson, 2005.
10. If this was not completely clear in Bateson then at least von Foerster picked it up and developed it further.

individuals to experience and creatively imagine. This is not only a biological, but also a psychological constraint, as it has to do with the complexity with which we are able to process meaning, a matter seldom touched upon by Luhmanian theorists.

But it is difficult to find out if Luhmann manages to rise above Bateson's problem with his cybernetic mind definition, which does not seem able to encompass emotions, qualia, and free will (Brier, in press). It seems safe to assume that the dynamics of meaning processing may be very different from the dynamics of information processing, since meaning often has an existential component and is connected to the life world of individuals, organizations, and cultures where myth, religions and political ideologies contribute to the possible frameworks of interpretation. While having specific meanings and communicating them can be considered as codifying information, and different meanings can be based on different codifications because they are communicated in different symbolic generalized media, then the ability to produce meaning in itself is not informational. As Luhmann also sees it, meaning is the field in which we make the significant differences (those that make a difference). I am asking if Luhmann has a theory for this personal and social ability to produce meaning that Gadamer sees as an inevitable part of being human, and that Peirce sees as part of being alive, an ability inherent in all living systems.

Luhmann is inspired by Husserl in thinking that the present actually gets its meaning from the potential. As such, meaning becomes a sort of probabilistic game. Social systems are meaning systems orienting themselves from the operative difference between what is communicated and what is not, in contrast with what was and what could have been, and from there to possible connection in the future to other differences and distinctions of meaning. But as Guenther Teubner[11] points out this cannot constitute a full human subject:

> An uncomfortable, but necessary, consequence of autopoiesis is its anti-individualistic view of contract making. Despite much rhetoric about the revival of an individual's autonomy in modern private law, an understanding of contract as an autopoietic system demonstrates that the individual subject is not the master of the contractual relation. Autopoiesis fragments the subjective actor's rich social fullness into diverse semantic artifacts. The rational economic persona thus created maximises efficiencies and utilities; the rule-bound legal subject fulfills contractual obligations; and the productive actor produces or consumes goods and services. None of these personae expresses the desires of the full human subject. (Teubner, 1997, n.p.)

As Teubner hints, this is not only a problem for system science but also for classical economic model theory, because this theory is a kind of impersonalized deterministic theory based on a first-order or classical system theory and cybernetics, where the subject model has a kind of artificial egocentric intelligence devoid of emotions and irrational beliefs.

---

11. I have used a lot of quotes from renowned Luhmann scholars that have used his theory for many years, in analyzing social phenomena, rather than from Luhmann's own theoretical work. This is done to show how the problems I identify are real for researchers that know Luhmann's theory very well and have tried to apply it for many years. I have, in my previous writings, made the more theoretical analysis also, but this paper constitutes a more pragmatic approach.

From the point of view of Luhmann and many other researchers, a human body-mind is not really a human being when it is without language. It is language that creates the reflective social self-consciousness, which takes us out of animal awareness. I agree with this theory, but it is also one of the reasons why there are no persons in his "systems theory" – understood as embodied subjects with a conscious free will, having causal influences on both natural and social systems in system science – as well as in so many other social sciences.

The human consciousness manifest to the individual[12]—and other observers—is a unity, but not in Luhmann's theory. There are no individual animal or human observers, conceived as souls, human essences, or as transcendent subjects such as Kant and Husserl work with. In systems science, there are only recursive self-organizing patterns of communication. Still a Spencer-Brownian[13]/Luhmann understanding must rest on the basic concept of an observer. Luhmann (1995) explicitly writes how his whole epistemology derives from the fact that all kinds of rational knowing are based on making a difference between the observing system and the environment, a theory derived in turn from Spencer-Brown's *Laws of Form*. But the concept of observation – What are the minimum requirements for a system to be able to observe? – is not consistently theorized in that volume. In Luhmann's theory it seems to be a common sense concept "smuggled" in, whereas in Peirce' s semiotics abduction and semiosis are central theoretical concepts connected to his philosophy of the three basic categories: Firstness, Secondness, and Thirdness.

But it is not clear if an observer needs to have feelings, free will, and qualia as minimum requirements in Spencer-Brown's theory. Spencer-Brown works in a logical framework and does not systematically discuss the ontology necessary to support the epistemology of differences and form that he promotes in *that* work.[14] Based, as it is, on observation or the process of knowing, like second order cybernetic and autopoiesis theory, it does reflect on the ontology of the observing as, Husserl, Heidegger, Merleau-Ponty, Peirce, and Bataille do (Sørensen, 2007).

There is a biological system in Luhmann's system theory, but I am not sure that you can call it *a body* or *the body*. Luhmann's revolutionary idea is to distinguish between biological, psychological, and social autopoiesis. Autopoietic operational closure creates a meaning world of its own that does not exclude outside influences, but selects them to have influence only according to the system's own inner world of meaning and survival. The deep meanings of an individual's psychic world should therefore not be lost within the social, as we often see in theories which seek to socialize the individual or deconstruct the subject through language-centered views

---

12. I am avoiding using the concepts of subject and person as Luhmann does not use the first one and has a special definition for the second.

13. I will use Spencer-Brown in my paper because that is the way he spells his name. I will disregard the fact that the name appearing on many of his books is Spencer Brown and that he has also used the pseudonym James Keys.

14. To my surprise I found he discussed it in other of his less scientific works, written under the name James Keys (especially *It takes Two to Play This Game),* which I will use in my argument.

like discourse theory, structuralism, or a combination of both. The individual should re-emerge in Luhmann's theory as an autopoietic system of its own. But how?

Luhmann essentially identifies two autonomous worlds of meaning based on different autopoietic systems (psychic and socio-communicative operations), which he writes, both operate in the medium of meaning, which is not culture; he has a different view of this term than the received sociological view. Thus psychic systems—which are not the same as classical subjects—have a competitor in the social system, which has the ability to cognize through communication. This latter ability is not available to the psychic system! It only has its own closed world of meaning, thoughts, and feelings.

But in Luhmann's theory it is not clear if there is a center there of free self-conscious will which would be what some theories would call a self-conscious subject. An attempted solution, that is not Luhmann's own, suggests that the self-conscious subject would be the interpenetrations between the psychic and the socio-communicative system. If one sees this connection as a special tight interpenetration one might distinguish it as a system in its own right. I got this idea from Qvortrup (2003) who suggests this solution. But you then have to find a way to integrate the systemic and cybernetic concept of mind with Husserl's and I see no efforts to deal with that deep problem. This makes one wonder what Luhmann's concept of person is and how it is connected to his concepts of psychic system, observer, and ego in his systems theory.

Luhmann's concept of person

Luhmann uses a concept of *ego* connected to a concept of an *alter* to characterize the psychic system, but his ego is observational and thus not a traditional subject It is nevertheless the basis for the creation of the *person*. The person, in Luhmann's systems theory, is only brought into existence as the social dimension of ego and alter. He writes:

> Finally, in the *social dimension* ego and alter are personalized for the purpose of attribution or are identities with specific social systems. Even though they always function as ego and as alter (for another ego), they retain their identities, names, and addresses. Nonetheless, the social schematism does not intend these systems as objective givens of the world; instead, it only concerns their functioning as ego or alter and the consequences that result. (Luhmann, 1995, p. 85)

This means, that in this theoretical framework, we do not have a personal core with a free will, and a communication-independent great variety of qualia that controls the communications and actions, and that further can be held responsible for them in the socio-communicative context. Rather it is the other way round, that the communication creates conditions to which the psychic system can make a structural coupling, through interpenetration. We are discussing an abstraction, in which one essentially separates out the communications that are occurring, as if nothing else existed except communications. Each autopoietic system can be seen as a unique ongoing dynamics that cannot be controlled from elsewhere. Functional differentiation can be understood as the emergence of a series of autonomous systems based on operations of their own. As psychic systems are autopoietic and silent they can only contact each other through social systems and these are communicative systems. "The system of society consists of communications. There are no other elements, no further substance but communications" (Luhmann, 1990, p. 100). The central assumption of his social theory is that society has to be interpreted as a system of communication and functional differentiation.

Luhmann also makes a clear distinction between social roles and personality (Luhmann, 1995, pp. 316-17). His concept of person is thus differentiated from the psychic system and the social roles and role expectations in other theories:

> We would like to call psychic systems that are observed by other psychic systems or by social systems *persons*. The concept of a personal system is thus one that involves an observer perspective, in which self-observation (so to speak, self-personalization) can be included. Because one can assume that any theory of psychic systems actualizes an observer perspective, one can speak of psychic and personal systems almost in the same sense. However, the conceptual distinction remains important because the concept of person emphasizes relevance for an observer ...We will not speak of psychic the "psychicalization" but of the "personalization" of social systems' reproduction on the personal attributions of the participants. (Luhmann, 1995, p. 109)

Thus Luhmann's concept of person manifests as a social function, an assembly of expectations inside from the ego and outside from other persons.

There is further a clear differentiation between consciousness and communication although they depend on each other. In fact, Luhmann suggests getting rid of *person* altogether, except as an attribution by an observer using *person* to notify a set of expectations from another assembly of biological, psychic and socio-communicative systems that other philosophies would call a human being. But the concept human being is one that Luhmann only uses when he slips into common-sense language. This is revealed in what Luhmann further writes about the concept of person:

> By *person* we do not mean psychic systems, not to mention human beings as such. Instead, a person is constituted for the sake of ordering behavioral expectations that can be fulfilled by her and her alone. One can be a person for oneself and for others. Being a person requires that one draws and binds expectations to oneself with the help of one psychic system and body, including expectations about oneself with regard to others. The more expectations and the more different types of them that are individualized in this way, the more complex the person ...With this concept of person and with the distinction between person and psychic system, sociology can gain access to themes that now have been reserved for the literary tradition, but that include typically modern experiences. ... no secure path of knowledge leads from the person into the depth of the psychic system, but that all attempts that are not contend with the person and really seek to know another sink into the abyss of the always-also-otherwise-possible. Furthermore, this explains why a person copies personality models or gestures (Stendhal), nevertheless with unique results: one copies a person as a model into a concrete, and therefore always distinctive, psychic system. (Luhmann, 1995, p. 315)

Thus Luhmann clearly wants to shift the weight from the inner psychic forces to the outer socio-communicative forces in creating the person. He is somewhat in line with

Peirce here as Peirce does not believe we have the ability of introspection or deep intuition.

It is clear that Luhmann's socio-communicative systems are not subjects or persons in themselves. Thus there seem to be no *locus observantis*. It is not that this problem debunks the theory as such. Bio-medicine does not have one either, but only sees the human subject as a physiological body and the agent as the brain. It is useful anyhow, but it has a problem of how to relate its description to the human subject as a legal and morally responsible person, not to mention the problem concerning what kind of causal influences this human subject can have on physiology and on communication. Unfortunately it has become more and more acceptable to refer to us, the subject or our consciousness, as the brain. Thus Luhmann—and most cybernetics and system theory—shares a deep problem with those that see ontology within the sciences as eliminative materialism.

The psychic system and meaning

Another problem is that first person experiences including emotions and qualia are principally accepted as real in the psyche in Luhmann's systems theory as inspired by Husserl's phenomenology, but he does not really seem to have a theory of consciousness.[15] The fact that the psyche is a closed system that thinks and feels, does not seem to violate Husserl's thinking, as he does not want to attend to any ontological questions outside consciousness as such, and prefers to address the unity of conscious being before subject and object. But, as I have shown above, these concepts have now real foundations in cybernetics and general system theory. Thus there seems to be a contradiction between some of the elements Luhmann tries to integrate to reach his new and transdisciplinary system theory.

Luhmann's system theory of social autopoiesis is supposed not to give primacy to either the individual or the collective, but to emergent communication systems. It is an important point in his system theory to realize that functional differentiation and autopoiesis mean that it is no longer possible to direct and control social systems to move along predetermined paths. Rather, movement can be the result of interventions from external systems, such as politics, the law, corporate management, or individual actors inside the system. Teubner 1997 writes:

> Social autopoiesis argues for the modern contract to be seen as being primarily about inter-discursivity, not the inter-personal relations between two actors with their own goals and resources. This means giving up the idea of the dominance of the psychic inner worlds of the actors and their subjective meanings and individual resources. Of course, a contract always needs an agreement between at least two actors, whether they are real people or fictitious entities, like an enterprise acting as a 'legal person'. But the unmediated relation of such contractual inter-subjectivity has been supplanted today by the greater complexities of inter-textuality between several functionally differentiated worlds of meaning.

---

15. Again, he does write about consciousness and emotions at the level of science, but he does not have a philosoph-ical framework, where he defines then as theoretical concepts.

The participants in this process can be considered as 'social homunculi of modernity', in that they are artificial personae arising purely from social discourse. The contract can then be seen as being not between physical beings but between highly artificial structures, whose interactions form an autopoietic system of contract that has a logic and dynamic of its own. The interests that people think they are realizing or exchanging through a contract are therefore not their personal interests, but are social or discursive products. (Teubner, 1997)

This clearly shows that emotions, judgment, and free will of individual subjects do not really have any causal influence on what is communicated. The subject can only be structurally coupled to it. Communication acts produce new artificial structures that have dynamics of their own and can self-reproduce through autopoiesis.

As in many other sociological and systemic-cybernetic-functionalistic systems, on the one hand, and, on the other, the biochemical, physiological and neurophysiological scientific understanding of the human, the idea of any causality stemming from a first person experiential subject would destroy the foundations of Luhmann's theory. This, then—like the theories of the natural sciences—gives us the problem of how to reintegrate the knowledge gained in and with the theory into a common-sense world of responsible persons and causal subject. But where natural science will not accept any concept of meaning, Luhmann builds his system theory in part on a Husserlian phenomenological foundation interpreted in a special way as communication. This seems to take the concept of meaning as given, but unaccounted for, though still not a primitive as one might say it is in Husserl's phenomenology, which theoretically explores the world before it is split into subjects and object as done by the sciences. Leydesdorff also sees this problem and quotes Habermas critical view on it:

From the perspective of cultural studies and critical theory, Luhmann's communication-theoretical approach in sociology can still be read as a meta-biology: while biologists take the development of life as a given, Luhmann tends to treat the development of meaning as a cultural *given*. Meaning is no longer considered as constructed in communication, but meaning processing precedes and controls communication as an independent variable. Habermas (1987) made the argument about this meta-biological foundation of Luhmann's systems theory most forcefully:

In this way, subject-centered reason is replaced by systems rationality. As a result, the critique of reason carried out as a critique of metaphysics and a critique of power, which we have considered in these lectures, is deprived of its object. To the degree that systems theory does not merely make its specific disciplinary contribution with the system of the sciences but also penetrates the lifeworld with its claim to universality, it replaces metaphysical background convictions with metabiological ones. Hence, the conflict between objectivists and subjectivists loses its point. (Habermas, 1987, at p. 385)

In other words, Habermas appreciates Luhmann's distinction between psychic and social systems, but he challenges us to bring the critique of metaphysical issues (of providing meaning to events in a dialectics) back into this metabiological perspective that processes meaning without intentionality, that is, as a scientistic objectivation. (Leydesdorff, in press, n.p.)

I agree with Habermas and with Leydesdorff here. Since we know that Luhmann is not one of those cybernetic information theorists that believe that information is an objective thing existing in both nature and culture by itself without any observers, then how is it possible to have meaning in socio-communicative systems without embodied cognitive intentionality? In his note to the text above the Habermas quote, Leydesdorff writes with great insight about the paradoxical nature of Luhmann's metaphysics:

> Luhmann alternates between this meta-biological model using concepts of functional differentiation and structural coupling for the explanation, and a meta-theological one where meaning seems to be given transcendentally as a substance analogous to life (Luhmann, 1986). The meta-theological metaphor is pursued by Luhmann by grounding his theory on the operation of the distinction (that is, on a paradox). The *first* distinction is then Lucifer's breaking away from God as the devil (Luhmann, 1990, at pp. 118 ff.) or, in other words, the problem of the Theodicy, that is, the origin of evil in the world (Leibniz, [1710] 1962). (Leydesdorff, in press, n.p.)

I agree with this analysis. Meta-biological theory here means that the system above the biological description level and/or ontological level has biological properties as life, cognition and purposefulness, which is clearly what is ascribed to the socio-communicative systems in a mysterious way in Luhmann's theory. This has always puzzled me. How can a communicative system have agency in itself? All there is are systems, and especially meta-biological communicative systems that seem capable of making distinctions. Therefore—I would claim—has agency in the form of being able to observe as observations and communications can only be inferred from actions. In Luhmann's system theory the socio-communicative does build on the biological and psychological systems in the usual understanding, because these are autopoietic and cannot therefore transfer any of their own agencies to the communicative system. They are only environments for the communication system, to which it can make both structural couplings and interpenetrations.

According to Luhmann meaning processing can be considered as providing social and psychic systems with the ability to distinguish between actual and possible states of the system in terms of expectations. Information is defined as a selection by the system, and not as uncertainty as in Shannon's information concept and theory. But we also know that the system in Luhmann's system theory, be it biological, psychic or socio-communicative, is defined as an operation at an interface with an environment. Luhmann writes:

> The three components – information, utterance and understanding – must ... not be interpreted as functions, as acts, or as horizons for validity claims (which is not to deny that these are also possible ways of applying the components). They are also not building blocks of communication that can exist independently and need to be put together by someone - by whom, the subject? Rather, it is a matter of different selections, whose selectivity and field of selection can be constituted only through communication. There is no information outside of communication; there is no utterance outside of communication; there is no understanding outside of communication. This is so not in a merely causal sense, according to which the information would have to be the cause of the utterance and the utterance the cause of understanding, but rather in the circular sense of mutual presupposition. ...A system of communication is therefore a fully closed system that generates the components of which it consists through communication itself. (Luhmann, 2002, p.160)

Luhmann defined social systems as consisting of communications and their attribution as action. He claimed that systems of communication reproduce by linking communications to one another over time. *Communications cannot directly be observed. Therefore they are theoretical explanatory concepts.* One can only make inferences about them on the basis of the observable interactions among the agents, which again are the communicative systems. Thus where is the phenomenological aspect? Where does first-order experience come in?

Phenomenology in an autopoietic system

It is well known that Maturana is not happy with what Luhmann has done with his biologically-based autopoiesis concept. To Maturana autopoiesis is a biological concept, not a general abstract formal concept from which one can form the idea of psychic and communicative systems (Mingers, 1995). Willke sees this problem, too, and describes it very precisely The model concept of autopoietic system originated in biology but was made into a general abstract concept by Luhmann, making it possible for him to distinguish between biological, psychic, and social autopoietic systems:

> Maturana tackles organised complexity by a concept of autopoiesis, which was derived from the workings of the brain, starting with the eye of a frog. His idea of operational closure is of a self-reproducing system within the clearly demarcated limits and boundaries of a cell across which there can be no instructive interaction or direct intervention. … Maturana (1982) argues that the only relation or connection between autonomous systems is through 'co-evolution', which is a kind of ecological niche that presents avenues of adaptation, development and reaction leading to new systems. However, Maturana is not very clear about how co-evolution actually happens. … Luhmann's definition of autopoiesis is very different to Maturana's. He starts from a viewpoint which regards Maturana's cell-inspired biological view as one which doesn't make sense for a social system (Luhmann 1983) and investigates what the idea of autopoiesis might mean as an analytical tool for building models to help in the observation of social systems. Maturana, on the other hand, rules out the feasibility of applying his model of autopoiesis to social systems, although he does implicitly discuss systems of higher social orders than the basic cell.
>
> Luhmann fits autopoiesis into a social science context that emphasizes the need for 'tools for thinking' to assist in the process of observing social systems and constructing models to analyze information gleaned from the observations. This version of autopoiesis transforms the notion of co-evolution into one of 're-entry', or reconstruction, between functionally differentiated and closed worlds of meaning. … Re-entry is not about adaptation or direct intervention, but is a complex process involving interaction between different logics, systems, firms, etc, which do not result in a 'meeting of minds'. Re-entry recognises how each autopoietic system uses its own logic to build its internal models of other systems. For example, a company builds an internal model of its market or the school system builds internal models of the economy, history, science, and so on." (Willke, 1997, n.p.)

Nevertheless a solution can be found to this problem by considering the psychic and the socio-communicative systems as self-organized systems with closure, or derived and dependant autopoietic systems, meaning that they depend on biological autopoiesis to be able to exist (cf. Mingers, 1995). In this way we can still make Luhmann's very useful idea work. But we have underlined communication's dependence on embodiment, more than Luhmann usually cared to do. Further we cannot call the psychic and socio-communicative systems second-order and third-order autopoietic systems as Maturana reserved that for the human body and then viewed society as a self-organizing conglomerate of interacting bodies, but refused to use the term autopoiesis for this system. But apart from this there seem to be no inconsistencies in the compatibility of the frameworks behind the two theories. Actually, they share the same faults of combining an evolutionary view with an open ontology and no explicit theory of mind (Brier, 2007) – or, at best, either relying on Bateson's theory of mind or just being compatible with it. Bateson, of course, did not include first-order experience.

In Brier (in press) I have demonstrated Bateson's ontology to be pure Wienerian cybernetics. This is a world view where the mind dimension is understood as consisting of information understood as neg-entropy. This is combined with a view of the material dimension as compatible with the probabilistic complexity view of thermodynamics as Boltzmann saw it and (after Wiener) it is further developed into non-equilibrium thermodynamics with dissipative structures by Prigogine. Luhmann has avoided being that explicit and instead adopted an open realistic ontology combined with an evolutionary and complexity view (Luhmann, 1995).

Many of my Luhmanian colleagues (e.g., Åkerstrøm, 2003[16]) seem to think that this is a smart move on Luhmann's part and argue that he does not have to say anything about ontology because his theory is second-order and therefore just observing observations. Still we agree that second-order observations are first-order observations too. Therefore one cannot escape an ontological background idea (a metaphysics) and there has to be a view of some possible categories of mind and matter or structure and processes in nature that makes cognition possible and of survival value.[17] Some basic categories—like the ones Aristotle and Kant work with and Peirce revised—need to be defined. That is a responsibility in science and scholarship one cannot reasonable avoid when forging a major system like Luhmann's.

This current perspective is based on Brier (2007) where I have developed, what I consider, a minimum ontology in order to make theories of information, cognition, and communication. In order to make (non-solipsistic) observations communicable in language you need at least:

1. an embodied observer,[18] and
2. some objects or differences outside one's individual mind to refer to or represent in[19]

---

16. I thank Professor Niels Åkerstrøm, with whom I share a department, for many engaging discussions on this subject where I think we end up agreeing to disagree.
17. A point also made by Ole Thyssen in his paper "Luhmann and Epistemology" (2004).
18. As we have no knowledge of unmanifest observers we can communicate with in unmanifest languages that we can then transfer between humans. Although the individual human being may have such internal experiences (of revelations and hearing inner voices), we yet have to see convincing evidence of direct (non-verbal, non-bodily) communication between consciousnesses of these and other experiences and emotions.
19. Or else one ends up in nominalism or radical constructivism or even solipsism as Peirce saw it around 1890, deciding that Secondness had to be real. From then he started changing his pragmatism into pragmaticism.

3. a system of signs for communication with other humans (as there are no private languages that we can know of); and

4. you must accept that these other humans are real (at least as real as you are),[20] and

5. are living in both nature, as well as

6. society and culture.[21]

All these elements have to be accepted as real in order to make a combined signification and communication theory relating back to social common sense. After the fact, I have realized that I am pretty much following Merleau-Ponty's (1945/2002, p. 421-25) argument in what one could call a ontologizing of phenomenology into the real world,[22] but I also have also been inspired by Lakoff and Johnson's (1999) embodied cognitive semantics.

This minimum framework is necessary if one wants to avoid the paradoxes in radical constructivism, in which we create the world through our individual and collective observation coined in the concepts of natural language.[23] In these radical constructivist theories there is a strong belief that we have no access to any structures[24] or partly structured processes outside the human mind and communication. I have developed arguments against these theories further in Brier (2007). Stjernfelt's (2001) argument on how iconicity works is also much in line with mine.

Kant (1990) saw the sense experiences as chaotic before being ordered by the categories of the human intellect and thought we cannot in historical time expect to know the thing in itself.[25] This claim of *chaoticy* cannot be the whole truth, since the perceptions must come from some differences whereby there is a certain stability in the world if we are to make sense and signs of them. There must be differences that can make a difference! As Peirce points out, then, order and understanding both belong to the same category; namely his category of Thirdness. They are interdependent. Total chaos makes no sense. A series of random numbers cannot be represented in any shorter form than it already has, as Chaitin (1988) points out. There has to be some sort of regularity in it for the human mind or the computer to make a representation of it. Von Foerster realized that:

> The second thing that I see: I have the theory of observing, I am myself an observer, so I am doing the observing, I am including myself into the loop of argumentation. And in which way can I handle that? So, my proposition here is now that in the second phase of cybernetic evolution a serious

---

20. This far I am in agreement with Thyssen's view (developed in Thyssen, 2006) and von Foerster.

21. A concept Luhmann wants to avoid but cannot. See Laermanns' article in this issue.

22. I thank my philosophical colleague, Asger Sørensen, for bringing this side of Merleau-Ponty to my attention. In my view Merleau-Ponty's development of phenomenology brings it closer to Peirce's phaneroscopy, because it is also both phenomenological as well as realistic in its epistemology and ontology.

23. This is what is often called cookie cutter realism, because the world is seen as undifferentiated dough, in which the word cut the forms. I would call this a kind of *non-essence magic*, in contrast to the theory of magic where the words work on things or can create them because they represent their (transcendental or immanent) essence.

24. In time and /or in space.

25. Still, as Peirce points out, that should be the leading goal of all science. It is the ideal we strive for.

attempt was made to cope with the epistemological and the methodological Grundlagen propositions that appear if you begin seriously to include the observer in the descriptions of his observations. With the first appearance of Maturana's autopoietic system for us all who were working in this field the suggestion was immediately made that for the first time we can start here with a biological theory of autonomy, because if we do not stipulate autonomy, observation is not an act of interaction or something like that, observation would just be a transducer kind of an idea, the concept of observation will not appear, only the concept of a transducer, a recorder. (von Foerster, 1981, p. 104)

Thus a biological autonomous body is needed, but also some structure in the environment. Von Foerster realized that to accept the reality of the biological systems of the observer lead into further acceptance about the structure of the environment.

I propose to continue the use of the term "self-organizing system, "whilst being aware of the fact that this term becomes meaningless, unless the system is in close contact with an environment, which possesses available energy and order, and with which our system is in a state of perpetual interaction, such that it somehow manages to "live" on the expenses of this environment. (von Foerster, 1984, p. 4)

As he also says (von Foerster, 2003 p. 1) "There are no such things as self-organizing systems!" That is because the second law of thermodynamics would lose its validity if the systems were not connected to the use of neg-entropy. So both the self-organizing system and the energy and order of the environment have to be given some kind of pre-given objective reality. Later in the same paper he goes on:

to show that there is some structure in our environment …by pointing out that we are obviously not in the dreadful state of Boltzmann's "Heat Death." Hence presently still the entropy increases, which means that there must be some order—at least now—otherwise we could not loose it.

Let me briefly summarize the points I have made until now:

1. By a self-organizing system I mean that part of a system that eats energy and order from its environment.
2. There is a reality of the environment in a sense suggested by the acceptance of the principle of relativity.
3. The environment has structure. (von Foerster 1984 p.8)

I find these arguments compelling and I do not understand[26] why they are not picked up in constructivist second-order cybernetics since von Foerster is the father of it and a great inspiration for Luhmann. Anyway, the same point was picked up by Peirce around 1890 when he left his nominalism and accepted the necessary independent existence of Secondness.

One needs a theory of those basic structures of order and concepts as Plato and Aristotle saw it, but without the ability to think in material evolution theory building on irreversibility. Time is brought in partly through thermodynamics and partly through the recursive operation of making observation by a living embodied system in

---

26. Except that they destroy the world view of so many radical constructivists.

language or sign play (Varela, 1975; Brier, 2002; Brier, 2000a). Peirce also realizes that we can only know though making signs and that we need a little time to make them thus our knowing is never about the immediate now. Further, one requires a theory of mind, consciousness and of their relation to matter and energy and of how forms and qualities come into existence. Here it is not enough to theorize how to order perception with categories as Kant did. This is why Peirce's metaphysics of Firstness, Secondness and Thirdness and it relation to Spencer-Brown's metaphysics behind his *Law of Forms* becomes so interesting. The way one conceptualizes categories is foundational to one's philosophical framework.

Luhmann attempts to solve this problem by combining his new concept of a psychic system with Husserl's phenomenological theory of the experiences of consciousness before any distinction is made between subject and object or between inside and outside! But like Maturana I think that Husserl would probably not be too happy with Luhmann reallocating Husserl's theory and concepts from the intentionality of consciousness and its field of meaning to the distinction between system and environment and communication between social systems. In general, Husserl only wants to address what appears in consciousness:

> We call experiences in an ego's experiential unity 'phenomena'. *Phenomenology* is accordingly the theory of experiences in general, inclusive of all matters, whether real (reellen) or intentional, given in experiences, and evidently discoverable in them. Pure phenomenology is accordingly the theory of the essence of 'pure phenomena', the phenomena of a 'pure consciousness' or of a pure 'ego': it does not build on the ground, given by transcendent apperception, of physical and animal, and so of psycho-physical nature, it makes no empirical assertions, it propounds no judgement which relate to objects transcending consciousness: it establishes no truths concerning natural realities, whether physical or psychic ... It rather takes all apperceptions and judgemental assertations, which point beyond what is given in adequate, purely immanent intuition, which point beyond the pure stream of consciousness, and treats them purely as the experiences they are in themselves: it subjects them to a purely immanent, purely descriptive examination into essence. This examination of essence is also pure in a second sense, in the sense of Ideation; this is an *a priory* examination in the true sense. ... did not speak of psychological facts and laws in an 'objective' nature, only of pure possibilities and necessities, which belong to any form of the pure 'cogito.' (Husserl, 1970/1921, p. 859)

Merleau-Ponty (1945/2002) points out in the foreword to his *Phenomenology of Perception* that Husserl's phenomenology is not a fully developed philosophy, as such. Husserl does not have a full fledged ontological theory of mind and meaning's place in the world and how consciousness, emotions, qualia and free will are produced related to an ontology and an epistemology. This is the case in the sense that he did not give a solution to the dilemma between realism and anti-realism in the problem of perception and knowledge. But that might not be quite true. What he did, though, was to assume that the spatio-temporal objects in one's own life world exist independently of one's subjective perspective and the particular experiences I perform. Not in some outside reality, but from the immanence of one's own experience, he deducts that they are part of an objective reality in that immanent perceptual objects have a transcendent origin (Husserl, 1977). Through the *epoché* method of variation and putting non-objective features in parenthesis, phenomenological analysis aims at specifying the *noema* or the common ground of both veridical perceptions and hallucinations. In any moment noema display an inexhaustible number of unperceived features, only some of which will be intuitively presented in one's observation. Husserl's notion of the intersubjectivity of spatio-temporal objects does not presuppose that any other subject can observe such an object from her own perspective (Husserl, 1999, pp. 122-127, 131-133).

This rather Platonic vision is a strange thing to most realists and scientific researchers, although these are often Platonist when it comes to the function of mathematics and logics in the mind and the universe, namely as that order and rationality (Logos) that unites subject and object. Here the analysis is based on an investigation of the outer world and an assumption that the order and dynamics of the material/energetic aspect of reality is what unites object and subject. But Husserl went within, to a world prior to the distinction of subject and object, claiming that to be foundational for any philosophy of being. He imagined that the transcendental patterns of perception would be the same for all[27] as foundational forms in the universal constitution. He believe that going in through the individual mind analyzing "up" to the general level of cognitive being before the split in subject and object, he can find the absolute ground of being or reality. But he does not deal with, nor approve of, the sciences' attempt at finding the basis of being by going through the "outer" reality using a combination of empirical and rational analysis to find "natural laws" and then making the connection back to consciousness through materiality. Luhmann does neither of these things, as he—inspired by Spencer-Brown—starts with observation and let the observational knowing make the distinction between system and environment. Thus it cannot be the system created in the distinction that makes the original observation! We are in a different setting than Husserl's! But which one?

Husserl does not work with a dual reality or the social-linguistic reality as a third intersubjective reality or a distinction between animate and inanimate nature. It is interesting that although C. S. Peirce starts in the same place as Husserl[28] he ends up in a very different metaphysics that reinstates science as the most important way to knowledge and he denies the possibility of direct introspection. This is one of what he call the the four incapacities of the human mind (Peirce, 1992, pp. 28-51). Husserl completely shies away from empirical scientific investigations on the object world as

---

27. This may be where his phenomenology, seen from the vantage point of Luhmann's system theory, can be related to Spencer-Brown's *Laws of Form*, as these forms could be the noema. But I have not found any text on this from either Spencer-Brown's or Luhmann's hand. But who has read all of Luhmann's writings?

28. Peirce's phaneroscopy differs from Husserl's phenomenology, with the former's three basic categories: "I use the word *phaneron* to mean all that is present to the mind in any sense or in any way whatsoever, regardless of whether it be fact or figment. I examine the phaneron and I endeavor to sort out its elements according to the complexity of their structure. I thus reach my three categories." (A Draft of a Letter to Calderoni, CP 8.213, c.1905). "The three categories are supposed to be the three kinds of elements that attentive perception can make out in the phenomenon." (A Letter to William James, CP 8.264-5, 1903). "After trying to solve the puzzle in a direct speculative, a physical, a historical, and a psychological manner, I finally concluded the only way was to attack it as Kant had done from the side of formal logic" (Comments on 'On a New List of Categories', CP 1.563, c. 1898). In 1903 (Peirce, 1997) developed his last version of pragma*t*icism (as he called it to differentiate it from James' utilitarian version of pragmatism).

leading into any kind of deep knowledge that can put us on the track of finding foundations for being and knowledge.

The question is, then, how Luhmann can use Husserl's phenomenology in his system theory, starting with the distinction between system and environment that Husserl wants to avoid in analyzing what was before. The paradigmatic distinction Husserl wanted to avoid was most of all in the form of the distinction between subject and object. Luhmann exchanges that for the distinction between (observing) system and environment. The problem is that Luhmann (1995) simply starts in his system theory in a way that is contrary to Husserl's the moment he begins using him. Luhmann is quite clear on this:

> Auf die frage, wie denn Erlebnis als Erlebnis möglich sei, hätte Husserl vermutlich mit Hinweis auf die Transzendentale Faktizität und Selbstzugänglichkeit des Erlebens geantwortet. Von hier aus (und ohne Widerspruch dazu) ist es kein weiter Schritt zu einer systemtheoretichen Reformulierung. Sie würde lauten: Erleben ist dadurch möglich, das eine rekursive Erzeugung und Reproduktion dieser Innen/Aussen-Differenz gelingt. (Luhmann, 1995, p. 33)

By making this reformulation with an inner/outer distinction basic he brings Husserl's phenomenology on the same footing as Spencer-Brown's *Laws of Form* along with his own claim that one must start with making a distinction, or a difference that makes a difference. Thus he chooses to start with the difference between system and environment. That distinction is the first vital one in order to create systems and forms at all for Luhmann and Spencer-Brown. But thereby he breaks with a fundamental idea in the foundation of Husserl's phenomenology. He also changes the ontological view on the transcendental analysis. By doing this Luhmann thinks he can then import Husserl's phenomenological view into his theory of an autopoietic psychic system and thereby use it in his overall theory and the idea of the silent psyche, where only communication communicates. Luhmann is very clear about this in *Social Systems*:

> Husserl described phenomenologically how the world, although an endless horizon guaranties its own determinability. This leads directly to the idea of the typology or the typological restriction of all experience and action with which phenomenological sociology has continued to work. A self-interference of infinity in the direction of specification, however, cannot be adequately understood as the mere content of experience and the condition under which experience can take place. The decomposition of the world into dimensions on the basis of meaning, including the ascription of a constitutive double horizon to every dimension, as presented here, makes possible a further step in the analysis; above all, it enables a clearer depiction of the conditions of possibility for determining meaning.

> In agreement with a basic premise of evolutionary theory, we do not assume that the world respecifies itself to determination. Instead we begin from the fact that there must be mechanisms that, regardless of what triggers them, produce adequate determinacy. The difference between meaning and the world is formed for those process of the continual self-determination of meaning as the difference between order and perturbation, between information and noise. Both are, and both remain, necessary. The unity of the difference is and remains the basis for operation. ... The typology of the essential forms that actually guide daily conducts results from previous determinations of meaning, which cannot be attributed to the world (in the sense of an ontology of

essential forms or to the subject (in the sense of a theory of its constitution). Instead, these forms follow from the fact that the meaning-related operations of self-referential systems are triggered by problems (primary disjunction, irreversibility, dissent) (Luhmann, 1995, pp. 82-83)

Like both Popper and Pierce, he claims that knowledge does not start with either sense experience in the form of data or rational thinking in the form of logic, or that it is based on transcendental ideas or immanent form that has always already made the vital and essential distinction. But there is a problem, a discrepancy—and if I understand him right—this leads to making a distinction on the basis of meaning that reduces the chaotic complexity of the world to something that observing-socio-communicative systems (they are not subjects!) can handle. Thus, in one elegant fell swoop Luhmann breaks both with the classical scientific belief in a world of "natural kinds" governed by universal laws as well as Husserl's rather Platonic form of consciousness. Like Kant, he breaks both with empiricism and rationalism. He clearly, then, connects to Spencer-Brown's paradigmatic reformulation of cognition and observing in the form of making a distinction, which then—in their view—leads to a general dynamic logic of form. Spencer-Brown writes in the foreword to his book *Laws of Form*:

> The theme of this book is that a universe comes into being when a space is severed or taken apart. The skin of a living organism cuts off an outside from an inside. So does the circumference of a circle in a plane. By tracing the way we represent such a severance, we can begin to reconstruct, with an accuracy and coverage that appear almost uncanny, the basic forms underlying linguistic, mathematical, physical, and biological science, and can begin to see how the familiar laws of our own experience follow inexorable from the original act of severance. The act is itself already remembered, even if unconsciously, as our first attempt to distinguish different things in a world where, in the first place, the boundaries can be drawn anywhere we please. At this stage the universe cannot be distinguished from how we act upon it, and the world may seem like shifting sand beneath our feet. … it becomes evident that the laws relating such forms are the same in any universe. It is this sameness, the idea that we can find a reality which is independent of how the universe actually appears, that lends such fascination to the study of mathematics. (Spencer-Brown, 1969, p. v)

Not that I disagree, but for one thing Luhmann cannot use Husserl on this basis and, second, he needs to establish some sort of ontology that explains why there is order rather than chaos in the world as such, when there are no basic structures or processes in his ontology.[29] It is inconsistent to work with an observer, a world, distinction and consciousness and claim that one's ontology is completely open and that there are no structures at all – and by the way: who is remembering? As we shall see later on, Luhmann's use of Spencer-Brown locks him in certain ontological limits.[30] From

---

29. See Qvortrup's article in this volume that analyzes and discusses aspects of this problem.
30. But let me just point out that Peirce gives a solution to this problem of the beginning of structures and concepts by operating with a concept of vagueness of forms and concepts in the beginning of evolution, and he further introduces his basic category of Firstness in his onto-epistemology which is a monistic hylozoist's theory of mind and matter as a continuum, where mind in the beginning is partly hidden inside matter (Brier, in press). He does not believe in these sharp distinctions. He writes: "I object to absolute universality, absolute exactitude, absolute necessity, being attributed to any proposition that does not deal with the Alpha and the Omega, in the which I do not include any object of ordinary knowledge" (CP 6.607, 1893).

Spencer-Brown's formulations it seems that his work is based in some sort of objective idealism or mystic vision of a one or one-ness that is dividing through an original act of observation. In *It takes two to play this Game* he write that *Law of Forms* is:

> An account of the emergence of physical archetypes, presented as a rigorous essay in mathematics.
>
> Starting with nothing and making one mark, we trace the first of all the eternal forms. From these we obtain two axioms, and proceed from here to develop theorems. (Keyes, 1971, p. 109)

The problem of the transcendental ego, subject or self

But there is also another problem. Husserl (1999) has a transcendental ego concept – with a monadic structure – that seems rather central to his theory structure as it was to Kant. It is the life world and the transcendental subject that creates that field of meaning, in which the intentionality of consciousness operate in the Husserlian phenomenology by being the center in which all perceptual data is conversing.

Luhmann takes Husserl's concept of meaning from this construction in the same move as he deconstructs it! It seems to me that Luhmann has not formulated anything like this in his theory, because he wants to work with autonomous autopoietic systems without centres. Although his psychic system is a kind of monad in its autopoietic self-constitution, then, it is not an ego and it does not participate in a life world. Its environment is the biological autopoietic system on the one hand and the socio-communicative system on the other. As the psychic system is an autopoietic system it is forced to interpenetrate it to create a functional relationship. The psychic system is an alter/ego which again has this inside/outside structure; Husserl wants to avoid this, but it guarantees dynamics in irreversible time in Luhmann's system theory. Luhmann (1995, p.80) writes:

> To begin with, it is important to avoid combining the social and facts dimensions. This was and is the cardinal mistake of humanities. Human kind was variously understood as distinct from animals, was equipped with sociality (animal sociale) and temporality (memoria, phantasia, prudential), and was finally declared to be the subject. Even today the theory of the subject still accepts a single internal/external relationship where object and social dimensions should de distinguish as different twofold horizons. But human subject always remains one privileged object among others – as can be seen in the tendencies to re-anthropologize transcendental philosophy. (Luhmann,1995, p. 80)

First, then, Husserl was reluctant to re-anthropologize transcendental philosophy. He wanted to build a theory that preceded any subject-object distinctions. As such, he did not enter upon any theory of the external world in the form of an ontology in which to place the mind or visa versa. In a way, both Luhmann and Spencer-Brown took the same route, but neither of them had the same framework as Husserl. One could say that Luhmann stayed inside the living observing systems through his use of autopoiesis theory. There is, in Luhmann's theory, no information transfer from the outer world into the autopoietic system. One could then say that by accepting and using a biological and a socio-communicative autopoietic system Luhmann's move comes close to Merleau-Ponty's. But, as far as I know, he never mentions that and he does not do the same painstaking work as Merleau-Ponty does with Husserl's phenomenological theory in order to make his enlargement of it as consistent as possible. To Luhmann this social aspect is what destroys Husserl's transcendental ego into the dynamic process of alter/ego. He writes:

> The social dimension concerns what one at any time accepts as like oneself, as an"alter ego," and it articulates the relevance of this assumption for every experience of the world and fixing of meaning. The social dimension possesses world-universal relevance, because if there is an alter ego, then he is, just like the ego, relevant to all objects and to all themes. (Luhmann, 1995, p. 80)

Thus, Luhmann establishes the social and its dynamism in a way quite different from Husserl and denies the social as a process of intersubjectivity. This is clear when he further writes (Luhmann, 1995, p. 81) that alter ego are two

> horizons that collect and bind together meaningful references. Thus the social dimension is also constituted by a twofold horizon; it is relevant to the extent that in experience and action it becomes apparent that the interpretative perspective a system relates to itself are not shared by others. Here, as well, the horizons of ego and alter means further exploration will have no end. Because a twofold horizon is constitutive of the independence of a meaning dimension, what is social cannot be traced back to the conscious performance of a monadic subject. This has been the downfall of all attempts to establish a theory of the subjective constitution of "intersubjectivity" ... If what is social in meaning themes is experienced as reference to (possible distinct) interpretive perspectives, then this experience can no longer be attributed to a subject." (Luhmann, 1995, p. 81)

It remains obscure to me what it is, then, that is that is capable of experiencing the social dimension of meaning. Yet, his theory seems only able to point at one thing, namely the socio-communicative system in itself as an autopoietic system. As his famous formulation goes: *Only communication communicates*,[31] although he does realize that an interpenetration with the silent psychic system, which only thinks, is necessary. Even so, to my knowledge Luhmann never really develops that point.

This is thus a special autopoietic version of system theory, as it was not Luhmann that invented system theory but Bertalanffy. But Luhmann added to Bertalanffy's idea of living systems as thermodynamically open the notion that they are also organizationally closed. Further he (Luhmann, 1995, chap. 3) then introduces the idea of double contingency between those two horizons that cannot really see each other as central to the emergence of social systems.

> Two black boxes, by whatever accident, come to have dealings with one another. Each determines its own behaviour by complex self-referential operations within its own boundaries. Each assumes the same about the other. Therefore, however many efforts they exert and however much time they spend, the black boxes remain opaque to one another. (Luhmann, 1995, p. 109)

---

31. It is on its way to becoming as famous as Spencer-Brown's *Make a distinction* as well as Bateson's *information is a difference that makes a difference*, on which Luhmann also builds. See his use of Bateson in Luhmann, 1995.

The social system as communication simply *emerges* from this double contingency. But how? *Emergence* is such a nice word to use when there is no precise description of the process and it preconditions, which is also a common critique of general system theory's use of this term. (Emergence is a central concept in Bertalanffy's general system theory).

But Luhmann has also redefined the general system theory of Bertalanffy in another way, in that he deals primarily with systems of socio-communication, where Bertalanffy's theory is much broader as it deals with all kind of systems, especially the living ones, and does not see communication as a system. Luhmann (1999) has further redefined autopoiesis in leaving the biological founded autopoiesis theory for a more general one including psychic and communicative systems.

This new system theory was then in need of a new foundation. Luhmann left the foundation for the other mentioned theoretical systems he drew on in order to transcend their subject areas to make a social system theory based first of all on analysis of social communication in an open ontology. He then chose to draw on Heinz von Foerster's second-order cybernetic constructivism of recursive cognition and communication (Brier, 2005a) and Spencer-Brown's *Laws of Form* (1969, 1972) and his theory of making distinction as well as Bateson's theory of information as "a difference that makes a difference" (Bateson, 1972, 1980).

As I have analyzed elsewhere, the ontological foundation of von Foerster's paradigm as well as Spencer-Brown's (Brier, 2005a), I here want to try to understand how Luhmann combines the two in establishing a new framework for socio-cybernetics. I observe the combination as an attempt to give a solution to theoretical problems of the origin and nature of the observer, consciousness, communication and meaning.

Socio-animism versus the emancipated person of the Enlightenment

One central problem in Luhmann's philosophy derives from the absence of objective idealism and a subjective core created as a part of that wholeness. It is this that attacks the core metaphysics in democratic societies after the Enlightenment, especially the emancipation of the individual subject as the a responsible decision maker, a process which was so important to Kant and to democratic society even today.

Although we believe in the social forces of language and its models of reality and social institutions, of coercion, group pressure, status and power, our society is still based on the belief that the individual is a responsible subject, able to make personal and individual decisions and taking political, moral and legal responsibility for them. Subjects are punishable for their acts which might violate the law, and their vote has political consequences that cannot be withdrawn. As the scientific world view develops, the problem of subjective consciousness as a causal factor becomes a major problem for consistency in the scientific grand narrative about the place of the human in an evolving material universe. The physical, chemical and bio-molecular view of the living human seen as a product of evolution has to deny any causal effects to first person experiences as such. It simply does not have any theoretical concepts for qualia, experience and free will or, if they did exist, how they should interact with the material body.

Thus, there seems to be a deep contradiction in metaphysics, especially the view of the human, between the self-conception of the researched society, and the paradigm in which the research is going on. Teubner makes this very clear:

> Promoting artificially constructed discourses to a key position in contractual autopoiesis reflects the split in modernity that distinguishes between personae as social 'masks' and the inner subjective thoughts and feelings to which the personae refers, but can never be a part of. These metaphors of personae and masks help to understand the role of actors in social worlds consisting only of communications.

> Actors as personae are secondary phenomena, given that it is the communication act which creates structures, which do not have an independent existence outside the system. Every communication invokes its structures explicitly or implicitly only by this ongoing process of invocation. ... A communication could be treated as a relation between two emergent structures or between individuals, as in Weber's theory of relation, which provided a bridge between the inner psychic worlds of individuals and social life by indicating that inter-subjectivity grows through relationships. However, relation theory papers over underlying difficulties in the way a relation oscillates between the 'inter' relations and the two entities of the relation. It isn't clear whether the relation is primarily the 'inter', the two points, or both. Social autopoiesis, on the other hand, focuses on actions rather than actors and relations. ... It would be wrong to interpret social autopoiesis as in some way giving meaning to the actors within the process. Instead, autopoiesis suggests that ongoing communication acts produce their own meanings in the form of semantic artifacts. Within the overall stream of talk in society, specialized languages emerge for each of the functionally differentiated systems. Each of these creates its own artificial 'Homunculi' actors, such as the 'legal person' or 'homo economicus'. (Teubner, 1997, n.p.)

Teubner very clearly summarizes the consequences of looking at social communication through Luhmannian system theory: Communication or discourse types create, for example, the juridical and the economical person. Many social science paradigms based on some kind of constructivistic metaphysics including discourse theory already doubt the idea of a stable subject with essential characteristics. They see the individual emerged in social and cultural meaning and power relations which the individual is not aware of, and which therefore control him/her – like the habitus concept of Bourdieu and discourse and power in Foucault. The individual is totally molded by social forces. Luhmann seems to share this view but in an open or empty ontology, which he claims is a realist one. But how can this be if there are no observer independent structures or forces? The world and society exist, but they do not have any specific form in advance, before human perception. Form is then determined through observation. This idea is again based on socio-communication. Luhmann writes on this question:

> The effect of the intervention of systems theory can be described as a de-ontologization of reality. This does not mean that reality is denied, for then there would be nothing that operated – nothing that observed, and nothing on which one would gain a purchase by means of distinctions. It is only the epistemological relevance of an ontological representation of reality that is being called into

question. If a knowing system has no entry to its external world, it can be denied that such an external world exists. But we can just as well – and more believably – claim that the external world is as it is. Neither claim can be proved; there is no way of deciding between them. This calls into question, however, not the external world but only the simple distinction being/non-being, which ontology had applied to it. As a consequence, the question arises: Why do we have to begin with precisely this distinction? Why do we wound the world first with this distinction and no other? Systems theory suggests instead the distinction between system and environment. (Luhmann, 1990, pp.132-33.)

Here one clearly sees the paraphrasing of Spencer-Brown in "Why do we wound the world first with this distinction." But, this way of operating with "empty ontologies" seems to be a kind of magical thinking: The world is created and formed by words or religion, the word of God: First was the word! In discourse theory the world only appears through discourse or only the discourse aspect of the world can be understood. The social system is both structurally and operationally coupled to human beings. The operational coupling is through language and higher-order media of communication, while the structural coupling is a priori.

When applying system theory, you have to be explicit about your own role as an observer. You have to make yourself visible and accountable so that other observers may be able to evaluate your observations. Luhmann never operationalized this as Bourdieu did in his method of also objectifying the observing subject as well as the social object.

On the basis of Thomas Kuhn's (1970) analysis of the conditions of incommensurability of the communication between different paradigms,[32] to which many of these scholars subscribe, one wonders how these researchers can feed back into society the results obtained in applied Luhmanian systemic investigation, in a way that is useful to a democratic society based on human rights. In general, Luhmann's theory is also considered difficult to apply, which is why we focus on this application problem in this special issue.

I also think that a non-theoretical notion of an observer is introduced covertly by Luhmann through the second order cybernetic theories of Heinz von Foerster, Maturana and Bateson, none of whom have a theory of first person consciousness either. The observer in these theories oscillates between a human observer and an abstract non-human cybernetic concept of observer as recursive differences, traveling information networks and loops. This is how I understand Bateson's *ecology of mind* based on his cybernetic idea of mind and information, as a difference that makes a difference as already mentioned (Brier, 2007; Brier, in press).

But in my theory (cybersemiotics), I see the embodiment of knowing in living systems as a prerequisite for the psychological, and that the psychological systems organization as a subject is a prerequisite for the socio-communicative, as they provide the very field of meaning that the socio-communicative feeds on and

---

32. Actually I think we can always return to natural language to discuss the definitions of concepts and /or the scientific or philosophical framework they are a part of and partially defined by; thus, I do not believe in any kind of absolute incommensurability in human communication, as I am not a radical constructivist.

manipulates!! Teubner sees this problem of the construction the social conscious in system theory very clear in the following quote, where he calls it *socio-animism*:

> Durkheim's concept of the 'collective consciousness' refers to the parts of our psychic lives which integrate into a social consciousness that is more than just individual motives and actions. In autopoiesis, however, meaning emerges in the social sphere as a way of processing information and putting it into a multitude of different contexts, then moving from one actualisation to another. This can be regarded as a form of 'socio-Animism'.
>
> When a lawyer or economist or poet creates a work of meaning, the important thing in an autopoietic system is not what that work means to its author's individual psyche, but the way the work gains in meaning when it moves through different worlds. This is similar to the way in which the legal world interprets a contract in terms of its observable meaning, rather than according to the subjective motivations of individual actors. ...Social autopoiesis based on Luhmann's principles creates a distance between real people and their engagement in social processes, which also makes clear we are dealing with profound and infinite dynamics that never intersect with each other. ... Husserl's notions about 'consciousness' initiated debates about the difficulty of integrating society into phenomenology. Wittgenstein and others replaced this with language theories in which the observer was no longer the conscious human, but the language game. Autopoietic systems theory reinstates Husserl's idea of consciousness, but this time parallel to - and in competition with - several autonomous 'language games'.
>
> To some extent, this reifies collectivities and deconstructs the reality of the actor through socio-Animism. It multiplies the number of observational perspectives as the observer is not identified just with the mind of an individual agent but with a 'chain of distinctions', which could be a human actor or an ongoing process of communication involving people. (Teubner, 1997, n.p.)

In many sociologies – from the Marxist inspired, through symbolic interactionism, to Parsons' and Luhmann's functionalism – we have this philosophy of a social reality almost completely independent of the individual psyche's first person experiences. Sociological models should not be micro-founded based on analysis of social-psychological meaningful interaction as in symbolic interactionism or modeled as an aggregate of *rational actors*, as in classical economical thinking and rational choice theory according to this theory. There is an independent social level, which is the subject-area of social science. Luhmann also claims that his program is aimed at *de-ontologization*, because the social systems do not exist in a sense similar to biological systems. They are not naturally given, but socially constructed. Still, Luhmann explains the construction at the social level in Darwinian terms, that is variation and selection. For instance, in science one's hypotheses are selected by a relevant scientific discourse and experimental practice. But this is actually a biological argument on a different time scale. Species are evolving constructions of the interactions between the gene pool and the changes in the surrounding ecology, or rather the individual's interpretation of their ecological niches.

Functionalistic meaning can probably be described for certain uses as an operator. But it is not an operator in itself. Generally Luhmann does not use the interpersonal phenomenological dimension he originally introduced from Husserl, because from a sociological point of view meaning cannot be seen, only inferred, as a dynamics from observed action. This means that you are observing observers constructing their reality, while being embedded in some reality you believe it is possible to observe, and you believe to be possibly different from the one constructed by the observers you observe. Second-order observations are, therefore, the basic concept of sociological system theory or socio-cybernetics. But how can human embodied beings be observers based on this theory in which no embodied subjects/persons make observations and choices?

Luhmann's idea of distinguishing between information and meaning only within meaningful communication is very good. Thus we can measure the bits in a message, whilst there is no direct connections between bits and meaning. But it does not make sense to count bits if the there is not a meaning content. Measurements in bits have no meaning.

This view, of course, makes me shy away from the idea that we should be able to define meaning primary on any mathematical level. That is why I want to semiotize Luhmann (Brier, 2002/2003). I see meaning as embodied related to the evolutionary fight for existence, and when awareness is added to the growth of self-preservation for the individual and its kin there is the beginning of the existential dimension of meaning. This leads to discussions of values, the good life, the meaning of life, religion and philosophy in the socially conscious human, as Heinz von Foerster saw it and Maturana still does. But all these aspects of reality are carried by signs.

The meaning of information can be ascribed only with reference to an embodied system that is able to organize the information through operating over time. That is, a system contains a medium for the communication that is the field of meaning. In humans it is generated by the embodied mind in living systems (Kirkeby, 1997). Un-embodied systems, like the computer as we know it presently, can therefore not really produce meaning that means anything to humans in any other form than by passing on or rearranging meaningful messages from other human beings, some of which can be faulty messages made by the system designer about the computers functioning.

I agree with Qvortrup (2003) that one compensatory way of getting out of this impasse of Luhmann's theory is to say that the psychic and the social communicative system has a much stronger mutual structural coupling than the other systems, and this is what makes them stand out as what we normally call persons or subjects. But I want to integrate the living body also, as it is the source of life. In biosemiotics, life and semiosis are co-extensive and together they are the source of meaning and evolution. Thus, the living body's cognitive system is sets up some essentials for the human being, and some limits to how far it can be psychically molded without the whole system – all three autopoietic systems – collapsing. But, still, the source of mind and consciousness and thereby feeling and will is obscure in Luhmann's theory, even while it is the foundation of Peirce's (See Sheriff, 1994; Innis, 1994; & Raposa, 1993)

The problem of transforming Husserlian phenomenology to a systemic communication theory

Luhmann's theory is not really phenomenological at all. His intersubjectivity does not occur in the experience of phenomena, but seems closer to Bateson's development of Wiener's informational world view and, like Bateson, he does not have a theory concerning to whom the difference makes a difference (Brier, 1992). Who makes the interpretation? On what background of reality is meaning created in a world without persons?

The answer from the social sciences is often that meaning is created in society. The counter answer is that a society is also based on the presence of biological systems and the physical environment of embodied conscious humans (Brier, 2007; Brier, in press). But cybernetics and system theory do not have a theory of embodied subjects capable of interpretations of meaning. In Brier (2005a, 2006c) I have contrasted von Foerster's, Bateson's and Luhmann's theories with Peirce's concepts of mind and the sacred. I am pointing out that Bateson's "Lonely Skeleton of Truth" (Bateson & Bateson, 2005) can never produce first person qualia, but its idea and dynamics – and thereby Luhmann's – can become meaningful within the frame of an embodied Peircean semiotic background. Willke comments on this problem in his characterization of the consequences of working with a theory of autopoietic systems. His third point addresses the role of Husserl's theory in Luhmann's socio-communicational paradigm.

> Phenomenological versus communicational. The autopoietic notion of basing social systems solely on a communicational paradigm is a totally different way of observing and reconstructing reality to phenomenological thinking, which starts with very concrete things, like real people performing real acts. However, Luhmann (1983) is imprecise in the way he deals with this strategic issue of phenomenological versus communicational system thinking. He uses 'sense' as a core term shared by both types of thinking, but gives it a very different meaning in each area. In one case he treats sense as being built into the process of doing real things, while in autopoiesis it derives from communication acts. (Willke, 1997, n.p.)

In my view, biology is foundational for a theory of meaning and signification. That was what Tom Sebeok saw when he started to develop biosemiotics! Embodiment has both a scientific and a phenomenological side to it. Merleau-Ponty (1945/2002) saw that too in his development of an embodied phenomenology. A baby is already structurally coupled to other people and its environment through its bodyhood before it has learned to speak. Language and other media add to the coupling, because there is an interface within language, which animals do not have. Language plays an eminent role in the coupling between the psychological system and the social system, and the structural coupling precedes linguistic capacities. It is my point of view that all meaning and value comes from our existential awareness of being an embodied openness in being, in relation to an apparent nothingness, a host of surrounding objects and other human beings, as Heidegger (1962) expresses it.

But in Luhmann's theory – as in so many other sociological theories – there is, on the level of biological autopoiesis, hardly any influence on actions that counts in sociological studies. Luhmann avoids the whole motivational psychology. But, in the ethology of Lorenz (Lorenz, 1970-71, 1973) and Tinbergen (1973), animals were seen as having developed refined and different sets of instinctual motivations governing their cognition and communication in hunting, mating, fights for rank, mates and territory, caring for the young, and so forth This can be connected to a biosemiotic theory (Brier, 1995, 1999, 2000a; Emmeche, 1998).There is a seemingly deep contradiction between this knowledge and Luhmann's lack of reflection on the consequences of embodiment Brier (2000b). Willke documents these problems of the embodiments and praxis of knowledge to get value in the human world:

> Information in itself is not knowledge. Information must be embedded in experience if it is to produce knowledge. That is why sharing common experiences is so important for the consultation system I have described. Without it, there will be large areas of ignorance and increased risks. Action learning, project learning and organisational learning are among the organisational strategies which can be used to produce knowledge from information.
>
> Intelligence can be derived from knowledge by embedding knowledge in decision-making processes, for example with the support of expert systems and intelligent decision support tools. At the highest level of cognition, reflexion connects expertise and observed effects through feedback, monitoring and supervision processes which return to observations of the 'facts'. (Willke, 1997, n.p.)

Consequences of the Spencer-Brownian foundation

Luhmann (1995) very clearly chooses to base his system theory on the philosophy that the first action in being is an observer making a distinction between system and environment, identifying only with the system. Thus, in von Foerster's terminology, it is an *observing system*. This leaves unanswered the question about which observer made the first distinction between system and environment and Luhmann does not mention Hegel here! Instead, he refers to Spencer-Brown's *Laws of Form* and he provides a modern alternative to Hegel's spirit and dialectics in a philosophy of distinction and form, which brings Luhmann's signification and communication close to semiotics.

George Spencer-Brown, the philosopher and logician who came to mean so much to second-order cybernetics and autopoiesis theory, actually provides the theological aspect that Leydesdorff mentions in the passage quoted earlier. But it is not explicitly used by Luhmann and often suppressed in the constructivistic interpretation of Luhmann. Spencer-Brown writes:

> Let us then consider, for a moment, the world as described by the physicist. It consists of a number of particles which, if shot through their own space, appear as waves... All these appear bound by certain natural laws which indicate the form of their relationship.

Now the physicist himself, who describes all this, is, in his own account, himself constructed of it. He is, in short, made of a conglomeration of the very particles he describes, no more no less, bound together by and obeying such general laws as he himself has managed to find and record.

Thus we cannot escape the fact that the world we know is constructed in order (and thus in such a way to be able) to see itself. This is indeed amazing.

Not so much in view of what it sees, although this may appear fantastic enough, but in respect of the fact that it *can* see *at all*.

But *in order* to do so, evidently it must first cut itself up into at least one state, which sees, and at least one state, which is seen. In this severed and mutilated condition, whatever it sees is *only partially* itself. We may take it that the world undoubtedly is itself (i.e., is indistinct from itself), but, in any attempt to see itself as an object, it must, equally undoubtedly, act so as to make itself distinct from, and therefore false to, itself. In this condition it always partially eludes itself.

It seems hard to find an acceptable answer to the question of how or why the world conceives a desire, and discovers an ability, to see itself, and appears to suffer the process. That it does so is sometimes called the original mystery. (Spencer-Brown, 1972, pp.104-105)

Spencer-Brown includes the process of observing as an important part of basic reality; this places him near Peirce, who includes feeling and qualia in his concept of (unmanifest) Firstness (Sheriff, 1994). Both are showing a way out of the phenomenological problem of the sciences that Husserl pointed out. In Brier (2006) I have argued that although Spencer-Brown seemingly only argues that in a logical universe, this process of breaking some kind of original wholeness demands a kind of objective idealism and monistic theory where mind is first and turns into matter in evolution, Peirce also theorizes this with his idea of pure feeling as the basis of Firstness and consciousness. There has to be some kind of transcendental awareness resting in itself that can make the first distinction and therefore the first system-environment difference – what Peirce calls Secondness – which is something else than the wholeness. It breaks the wholeness and makes space and time appear. This is what Leydesdorff in the quote above called Lucifer's breaking away from God. It is an interesting Gnostic view that the world is actually created by the devil through the breaking of the wholeness of God. Another conception in much mysticism is that it is the Godhead that in the break makes God and the world.

It is not clear if an observer needs to have feelings, free will, and qualia as minimum requirements in Spencer-Brown's theory, but in cybernetics, as we have underlined, it is not a requirement. I find that strange, since I am convinced that we need living feeling flesh for conscious observation. Spencer-Brown most of all works in a logical framework and does not systematically discuss the ontology necessary to support the epistemology of differences and form that he promotes. The problem is that "the observer" seems to be smuggled in from a world view that operates with a rather abstract subject or observer. It is not biologically connected, nor is it religiously connected to the concept of a soul. It is neither body nor soul! How can that be explained? I have discussed this at length with Louis H. Kauffmann who is acknowledged as one of the leading specialists in Spencer-Brown's theory. His interpretation[33]—with which I agree—is that Spencer-Brown addresses the emergence of form at that level where the observer, the universe and the distinction between universe and observer occur at once/together from the void. This places emptiness and the void on as central a place in Spencer-Brown's metaphysics as it is in Buddhism. A confirmation that can be found in Keyes/Spencer-Brown (1974). He writes:

> Space is a construct. In reality there is no space. Time is also a construct. In reality there is no time. In eternity there is space but no time. In the deepest order of eternity there is no space. It is devoid of any quality whatever. This is the reality of which the Buddhas speak. Buddhists call it Nirvana. Its order of being is zero. Its mode is completeness. (Spencer-Brown, 1974, p. 127 note 1) [34]

This points to a Buddhist philosophy as the framework for Spencer-Brown's theory, an influence he shares with Peirce.[35] The concepts of nothingness and emptiness are central to Spencer-Brown's – and Buddhist philosophy's – evolution theory of how form or the basic categories come into existence. Kauffman points to two quotes from Spencer-Brown (1972): "The form we take to exist arises from framing nothing"; and "We take, therefore, the form of distinction for the form" as being central to the understanding of Spencer-Brown's metaphysics. One can then point to the famous quote from the Heart Sutra that is a central text in Mahayana Buddhism's ontology: "Form is emptiness, emptiness is form."

> Form is emptiness and the very emptiness is form; emptiness does not differ from form, form does not differ from emptiness; whatever is form, that is emptiness, whatever is emptiness, that is form, the same is true of feelings, perceptions, impulses and consciousness. ... in emptiness there is no form, nor feeling, nor perception, nor impulse, nor consciousness; No eye, ear, nose, tongue, body, mind; No forms, sounds, smells, tastes, touchables or objects of mind; No sight-organ element, and so forth, until we come to: No mind-consciousness element; There is no ignorance, no extinction of ignorance, and so forth, until we come to: there is no decay and death, no extinction of decay and death. There is no suffering, no origination, no stopping, no path. There is no cognition, no attainment and non-attainment. (The Heart Sutra)[36]

Like Peirce, Spencer-Brown was heavily influenced by transcendentalism and mysticism of both Christian and Buddhist nature as can be seen in Daisetz Teitaro Suzuki's *Mysticism: Christian and Buddhist* (1957/2002)[37]. Spencer-Brown was further influenced by Chinese Taoist mystic philosophy. He writes:

> It is known to western doctrine, sometimes as the Godhead, sometimes as IHVH, or that which was in the beginning, is now, and ever shall be. This way of describing it, like any other, is misleading, suggesting that it has qualities like being, priority, temporality. Having no quality at all, not even

---

33. From an e-mail discussion.
34. All quotes are taken from http://www.uboeschenstein.ch/texte/spencer-brown-onlytwo127.html 5.April 07 and checked in the printed book.
35. Peirce saw Buddhism and Christianity melting together with transcendental religious views of empathy and love as the foundation of reality; hence his idea of Firstness as pure feeling and an emptiness behind it.
36. (Translation by Edward Conze) http://www.thebigview.com/buddhism/emptiness.html
37. The whole text of this classic work can be found on http://boozers.fortunecity.com/brewerytap/695/Suzuki-myst.htm

(except in the most degenerate sense) the quality of being, it can have none of these suggested properties, although it is what gives rise to them all. It is what the Chinese call the unnamable Tao, the Mother of all existence. It is also called the Void.

In a qualityless order, to make any distinction at all is at once to construct all things in embryo. Thus the First Thing, and with it the First Space and the First Existence and the First Being, are all created explosively together. (Spencer-Brown, 1974, p. 127)

The way he goes between these various versions of mysticism as representing the same thing seems to indicate thinking from the framework of the *Perennial Philosophy*[38] (Stace, 1960), seeing the mysticism from different cultures and historical periods as an expression of the same phenomenon. Spencer-Brown here exceeds the standard cybernetic world view of Wiener that is based on thermodynamics, as we also saw it in von Foerster's view in the quotes above, and as I have shown (Brier, in press), is also Bateson's view. Spencer-Brown thus provides a source of mind as first person experience.

But Spencer-Brown further makes the connection between mystical views and Western physics' struggle with the big bang theory of creation in a way that shows its compatibility with Christian thinking:

This does not of course mean that the "big bang" theory that cosmologists suggest for the creation of the universe is the true one. The "explosion" into existence does not take place in time, and so from the point of view of time is a continuous operation. Thus the "big bang" theory and the "continuous creation" theory, like all famous "rival" theories in western culture, are both equally true.[39]

This First Creation, or First Presence, is the order of which the Christ speak. Christians call it God. Its order of being is unity.[40] Its mode is perfection. ... It is known to eastern doctrine, as it is to western, as the Triune God or Trinity.[41] ... In China it is called the namable Tao. In Tibetan Buddhism it is called the densely-packed region. (Spencer-Brown, 1974, p. 127)

From here he continues in a description of *the densely packed region*'that is very similar to Peirce's description of Firstness. As Peirce also has a void – or a Tohu Bohu – behind his Firstness, their basic ontology seems to have a great deal in common:

---

38. According to the tenets of the perennial philosophy, people in many cultures and eras have experienced and recorded comparable perceptions about the nature of reality, the self, the world, and the meaning and purpose of existence. These similarities point to underlying universal principles, forming the common ground of most religions. Differences among these fundamental perceptions arise from differences in human cultures and can be explained in light of such cultural conditioning. The German mathematician and philosopher Gottfried Leibniz, used the term to designate the common, eternal philosophy that underlies all religions, and in particular the mystical streams within them. The term was popularized in more recent times by Aldous Huxley in his 1945 book: *The Perennial Philosophy* (taken from http://en.wikipedia.org/wiki/Perennial_philosophy)

39. Again, a view Peirce shares: evolution is creation. Physically there is also the interesting discussion of whether the universe has a time, since in relativity theory each system within the universe travels with its own time. Further, if the time we have now is the same as the beginning of the universe, is the first second the same as a second now?

40. This is the unity that is broken by the first indication creating the first distinction.

41. See Qvortrup's article in this volume about the idea of this fourth order knowledge form.

This last name is most vividly expressive, it being the region of the creating or seeding-out of all qualities from no quality: it is, in other words, the place where every blade of grass and every grain of sand are numbered, the place where nothing is forgotten. It is the place where all is still "small "enough to be reviewed together. The quality of being in nascent existence, and as yet without any size, is what makes the densely-packed region the region of omniscience. Unlike the Void, which is the place without quality, the densely-packed region is the place where all qualities can be seen at once to be capable of infinite variety and extension. How they may become extended is of course how, in some universe or other, they actually are extended. It is here that every universe is worked out from first principles, except that the "working out" does not take place mathematically step by step as it is done on Earth, or at the physical level of one of the other universes so constructed, but is all at once obvious and immediate, as there is no time. Hence the omniscience. (Spencer-Brown, 1974, p. 128)

Finally he gives a triadic explanation on the form of the distinction that brings him even closer to Peirce's semiotic philosophy (Brier, in press). This is surprising, because Spencer-Brown, Luhmann and Bateson are considered to be a rare type of dualists in that they only work with distinctions or differences. But it turns out that Spencer-Brown has a triadic view of the distinction, especially when drawn as a circle. Further he makes comparisons – like Peirce – to the Holy Trinity of Christian thinking:

The **explanation of the Trinity** in fact turns out to be simple enough. When you make a distinction of any kind whatever, the easiest way to represent its essential properties mathematically is by some sort of closed curve like a circle. Here the circumference **distinguishes two sides, an inside and an outside. The two sides, plus the circumference itself, which is neither the inside nor the outside, together make up three aspects of one distinction. Thus every distinction is a trinity. Hence the First Distinction is the First Trinity.**

We can even go so far as to identify, in this mathematical representation, which aspect represents what. The inside represents the aspect where the Void or IHVH remains undisturbed and undistributed. It is, in other words, the aspect of the Godhead in the God, and is called, when considered as an aspect of the Trinity, God the Holy Ghost...

Next we have the "line" of distinction itself – the circumference of the circle in the mathematical representation. This line ... is actually the "seeding" of the densely-packed region, the embryonic outline of all things. In the Christian Trinity it is what is called God the Father: first in creation, second in seniority.

Finally we have the outside. The first distinction may be regarded as cleft into and projects out of the Void, and this outer projective region, before it becomes further differentiated, as it does in the rest of creation, is the aspect known to western doctrine as the Word or First Message. In the Trinity it is the junior partner, God the Son. (Spencer-Brown, 1974, pp. 128-129)

Thus, in Spencer-Brown's philosophy, we have a rephrasing of a Hegelian philosophy, but replacing dialectics and determinism with his dynamics of distinction making and the laws of form. This is what is behind Luhmann's open ontology and gives life to his communication systems. It is actually not a meta-biology, if Luhmann respects the full Spencer-Brownian foundation.[42]

For Peirce this creational understanding means that subject/persons are elements in the super mind and that they discover themselves as partly ignorant beings through their own mistakes. They come to know themselves as individual selves or egos because they lack knowledge of the whole. They realize that they are not the whole and are therefore imperfect and distinct from the whole. Peirce (1868) sees introspection as one of the four incapacities of the human being. To him, introspection is wholly a matter of inference by the way of sign making. The human self can only be inferred (CP 5.462), and, surprisingly, it is inferred from our mistakes, from realizing that we are not the whole (we are not the Godhead). Human individuation is found in ignorance and error. Peirce says that "Ignorance and error are all that distinguish our private selves from the absolute ego of pure apperception" (CP 5.235). Peirce's argument concerning the self was developed in his discussion of the dawning of self-consciousness in children:

> It must be about this time that he [the child] begins to find that what these people about him say is the very best evidence of fact. So much so, that testimony is even a stronger mark of fact than the facts themselves, or rather than what must now be thought of as the appearances themselves. (I may remark, by the way, that this remains so through life; testimony will convince a man that he himself is mad.) A child hears it said that the stove is hot. But it is not, he says; and, indeed, that central body is not touching it, and only what that touches is hot or cold. But he touches it, and finds the testimony confirmed in a striking way. Thus, he becomes aware of ignorance, and it is necessary to suppose a self in which this ignorance can inhere. So testimony gives the first dawning of self-consciousness. (CP 5.233)

Thus children "infer from ignorance and error their own existence. Thus we find that known faculties, acting under conditions known to exist, would rise to self-consciousness" (Peirce CP 5.236).

I think this is compatible with the Spencer-Brownian foundation for Luhmann's ontology and would repair the break with the wholeness in Husserlian phenomenology that Luhmann made when he imprisoned intentional consciousness in an autopoietic system by the name *the psychic system* without taking into account the full consequences of it. It also gives an inner side to the socially constructed persons that system theory lacks. But neither Spencer-Brown nor Luhmann has worked through this idea. Thus, it is the imperfection of the autopoietic psyche and its closure that makes it a self in Peirce's view. But this self or subject is an idea and in its general form a sign or rather a symbol in Peirce's semiotic philosophy. All general ideas and signs are in development through the all-pervading process of evolution. Thus, this concept of subject and self is different from both the Kantian and the Husserlian idea of the transcendental concept in a way that seem compatible with Luhmann's general idea, because the creation of a self is the distinction between the observing system and its environment.

Then there is a first observer and it is this very abstract observer which we see in Spencer-Brown's philosophy that is cut up as the first system, is made part of it, is left

---

42. Philosophically he needs to, but he never did in practice.

as the unmarked site of the distinction, and therefore as environment. The system as a whole – the form in Spencer-Brown's philosophy – is form or sign producing and now has produced that inherited agency that was not accounted for in Luhmann's system theory. To Peirce cognition is sign producing (signification) and therefore the production of signification and meaning. Viewed as such Spencer-Brown's theory is also a semiotics.

I am sure this is a surprising discovery for most researchers using Luhmann in sociological analysis and who view his second order system theory as pure epistemology with an open ontology freeing them from any metaphysical speculations. Yet, it is not so, as I have argued. Only with reference to the subject and sign production could Luhmann arrive at a consistent foundation for his transdisciplinary information, cognition and communication theory. It is an even bigger surprise that he ends up so close to Peirce's foundation for his semiotics and pragmaticistic philosophy as, for many years, they have been considered adversaries or at least representing incompatible paradigms. I therefore find the results of this analysis supportive of my attempt to unite Luhmann and Pierce's theories in, what I (Brier, 2007) call cybersemiotics.

References

Åkerstrøm, N. (2003). *Discursive analytical strategies: Understanding Foucault, Kosselleck, Laclau, Luhmann.* Bristol: The Policy Press.

Apel, K.-O. (1995). *Charles Peirce: From pragmatism to pragmaticism.* Atlantic Highlands, NJ: Humanities Press International.

Bateson, G. (1973). *Steps to an ecology of mind.* Boulder, CO: Paladin Press.

Bateson, G. (1980). *Mind and nature: A necessary unity.* New York: Bantam Books.

Bateson, G., & Bateson, M. C. (2005). *Angels fear: Towards an epistemology of the sacred.* Cresskill, NJ: Hampton Press.

Brier, S. (1992). Information and consciousness: A critique of the mechanistic concept of information. *Cybernetics & Human Knowing, 1* (2/3), 71-94.

Brier, S. (1993). A cybernetic and semiotic view on a Galilean theory of psychology. *Cybernetics & Human Knowing, 2* (2), 31-45.

Brier, S. (1995). Cyber-semiotics: On autopoiesis, code-duality and sign games in bio-semiotics. *Cybernetics & Human Knowing, 3* (1), 3-25.

Brier, S. (1999). Biosemiotics and the foundation of Cybersemiotics. Reconceptualizing the insights of Ethology, second order cybernetics and Peirce's semiotics in Biosemiotics to create a non-Cartesian information science. *Semiotica, 127* (1/4), 169-198.

Brier, S. (2000a). Konstruktion und Information: Eine semiotische re-entry in Heinz von Foerster's metaphysische Konstruktion der Kybernetik zweiter Ordnung. In O. Jahraus, N. Ort, & B. M. Schmidt (Eds.), *Beobachtungen des Unbeobachtbaren* (pp. 254-295). Weilerswist: Velbrück Wissenschaft.

Brier, S. (2000b). On the connection between cognitive semantics and ethological concepts of motivation: A possible bridge between embodiment in cognitive semantics and the motivation concept in ethology. *Cybernetics & Human Knowing, 7*(1), 57-75.

Brier, S. (2002/2003). Luhmann semiotized. *Journal of Sociocybernetics, 3* (2), 13-22. (Available online at http://www.unizar.es/sociocybernetics/Journal/dentro.html)

Brier, S. (2005a). The construction of information and communication: A cybersemiotic re-entry into Heinz von Foerster's metaphysical construction of second order cybernetics. *Semiotica, 154* (1/4), 355-399.

Brier, S. (2005b). Third culture: Cybersemiotic's inclusion of a biosemiotic theory of mind. *Axiomathes, 15,* 211-228.

Brier, S. (2006). The necessity of trans-scientific frameworks for doing interdisciplinary researc. *Kybernetes, 35* (3-4), 403-425.

Brier. S. (2007). *Cybersemiotics: Why information is not enough.* Copenhagen: Icon. (ISBN 87-593-9986-4, pp. 554. Danish post-doctoral thesis defended and approved 6. March 2006 at CBS by professors Ole Fogh Kirkeby, Dirk Baecker and John Deely. In English with a Danish summary. A further revised and extended edition to be published by Toronto University Press, March, 2008.)

Brier, S. (in press). Bateson and Peirce on the pattern that connects and the sacred. In J. Hoffmeyer (Ed.), *Gregory Bateson as a precursor to biosemiotics*. New York: Springer.

Bertalanffy, L. Von. (1968). *General system theory*. New York: George Braziller.

Chaitin, G. (1988). Randomness in Arithmetics. *Scientific American*, (July), 52-57.

Chaitin, G. (2005). *Meta math: The quest for omega*. New York: Pantheon.

Deacon, T. W. (1997). *The symbolic species: The co-evolution of language and the brain*. New York: Norton.

Deely, J. (2001). *Four ages of understanding: The first postmodern survey of philosophy from ancient times to the turn of the twenty-first century*. Toronto: University of Toronto Press.

Emmeche, C. (1998). Defining life as a semiotic phenomenon. *Cybernetics & Human Knowing, 5* (1), 3-17.

Foerster, H. von (1981). On cybernetics of cybernetics of cybernetics and social theory. In *Self-organizing systems: An interdisciplinary approach* (pp. 102-105). Frankfurt: Campus.

Foerster, H. von (1984). *Observing systems*. Seaside, CA: Intersystems Publications.

Foerster, H. von (2003). On Self-Organizing Systems and their Environment. In *Understanding understanding: Essays on cognition and cybernetics* (pp. 1-20). New York: Springer.

Fuller, S. (1998). An intelligent person's guide to intelligent design theory. *Rhetoric and Public Affairs, 1*, 603-610.

Hayles, N. K. (1999). *How we became posthuman: Virtual bodies in cybernetics, literature, and informatics*. Chicago: University of Chicago Press.

Heidegger, M. (1962). *Being and time* [Sein und Zeit]. New York: Harper & Row.

Heims, S. J.(1991: *Cybernetics group*. Boston: The MIT Press.

Husserl, E. (1977). *Fænomenologiens idé*. Copenhagen:Hans Reitzels Forlag. (Translation of *Die Idee der Phänomenologie*, Kluwer Academic Publishing 1950 and 1973.)

Husserl, E. (1999). *Cartesianske meditationer*. Copenhagen: Hans Reitzels Forlag.

Innis, R. E. (1994). *Consciousness and the play of signs*. Bloomington, IN: Indiana University Press.

Kant, I. (1990). *Critique of pure reason,*(J.M.D. Meiklejohn, Trans.) Buffalo: Prometheus Books

Keys, J. /Spencer-Brown, G. (1974). *Only two can play this game*. Cambridge: Cat Books.

Kirkeby, O. F. (1997). Event and body-mind: An outline of a post-postmodern approach to phenomenology. *Cybernetics & Human Knowing, 4* (2/3), 3-34.

Kuhn, T. (1970). *The structure of scientific revolutions* (rev. ed). Chicago: University of Chicago Press.

Lakoff, G. (1987). *Women, fire and dangerous things: What categories reveal about the mind*. Chicago: University of Chicago Press.

Lakoff, G., & Johnson, M. (1999). *Philosophy in the flesh: The embodied mind and its challenge to western thought*. New York: Basic Books.

Leydesdorff, L. (in press). Luhmann's communication-theoretical specification of the "Genomena" of Husserl's Phenomenology. In E. B. Pires (Ed.), *Espaço público, poder e comunicação* [Public space, power and communication]. Porto: Afrontamento. (Quotations retrieved from: http://users.fmg.uva.nl/lleydesdorff/coimbra/index.htm January 8, 2007.)

Luhmann N. (1983). The improbability of communication. *International Social Science Journal, 23* (1), 122-132.

Luhmann, N. (1990). *Essays on self-reference*. New York: Colombia University Press.

Luhmann, N. (1995). *Social systems*. Stanford, CA: Stanford University Press.

Luhmann, N. (1996). *Die Neuzeitlichen Wissenschaften und Die Phänomologie*. Berlin: Picus Verlag.

Luhmann, N. (2002). *Theories of distinction*. Stanford, CA: Stanford University Press,

Lorenz, K. (1970-71). *Studies in animal and human behaviour I and II*. Cambridge, MA: Harvard University Press.

Lorenz, K. (1973). *Die Rückseite des Spiegels: versuch einer Naturgeschichte menschlichen Erkennens*. München:Piper.

Maturana, H & Varela, F. (1980). *Autopoiesis and cognition: The realization of the living*. London: Reidel.

Merleau-Ponty, M. (2002). *Phenomenology of perception* (C. Smith, Trans.). London: Routledge & Kegan Paul. (Originally published as *Phenomenologie de la Perception*, by Callimard of Paris, in 1945).

Mingers, (1995). *Self-producing systems-implications and applications of autopoiesis*. London: Plenum Press.

Peirce, C. S.(1868). Some consequences of four incapacities. *Journal of Speculative Philosophy, 2*, 140-157. Available online http://www.peirce.org/writings/p27.html .

Peirce, C. S. (1931-58). *Collected Papers of Charles Sanders Peirce, vols. I-VI* (C. Hartshorne and P. Weiss, Eds.),*vols. VII-VIII* (A. W. Burks, Ed.). Boston: Harvard University Press. (citations use the convention CP: Volume.Paragraph)

Peirce, C. S.(1992).*The essential Peirce, Volume 1, 1867-1893* (N. Houser & C. Kloesel, Eds.). Bloomington, IN: Indiana University Press.

Peirce, C. S. (1994). T*he Collected Papers of Charles Sanders Peirce*. Electronic version (J. Deely, Ed.) reproducing Vols. I-VI edited by Charles Hartshorne & Paul Weiss (Harvard University Press, 1931-1935), and Vols. VII-VIII edited by Arthur W. Burks (Harvard University Press, 1958). Charlottesville: Intelex Corporation.

Peirce, C. S. (1997). *Pragmatism as a principle and method of right thinking, the 1903 Harvard lectures on pragmatism*. Albany: State of New York University Press. (Edited and introduced with a commentary by Patricia Ann Turrisi)

Plato (2004). *Classics in the history of liberty, Plato, The dialogues of Plato in five volumes (1892), volume III: Timaeus*, The Online Library Of Liberty. Updated: April 20, 2004. URL: http://oll.libertyfund.org/Texts/Plato0204/Dialogues/HTMLs/0131-03ÅPt03ÅTimaeus.html#hdÅlf131.3.head.034

Raposa, M. (1989). *Peirce's philosophy of religion,* Peirce Studies number 5. Bloomington, IN: Indiana University Press.

Qvortrup, L. (1993). The Controversy over the concept of information: An overview and a selected and annotated bibliography. *Cybernetics & Human Knowing, 1* (4), *3-26.*

Qvortrup, L. (2003). *The hypercomplex society.* New York: Peter Lang.

Sebeok, T. (1976). *Contributions to the doctrine of signs.* Bloomington, IN: Indiana University Press.

Sheriff, J.K. (1994). *Charles Sanders Peirce's guess at the riddle: Ground for human significance,* Bloomington, IN: Indiana University Press.

Spencer-Brown, G. (1969). *Laws of form.* London: Allen and Unwin.

Spencer-Brown, G. (1972). *Laws of form* (2nd ed.). New York: Julien Press.

Spencer-Brown, G./James Keys (1974). *Only two can play this game.* Cambridge: Cat Books.

Stace, W. T. (1960). *Mysticism and philosophy.* London: Macmillan and Co.

Stjernfelt, F. (2001). Review of Umberto Eco: Kant and the Platypus. Essays on Language and Cognition. *Recherches Sémiotiques/Semiotic Inquiries, 21* (1-3) 309-322.

Sørensen, A. (2007). The inner experience of living. *Philosophy & Social Criticism, 33* (5), 587-615.

Suzuki, D. T. (2002). *Mysticism: Christian and Buddhist.* Routledge Classics, London. (Originally published by George Allen & Unwin, Ltd of London in 1957.)

Teubner, G. (1997). *Law as an autopoietic system.* LSE Complexity study group, meeting no 3. London School of Economics and Political Science. Retrieved January 3, 2007 from http://www.psych.lse.ac.uk/complexity/StudyGroups/report97june.htm

Thyssen, O. (2004). Luhmann and epistemology. *Cybernetics & Human Knowing, 11* (1), 7-22.

Thyssen, O. (2006). Epistemology as communication theory: A critique of Niklas Luhmann's theory of the vanished world. *Cybernetics & Human Knowing, 13* (2), 7-24.

Tinbergen, N. (1973). *The animal in its world.* London: Allen & Unwin.

Willke, H. (1997). *Autopoiesis and organised complexity.* LSE Complexity study group, meeting no 3, London School of Economics and Political Science. Retrieved January 3, 2007 from http://www.psych.lse.ac.uk/complexity/StudyGroups/report97june.htm .

Wiener, N. (1954). *The human use of human beings: Cybernetics in society.* Boston: Houghton Mifflin.

Wittgenstein; L. (1958). *Philosophical investigation* (3rd ed., G. E. M. Anscombe, Trans.). New York: Macmillan .

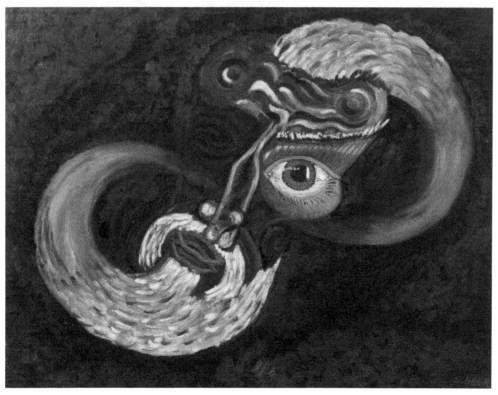

Beer, S. (n.d.). *Job of Uz.*

Beer, S. (n.d.). *Relativity.*

Cybernetics And Human Knowing. Vol. 14, nos. 2-3, pp. 67-83

Theorizing Culture, or Reading Luhmann Against Luhmann

Rudi Laermans[1]

This article tries to counter Niklas Luhmann's outspoken theoretical scepticism about the notion of culture. In the first part, it is argued that Luhmann devised at least three culture-related concepts: memory, semantics or semantic structures, and knowledge. After a short presentation of Luhmann's explicit considerations on the notion of culture, these conceptual equivalents are briefly clarified and discussed. In the second section, the interrelationships between Luhmann's culture-related notions are analyzed. More particularly, it is shown that they all point to the double process of condensation and confirmation of meaning or Sinn (in the phenomenological sense). Within communicative or social systems, this process explains the unintended production of what Luhmann terms *meaning kernels*, symbolic generalizations, schemes or identities. As Luhmann himself admits, communication cannot do without symbolic generalizations or meaning-identities. This necessitates a re-evaluation of the notion of culture from a systems theoretical point of view. The closing section offers a first step in this direction. It is argued that condensed and therefore typified forms or meaning-identities can be regarded as the elements of culture considered as a medium. According to this view, culture is a more specific articulation of the overall medium of meaning or Sinn and has a temporal, factual and social dimension. The primary function of the medium of culture is to ensure the structural coupling between social and psychic systems. Social systems therefore presuppose that condensed forms, or cultural elements, are always already known by all participating psychic systems. In order to underline this assumptive nature, the author proposes the notion of operative fiction.

Introduction

In more than one way, the work of Niklas Luhmann is a sustained provocative challenge to sociology and the social sciences in general, and to cultural sociology and the cultural sciences in particular. Indeed, it invites us to observe the social solely in terms of communications, or the selective uttering of selected information that is selectively understood, and proposes to analyze the self-referential enchainment of communications in terms of self-productive or autopoietic systems. Also, it urges us to give up the well-established idea that we cannot understand communication or social reality without invoking the notion of culture. Precisely this latter claim, which is anything but self-evident in the light of canonical social science, let alone in the context of the cultural sciences, will be scrutinized in a more in-depth manner in what follows.

Luhmann was quite outspoken on his theoretical scepticism about the notion of culture. In *Die Kunst der Gesellschaft* [The Art of Society], he speaks of "one of the most dubious concepts ever coined" (Luhmann, 1995a, p. 398); and in *Die*

---

1. Catholic University of Leuven, Centre for Sociological Research, Parkstraat 45 – box 03601, B-3000 Leuven, Belgium. Email: rudi.laermans@soc.kuleuven.be

Gesellschaft der Gesellschaft [The Society of Society], he declares that "the systems
theoretical approach has ... the advantage to make the unclear concept of culture
superfluous" (Luhmann, 1997, p. 109). Yet, in that very same book, as well as in some
other publications, he does make use, be it marginally, of this rejected concept. In a
characteristically ironical mode, he therefore notes that the notion of culture "only
lives on because a proposal to give it up will have little success as long as no
successive conceptualization is offered together with it" (Luhmann, 1997, p. 881). For
that matter, it remains to be seen if Luhmann's skepticism towards the concept of
culture was inspired only by the vagueness of that notion. Much can be said for the
thesis, convincingly argued by Dirk Baecker (2000, pp. 133-160), that Luhmann
deliberately tried to avoid the overall theory design of Talcott Parsons (1951, 1978), in
which culture is not only conceptualized as a separate system but is also given a
central place in the solution of the problem of double contingency (compare the
comments in Luhmann, 1995, pp. 103-136 & 2002, pp. 11-40)

As has been said, Luhmann does use the notion of culture in his writings now and
then. Moreover, his work contains several *conceptual equivalents* for the concept of
culture, which I provisionally define here in a loose and inclusive way as having to do
with meaning or signification – that is, its production, transmission, symbolization –
in order to avoid any commitment to a more specific theoretical approach (compare
Hall, 1997; Reckwitz, 2000). Therefore, Luhmann's oeuvre can be read as an at once
systematic repression of the notion of culture and a symptomatic conceptual return of
the repressed. Indeed, in Luhmann's writings, the notions of semantics, self-
description, knowledge or cognition, and particularly memory, all point to the idea of
meaning (see also Burkart, 2004). Yet, with the notable exception of the more general
phenomenological conception of meaning or *Sinn* as such, these concepts only play a
rather minor role vis-à-vis the central concepts of communication and social system
within the overall architecture of Luhmann's theory. In a word, Luhmann's culture-
related notions, such as semantics or memory, seem to function primarily as
conceptual supplements to more essential concepts. If this is indeed the case, a
Derridian (e.g., Derrida, 1972) or deconstructive reading of Luhmann's texts may try
to reverse this logic of supplement and essence by showing that the proverbial social
essence (communication, social systems) cannot be described or analyzed without
implicit references to the cultural supplement(s) (for a first attempt in this direction,
see Stàheli, 2000).

I will not indulge here in radical philology or "Deconstruction as Second-Order
Observation" (Luhmann, 1995c). In what follows, I shall first succinctly present
Luhmann's explicit considerations on, and conceptual equivalents for, the notion of
culture. In the next section, I will argue that they all point to one and the same
mechanism of condensation and confirmation of meaning or *Sinn* (in the
phenomenological sense) within social systems into what Luhmann terms symbolic
generalizations, schemes or identities. In order to grasp the precise scope of this
thesis, I will briefly clarify Luhmann's view on meaning. In the closing section, I shall
develop the thesis that condensed and therefore typified forms or identities can be

regarded as the elements of *the medium called culture*. According to this view, which is hinted at in just a few sentences by Luhmann (1997, p. 409) himself, culture is a more specific articulation of the overall medium of meaning or Sinn that has generalized and reiterated meaningful forms as its basic elements (cf. Hahn, 2004). This conceptualization is broader than a semiological approach to culture, yet it can incorporate the latter since signs—in the Saussurian sense—are one particular sort of symbolic generalizations. The primary function of the medium of culture, I will thus argue in the closing paragraphs, is to secure the structural and operative coupling between social and psychic systems. I shall discuss this function in some detail and argue that typified forms, or cultural elements, are usually used within communication as always already known by all participating psychic systems.

Luhmann's explicit statements on and "around" culture

Luhmann was a very productive author, yet he devoted only one article to the notion of culture (Luhmann, 1995b). The essay "Kultur als historischer Begriff" [Culture as historical concept] does not offer a straightforward conceptual clarification but relates the discussed term to the heightened intellectual interest during the second half of the 18th century in the comparison of different languages (linguistics), various historical periods (historiography) or contrasting ways of life within different places or territories (proto-anthropology). Thus, the notion of culture first and foremostly points to the observation of differences. Seen in the more abstract way advocated by Luhmann himself, the observed differences have to do with differences in making and using … differences or, to be more precise, of distinctions or forms (e.g., of linguistic forms or words). In Luhmann's view, which is much indebted to G. Spencer-Brown (1969), a *form* is a two-sided distinction that is used one-sidedly in order to indicate or mark something as *this* (and not *that*), thus making observations possible. All distinctive and distinguishing material, be it words or lines, pixels or tones, even clothes or ways of doing, can be regarded as consisting of nothing more than forms— when observed! Precisely this happens in the comparison of languages or ways of life, for that is when one observes how others observe the world by means of specific linguistic forms, particular myths and rituals, and so forth. "All in all: culture is a perspective for the observation of observers," Luhmann (1995b, p. 54) concludes. The notion of culture therefore points to the more general mechanism—first analyzed by Von Foerster (1981)—of so-called *second-order observation*, or the observation of observations, the distinguishing of distinctions or forms.

Luhmann's characterization of the overall function of the modern concept of culture is in line with his stress on the institutionalization of second-order observation – or in more traditional terms: of reflexivity – within modernity (see esp. Luhmann, 1992). This generalization of second-order observation implies that not only a distant culture but also one's very own language or ways of doing can be marked as culturally specific or culture-bound. "Like before, one can cut with a knife, can pray to God, drive to the seaside, sign treaties or embellish objects. But in addition, all this can be observed and described a second time when one conceives it as a cultural phenomenon and exposes it to comparisons," Luhmann writes (1995b, p. 42). The second-order observations of the forms or distinctions that are regarded as constitutive for one's own first-order observing are per definition synonymous with self-observations or, when the latter have a textual character, self-descriptions (see esp. Luhmann, 1997, pp. 880-881). Within every society, one can of course always find interpretations of the basic characteristics of that very same society. Yet, only within modernity these self-observations are once again observed and reflexively processed. Thus, a modern society explicitly – read: reflexively – describes itself as modern or, more recently, as postmodern, risky, or globalized. One may therefore speak of a *reflexive second-order observation*, a *modernization of societal self-descriptions* resulting in *reflexive self-descriptions* (Kneer, 2003). Once again, this is made possible via the notion of culture. The latter concept, thus Luhmann argues (1997, p. 880), "holds the place where self-descriptions are reflected. Culture in the modern sense is always culture that is reflected upon as culture."

In the very same essay in which he introduces the idea of culture as "a perspective for the observation of observers," Luhmann also speaks of *memory* (Gedàchtnis) (Luhmann, 1995b, pp. 42-47). Particularly in *Die Gesellschaft der Gesellschaft*, the notion of memory is even more explicitly linked with the concept of culture, albeit in a rather loose way (Luhmann, 1997, pp. 576-594). Memorizing is not synonymous with remembering, let alone with the selective retrieval of experiences or artifacts from the past. In Luhmann's view, the notion of memory is a conceptual form or distinction in which forgetting is the logical counterpart of remembering. Thus, memorizing is the unity of the difference between forgetting and remembering. Yet, the real point of Luhmann's considerations, which can be read as a dialogue with the work of Jan and Aleida Assmann on social and cultural memory, is the operative and functional nature of memorizing within social systems (cf. Esposito 2002; Holl, 2003). Social systems consist of recursively enchained communications, or utterances of information that are understood as such—and not for instance as just sounds or "noise"—by later communications (I will return to the notion of recursivity later). Indeed, within a social system, every new communication at least implicitly confirms that information has been uttered previously. This loop not only implies a basic form of self-referentiality—a later communication refers to a previous event as a communication—but also that all new information is constantly tested in view of its consistency with already uttered information. This testing happens implicitly and is of course only possible thanks to the structural coupling of communication with psychic attention (cf. Luhmann, 1996a on the structural coupling of social and psychic systems, see also the last section). The net result, Luhmann writes, is

> on the one hand … the formation of a compact-impression, of being known, of familiarity, … and on the other hand, precisely for that reason, it is left to forgetfulness how it was before, when particular impressions or demands and irritations came as new, unexpected, unfamiliar surprises. (Luhmann, 1997, pp. 579-580)

On the level of our contemporary world-society, which is the most encompassing social system, the mass media function as the principal social memory (Luhmann, 1996). They inform *in* society *about* society by means of news reports that are constantly renewed, which illustrates the more general primacy of forgetting above remembering within modernity (cf. Laermans, 2005). Yet, every kind of social system – so also every interaction system and organization – constantly memorizes: New information is again and again observed in the light of previous information. To a great extent, this general memory function within social systems comes down to recognizing, and re-recognizing (and re-re-recognizing, and so on), new information. The recognition, which like all memorizing is an actual happening in the present, is synonymous with temporarily observing that information is repeated. Or as Elena Esposito (2002, p. 25) aptly remarks: "Memory thus concerns the genesis of redundancy, and the [historic] changes of memory are changes of the form of the relationship between redundancy and variety." The produced redundancy is the unintended, and also unavoidable, side-effect of the recursive character of communication as the basic operation of social systems. An operation is recursive when it takes the outcome of one or more previous operations as its proverbial starting point. Thus, within communication processes, already uttered information is referred to in new communications. This normally goes hand in hand with confirming not only the theme under discussion, but also with the at least partial repetition of the particular forms or distinctions that were previously used in order to inform. Indeed, information is an observation *of something*—but the designation of something, for instance as a table, or even as some thing, is again the result of the one-sided use of a two-sided form (for instance of a linguistic form, such as the words *table* and *some thing*) (see *inter alia* Luhmann, 1995, 1997; cf. Laermans, 1999, pp. 85-90). Precisely the observed reiteration of already communicatively used distinctions is synonymous with memorizing – with their remembering and (eventual) forgetting.

The concept of memory only turns up in Luhmann's later writings of the 1990's. Yet, the earlier concept of *semantics* – or semantic structures – a notion that Luhmann has also explicitly linked to the idea of culture, already acknowledged the function of memorizing, be it with a clear stress on remembering. Thus, in *Soziale Systeme* [Social Systems], Luhmann casually introduces both the terms *culture* and *semantics* when discussing the distinction between themes and contributions (to themes) in communication processes. Within the context of face-to-face communication or interaction systems, but also in written communication, specific themes can be taboo or, on the contrary, they can be preferred. They are repeatedly avoided or taken up, which results in a range of possible themes that can be quickly mobilized in an unobtrusive way within communication. "We would like to call this supply of themes *culture*, and, if it is reserved specifically for the purposes of communication, *semantics*" (Luhmann, 1995, p. 163). "Culture is not necessarily a normative content for meanings; perhaps it is more like a limitation of meaning (reduction) that makes it possible to distinguish appropriate from inappropriate contributions or even correct from incorrect uses of themes in theme-related communication" (Luhmann, 1995, p. 163 or, in the original German edition: 1984, pp. 224-225, italics by Luhmann).

Luhmann's notion of semantics is much indebted to the work of the German historian Reinhard Koselleck (e.g., 1979) on "Begriffsgeschichte," or the historical role and impact of concepts. The sometimes lengthy articles collected in the four volumes of the series *Gesellschaftsstruktur and Semantik* [Societal Structure and Semantics] all circle around textually traceable evolutions in general notions or theoretical concepts that hang together with transformations in the primary form of societal differentiation, particularly the definitive institutionalization of functional differentiation within modern society during the second half of the 18th century. More specifically, the studied shifts indicate another way of observing by means of new conceptual forms or distinctions. Yet, the distinctive feature of the forms which Luhmann describes as semantics is their typified nature. Indeed, a society's semantics specifies, retains and stabilizes meaning—and not only themes!—by way of *typical forms*. They have a general nature and can therefore be used, and eventually re-articulated, within various communicative contexts. In a word, the concept of semantics refers to "a present stock of types, ... a highly generalized, relatively situation-independent available meaning" (Luhmann, 1980, p. 19). Luhmann also speaks of semantic structures, which is in line with his more general definition of the notion of structure in terms of a limitation or reduction of possibilities on the one hand and, within social systems, of expectations—and reflexive expectations of expectations—on the other hand (see esp. Luhmann, 1995, pp. 285-290). Indeed, semantic forms reduce the possible meaning of, for instance, a word, and this reduced meaning or—as Luhmann sometimes formulates it—*meaning kernel* induces expectations, particularly about subsequent meaningful communications. For that matter, Luhmann clearly tends to underestimate the structuring capacity of semantic forms within communication or social systems, a point which I shall not further elaborate here (cf., Martens, 2004; Stäheli, 2000, pp. 184-229).

For the sake of completeness, one may observe that the idea of typical forms is taken up in a slightly different way, and under another conceptual heading, in Luhmann's voluminous treatise on science. In *Die Wissenschaft der Gesellschaft* [The Science of Society], the author does not explicitly discuss the concept of semantics but coins the concept of *knowledge* (Wissen). "Knowledge is (the) condensation of observations," Luhmann (1990, p. 123) states. He stresses that not only in science but also in daily life, knowledge is produced again and again via repeated observations. As said, an observation consists of one or more distinctions or forms that are one-sidedly used in order to indicate something as *this* (and not *that*). Repeated observations by means of the same forms result in the knowledge that *something is this*. Such knowledge necessarily has a general, situation-independent character: Repeated observations condense into reproducible forms that can be used in various situations or with reference to heterogeneous particulars. Thus, the observation "this is an apple" invokes the notion of apple as a type or general category that disregards the specific qualities of the observed thing. Given the type-like nature of knowledge and semantic forms, both notions seem to imply each other. In passing, Luhmann (1990, pp. 107-108) confirms this immanent link and explicitly relates his notion of knowledge to the concept of semantics. Although he does not go into it, the different conceptualization in *Die Wissenschaft der Gesellschaft* of the process of generalization or typification, probably has everything to do with the fact that, in line with the subject of the book, the principal point of reference is the concept of observation and not the notion of meaning.

On meaning and identities

There are at least four obvious interrelationships between the notions that have just been presented, and which all have the explicit function to act as equivalents for the concept of culture within Luhmann's systems theory. First, (reflexive) self-descriptions consist of particular semantic forms by means of which a culture and/or society is literally typified. To give just one example: the semantics of subjectivity, modernization, class, and risk play a key role in the reflexive self-descriptions of modernity (Luhmann, 1997, pp. 866-1150). Of course, the notion of culture, understood as the invitation to compare differences or observe in a second-order way, is also a central part of modern semantics, or self-descriptions, witness the popularity of the distinction between traditional and modern culture within and outside the social sciences. Second, and of probably more importance, there exists an intrinsic relationship between semantic forms or structures and the memory-function within social systems. Indeed, as we have seen and Luhmann himself also regularly stresses, the first are nothing more than by-products of memorizing within communication. More particularly, semantics are forms which are repeatedly used and thus recognized namely remembered—or not!—in the actual operations of social systems. Or, as Luhmann (1997, p. 538) writes: "semantic structures identify, hold, remember or leave to forgetfulness meaning that is valuable to retain." The remembering or forgetting happens blindly: no consciousness or cultural steering is implied—at least according to Luhmann (for one can, inspired for instance by the work of Pierre Bourdieu or Ernesto Laclau, also observe semantic struggles and dominant or hegemonic forms; see Nassehi & Nollmann, 2004; Stàheli, 2000).

Third, the notion of memory is also intrinsically linked to the more general concept of structure, or the reduction of communicative possibilities over a certain period of time. Structures are memorizing devices since they foresee social systems with generalized expectations (social structures) or typified meanings (semantic structures) that emerged out of previous communications and are operative within actual operations. Therefore, both the concept of structure and memory, and *a fortiori* the notion of semantics, have a certain affinity with Parsons' characterization of the primary function of the cultural system in terms of latent pattern maintenance (see Hahn, 2004; & esp. Martens, 1999). Fourth, and lastly, we can observe that all the notions with which Luhmann encircles "the question of culture" point to the same process, that is the unavoidable mechanism that reduces and stabilizes meaning, in the phenomenological sense (see below), within recursively and self-referentially operating systems. It is therefore all the more striking that one of the many asides in *Die Gesellschaft der Gesellschaft* reads as follows:

> In the cooperation between all communication media – language, distributing media [like writing and printing—RL] and symbolically generalized media [or success media that regulate the acceptance of communications within certain domains, such as money within the economy or truth within science—RL] – condenses that what is called with an overall expression *culture*. Condensation should be understood here in the sense that, on the one hand, meaning (Sinn) that is used once, through its re-use in various contexts remains the same (for otherwise it would not be a re-use), but confirms itself, on the other hand, and enriches itself with significations ("Bedeutungen") that can no longer be lumped together (Luhmann, 1997, p. 409).

How do we have to understand this compact assertion, which reads as a meta-theoretical articulation of the various notions that Luhmann presents as equivalents for the concept of culture, and simultaneously introduces—be it casually and without further elaboration—a general notion of culture as such?

In order to unpack the just quoted statement, the overall notion of meaning or Sinn is a useful starting-point. In Luhmann's view, both social and psychic systems operate in a literally meaningful way: Meaning, in the Husserlian sense, is their basic medium. For this reason, meaning is sociology's basic concept (Luhmann, 1990). According to Luhmann's appropriation of Husserl's phenomenology, meaning is not synonymous with signification in the strict textual or semiological sense. "Instead, we would like to begin from the fact that a *difference* is contained in every experience of meaning, namely, the difference between what is *actually given* and what can *possibly* result from it" (Luhmann, 1995, p. 74 or, in the original German edition, 1984, p. 111 – italics by Luhmann). Thus, every actual thought or mental representation (psychic system) and every actual communication (social system) appears against a horizon of possibilities – of possible other thoughts or communications. A next thought or communication is a selection out of this horizon and thus contingent, in the sense of modal logic: It is not impossible and not necessary, and thus possible (for what follows, see Luhmann, 1995, pp. 59-102, 1990, 1997, pp. 44-59). More particularly, an actual communication is a threefold selection: Selected information is selectively uttered and selectively understood. Within a communication process, the horizon of possible selections is of course constantly renewed. Every new utterance of information makes certain former possibilities implausible and simultaneously opens up new ones out of which a next communication is selected. Thus, meaning or the unity of the difference of actuality and virtuality (possible possibilities) is constantly re-articulated within social systems. At the same time, it is the fundamental medium of both social and psychic systems since only the ever-present horizon of virtual communications or thoughts makes it possible to go on – to select a next communication or thought, and thus to reproduce the basic operation that makes up social or psychic systems.

Within thinking or communicating words, observed objects, payments, sounds … or whatever contingent form can all be taken up once again or re-used. If this is done repeatedly, the result is *an abstract scheme, a symbolic generalization or an identity*—Luhmann's vocabulary tends to shift here—that reduces the meaningful horizon of possibilities opened up by the form in question, for instance by a linguistic signifier. From the above considerations on semantics as typified forms, it may already have become clear that the notion of identity does not point at all to given substances or a univocal relationship of self-transparency, but rather to reductive self-relations (Luhmann, 1995, pp. 93-94). Thus, a word with a so-called identical meaning—one may think here of the semiotic notion of denotation—is a linguistic form in which a sound or a combination of letters is coupled with a "meaning kernel." Hence de Saussure's famous conceptualization of the sign as a particular distinction, i.e. as the unity of the difference between a signifier and a signified (cf. Luhmann, 1993). Yet, a typified or abstract meaning namely signified is not univocal or proper, in the strict sense, but a temporarily stabilized reduction of the possible significations it could also have. What may this imply?

We already noticed that Luhmann tends to refer to stabilizing namely temporally stabilized meaning kernels in terms of condensed observations or forms. Yet, not one but two mechanisms, *condensation* and *confirmation*, are involved in the process of producing identities, symbolic generalizations or abstract schemes (for what follows, see esp. Luhmann, 1990a, and Spencer-Brown, 1969, p. 10). Precisely this double logic is also hinted at in the just quoted aside in *Die Gesellschaft der Gesellschaft*, in which Luhmann evokes the possibility of a general concept of culture. On the one hand, there is the taking up again of an already actualized possible meaning or identity of a form via its re-use in later operations (A' = A). In this way, the signification of the form in a previous operation is condensed into its re-use, which is again condensed in the third re-use, and so on. Thus, every identity or meaning-kernel is the condensation of a plurality of operations. On the other hand, every new operation is also a singular confirmation of the already condensed identity. This singularity implies that the operation always takes place in a specific context that differs from the previous contexts in which the meaning-kernel concerned was already condensed. It is therefore impossible to re-use a scheme in a schematic way, or to stick to the mechanical duplication of the so-called literal or denotative meaning of a word within whatever kind of sentence. On the contrary, an identity or meaning-kernel is again and again slightly transformed with every re-use, but these specific contextual enrichments are not taken up in a next operation. Thus, an identity is an abstraction or generalization – a typified form – that on the one hand remains the same within different situations (condensation), but on the other hand refers to a never extinguishing horizon of virtual possibilities, of which one or more are contextually activated (confirmation). Yet, this is precisely the meaning ... of meaning! In Luhmann's (1990a, p. 22) own words: "the simultaneous processing of condensation and confirmation produces the difference of actuality and possibility, which we regard as the constitutive difference of the medium of meaning."

In *Die Gesellschaft der Gesellschaft*, Luhmann invokes the double logic of condensation and confirmation more than once in order to explain the production of the relatively stable meanings attached to words, resulting in linguistic forms (see Luhmann, 1997, pp. 205-229). The latter consists of sounds (verbal language) or letters (written language) which are coupled to at once specific and generalized significations or meaning-kernels that can be re-used or re-actualized. Like all identities or symbolic generalizations, linguistic forms combine determinateness and indeterminateness, particular significations and the reference to an open horizon of possibilities. According to a by-now well-established tradition already hinted at, they are usually described—and more recently: deconstructed—as signs. Yet, not all typified forms are signs, since, for instance, also objects or perceptual schemes are condensed distinctions or generalized forms. On the contrary, a sign is a particular form, that is the unity of the difference between a signifier and a signified (which Luhmann sometimes mistakenly identifies with the referent; see Luhmann, 1993). The relationship between signs and typified forms in general may be left open here, but it is immediately clear that the use of distinctions as signs implies that their designative side changes into a signifier that signifies a meaning or signification. Thus, signs are forms which reflexively indicate their primary status as vehicles of meaning. The net outcome of sign-use is therefore the emergence and institutionalization of the specific difference between the "real reality and semiotic reality," or the "imaginary space of significations" (Luhmann, 1997, pp. 218-219).

There are evident links between Luhmann's approach of meaning-identities or condensed forms in general, and of (linguistic) signs in particular, and Jacques Derrida's view on the impossibility of a proper meaning or a transparent signified (e.g., Derrida, 1967) on the one hand, Gilles Deleuze's considerations on difference and repetition as the proverbial hard kernel of every identity on the other hand (Deleuze, 1968). Also, the way Luhmann describes the emergence and stabilization of typified forms is comparable to Derrida's notion of iterability (Derrida, 1988). Actually, the blind—in the sense of unplanned and unforeseen (and thus: "unwilled")—and simultaneously unavoidable operative repetition or iteration of forms in an at once determinate and indeterminate way within social (or psychic systems) is the proverbial force behind the double process of condensation-confirmation. There is nothing mysterious about this since social systems operate in a recursive way. Actual communications take into account the results of former communications, and therefore also the specific ways in which forms or distinctions were previously actualized. Seen in this light, condensed-confirmed forms are an illuminating illustration of self-referentiality: A determinate form is what it is because of the reference to what it always already was. In addtion, this condensed identity only exists if it is condensed-confirmed once again in a next operation. There exists a French neologism to designate this strange loop: *différance,* indeed (Derrida, 1972a).

Culture as medium and operative fiction

The above digressions open up interesting perspectives for the comparison of Luhmann's systems theory with French post-structuralism—yet, let us return to the overall question that motivated my selective reading of Luhmann's writings: can social systems theory outdo the notion of culture? To be sure, Luhmann sometimes explicitly acknowledges the constitutive role of meaning-identities or symbolic generalizations for the functioning of social systems. He thus opens his discussion of knowledge or condensed observations in *Die Wissenschaft der Gesellschaft* with the brief remark: "No communication without assumable knowledge" (Luhmann, 1990, p. 122). And speaking of semantics, he stresses that "without any link to types, meaning ... would be underdetermined, incomprehensible, incommunicable [sic! – RL]" (Luhmann, 1980, p. 18). These kinds of statements do not abound in Luhmann's work. Nevertheless, they indicate that condensed meaning is indeed an essential supplement (Derrida, 1972) or, to borrow an apt expression from Henry Staten (1985), *a constitutive outside* of social systems (and of psychic systems, which also operate in a literally meaningful way). One cannot analyze the functioning of social systems without taking into account the reiteration as well as the renewal and creation of condensed meanings or significations (in the ongoing semiological sense: a condensed meaning!) namely of condensed forms. And yet, in Luhmann's own theory design, their enabling role is repeatedly neglected. Indeed, his social systems theory rather systematically relegates meaning-identities to the periphery, probably because of the author's skeptical attitude towards the concept of culture.

Given the constitutive role of condensed-confirmed meaning for the functioning of both social and psychic systems, I propose to take up Luhmann's own casual and already quoted suggestion in *Die Gesellschaft der Gesellschaft* that "in the cooperation between all communication media – language, distributing media and symbolically generalized media – condenses that what is called with an overall expression *culture*" (Luhmann, 1997, p. 409). In line with this remark, culture may be provisionally defined as *the available stock of condensed meanings, symbolic generalizations or typified forms* (cf., Hahn, 2004). Yet, a still more nuanced conceptual elaboration is possible in the light of the notion of *medium* (see esp. Luhmann 1995a, pp. 165-214; cf., Brauns, 2002; Schiltz, 2003). According to Luhmann, who re-interprets the initial considerations of Fritz Heider (1993) regarding the notion, a medium consists of loosely coupled elements. Language, for instance, is a specific medium in which words are the primary elements. Words are forms or distinctions since they combine sounds or letters with a condensed meaning. More generally, the elements of a medium are forms within another medium, for example, within perceivable sound or the alphabet. At the same time, every actualization of medial elements also results in forms, their tight and temporal coupling. Thus, words are selectively combined into sentences – and only within these momentary couplings or forms, or actualizations, a medium makes itself indirectly observable. Indeed, one never observes a medium as such but only its current realizations: A medium such as language makes observations possible but is in itself unobservable. Or as Michael Schiltz (2003, n.p.) aptly states: A medium is "ever present, yet not actual." Following these considerations, culture can be conceptualized as *a specific medium within the overall medium of meaning*. More particularly, condensed meanings or typified forms are the loosely coupled elements of the medium called culture. As such, culture is simultaneously an enabling and a (re)produced resource of both communication and thinking, or social and psychic systems. With every social or psychic operation, the elements of culture are contextually re-affirmed (condensed) and re-interpreted (confirmed).

In line with Luhmann's overall distinction between the three primary dimensions of meaning, the medium of culture can be described from a threefold point of view (on these dimensions, see e.g., Luhmann, 1990, 1995, pp. 74-82, 1997, pp. 44-59). Within the *temporal dimension*, culture is synonymous with the stabilization of meaning via the mechanism of forgetting and remembering. Culture is indeed a memory, or rather: a memorizing medium, since cultural forms are continuously re-used and therefore remembered significations. Usually, this goes unnoticed: the remembering is not observed, marked or designated as such within communication or thinking. Thus, culture can be defined as *the primarily non-reflexive remembering of (re-)condensed meanings or forms*. Of course, the reflexive use of such forms also belongs to the realm of culture. Following a suggestion made by Baecker (2000, pp. 11-32), one may refer to these second-order observations as instances of meta-culture. As Baecker rightly stresses, within contemporary or so-called postmodern culture a reflexive meta-stance has become institutionalized, as in, for instance, the mass-mediated impact of (communicated) life-styles on self-descriptions.

The *factual dimension* of the medium of culture follows from the proverbial nature of meaning-identities: They are condensed forms or distinctions which make observation possible. As Luhmann (1990) himself suggests, the iterative use of typified and stabilized forms results in the production of knowledge (Wissen), in the broad sense. Yet, every kind of knowledge is also by definition a *reality construction* – and precisely in this respect, culture has a factual dimension. When used, condensed forms indeed produce again and again a reality, or better: the reality of an observed reality. A second-order observer, such as an anthropologist or a sociologist doing ethnographic fieldwork, may observe distinctive patterns in the overall way that symbolic generalizations are communicatively used. Taken together, they form what is commonly called a worldview. As such, a world view does not exist, of course. It is a second-order construct, and thus also a reality construction. Or to phrase this in another way: when observing the factual dimension of (a) culture, one necessarily does what one is looking at.

The *social dimension* of culture is undoubtedly the most discussed, researched and known one. Within the social sciences, it is indeed proverbial wisdom that culture is shared. This premise is often interpreted in a psychological sense, so that shared culture equals internalized culture and culture as such equals a collective consciousness (*dixit*, of course, Emile Durkheim). Yet, as for instance the anthropologist Clifford Geertz rightly stresses, "Culture is public because meaning is. … [Culture] consists of socially established structures of meaning" (Geertz, 1973, p. 12). More particularly, from a social systems point of view, culture is first and foremost recursively produced and reproduced in communication. Social systems cannot function without typified meaning or condensed forms, which they also blindly create and re-create; conversely, cultural elements are only observable when used in communication. This is of course not to say that psychic systems do not make use of culture, quite the contrary. Via their participation in social systems, they are constantly socialized – and not only during early years! – in the communicatively used forms or meaning-identities. This does not imply that the so-called members of a culture think or valuate in a similar way. Within both social and psychic systems, culture just foresees the operations with reduced meaning or condensed forms that are temporally combined into a communication or a mental representation. How to think this double logic in a more precise way?

In Luhmann's view, social and psychic systems are structurally coupled to each other. This coupling is nothing more than a necessity, since "without consciousness, communication is impossible. Communication is *totally* (*in every* operation) thrown onto consciousness – if only already because only consciousness, but not communication itself, can observe sensorily and neither oral nor written communication can function without sensory performances" (Luhmann, 1999, pp. 103, italics in original). As Luhmann (e.g., 1995d, 1997, pp. 92-119) stresses more than once, the concept of structural coupling does not imply a merging or an operative overlapping of the coupled systems. Both social and psychic systems are operatively closed and therefore do not share, let alone exchange, their elements. Structural coupling only implies the operative synchronization of the functioning of the coupled systems. Thus, psychic systems must be attentive to communication when participating in a social system, which by definition implies the risk of becoming irritated by the uttered information. The latter is psychically understood – meaning thoughtfully understood – and this suffices for smooth functioning of the coupling. Conversely, the communication may for instance notice that a participating psychic system is indeed irritated by what has been said previously. Yet, neither the other participants, nor the communication process as such can directly enter the irritated consciousness and observe why formerly uttered information elicited irritation.

According to Luhmann, language and different kind of schemes, such as the temporal distinction past/future or the moral form good/bad, are the two basic mechanisms that ensure the structural coupling between social and psychic systems (see Luhmann, 1997, pp. 92-119). He never clarified the relationship between both, which is all the more striking since he also describes condensed linguistic forms – or signs – as schematizations or generalizations of meaning. In addition, Luhmann never systematically addressed the question of how social and psychic systems are coupled when the communication has a visual nature (this point is, for instance, omitted in the discussion of the visual arts in Luhmann, 1995a). Both problems are avoided when one describes all condensed forms or instances of typified meaning, including visual schemes, as being the elements of a specific medium, that is, a culture. In line with this view, *the medium of culture secures the structural coupling between social and psychic systems*. This approach has the advantage of being conceptually simple: one, and only one medium, structurally couples both kinds of meaning-based systems. A similar line of argument is unfolded by Siegfried Schmidt (1996), who also considers culture to be ensuring structural coupling, but in combination with technical media-offers and on the basis of a Parsonian definition of culture (which contradicts the basic assumptions of Luhmann's systems theory).

The principal hallmark of the structural coupling between psychic and social systems is the way in which condensed forms, or cultural elements, are used within communication, that is, as always already known by all participating psychic systems. What Luhmann remarks about so-called abstract schemes may indeed be given a more general purport:

> When using schemata [cultural elements – RL], communication assumes that every participating consciousness understands what is meant, but that on the other hand it is not determined how the conscious system deals with the schema, let alone: which connecting communications follow from the use of the schema. (Luhmann, 1997, p. 111)

For that matter, both Luhmann's early considerations on implicit consensus (in Luhmann, 1972, pp. 67-68) and his scattered remarks on organizational culture as the necessarily implicit fund of "non-decidable decision premises" (in Luhmann, 2000a, pp. 241ff) go in the same direction. They also suggest that social systems take up always specific forms of typified meaning and simultaneously presume that the participating psychic systems are familiar with it. As Luhmann himself has pointed out, familiarity is the defining feature of what is called the life-world within the phenomenological tradition. Yet, communication is not "really" situated within the life-world—as Jürgen Habermas (1981) has argued—but rather uses the existence of a life-world in which meanings are familiar as an assumption in every of its operations.

In order to underline the assumptive nature of the familiar character of typified forms or symbolic generalizations within communication, I propose the notion of *operative fiction* (Laermans, 1999, pp. 98-100, 178-179). The concept refers to the fictitious – in the sense of not verified and also non-verifiable – assumption of psychically well-known or evident meaning-identities that is operative within communication, thus facilitating the structural coupling with the participating psychic systems in the environment. As Harold Garfinkel's famous breaching experiments have clearly demonstrated, the operative fiction of *being familiar with* gives also rise to the corresponding normative expectation that the participants are indeed acquainted with the condensed meaning-identities used in a statement or whatever communication (Garfinkel, 1984). More generally, social systems theory can still learn quite a lot from early ethnomethodology and its later avatar, conversation analysis, for the study of culture within interaction systems.

Concluding remarks

This article started from the observation that Niklas Luhmann was highly skeptical about the theoretical usefulness of the notion of culture. At the same time, he could not negate the more general theoretical problematic of meaning or signification and, more particularly, the structuring and therefore operative role of stabilized meanings or identities within communication and social systems. Therefore, Luhmann devised at least three conceptual equivalents for the notion of culture: memory, semantics or semantic structures, and knowledge. They all point to the very same mechanism of the condensation and confirmation of meaning, in the phenomenological sense (Sinn), within social systems. According to Luhmann, repeatedly condensed and confirmed meaning results in symbolic generalizations or identities, or typical forms or schemes, that are taken up for granted, or always already known by the participating psychic systems, within communication. Given their pivotal role in social systems, in which they reduce semantic possibilities and produce normative expectations about "the correct meaning" (of a word, a picture, a piece of clothing, etc.), it seems plausible, even necessary to give meaning-identities more theoretical prominence within social systems theory. One way to do this is to take up a casual suggestion made by Luhmann (1999, pp. 409) himself and to conceptualize typified forms or meaning kernels as the basic elements of culture. Within the overall architecture of Luhmann's systems theory, the notion of medium perfectly fits this approach. Thus, condensed meanings or typified forms – or symbolic generalizations or identities – can be considered to be the loosely coupled elements of the medium called culture, which is itself a specific medium within the overall medium of meaning, in the Husserlian sense of Sinn or the unity of the difference between actuality and virtuality (possible possibilities), what is and what could also be.

The direct theoretical gain of the proposed conceptualization of the notion of culture for a social systems theory that tries to remain loyal to Luhmann's overall intuitions, is the possibility to re-think the structural coupling between social and psychic systems in simultaneously medial and cultural terms. The medium of culture, it was thus argued, ensures the coupling between both kinds of systems because typified forms or meaning kernels are used as such in communication vis-à-vis the participating psychic systems. Acquaintance or familiarity is counter-factually presupposed, which not only legitimates the notion of operative fiction but also opens up a vast area of possible empirical research. As said, ethnomethodology and conversation analysis are evident partners here as far as interaction systems of face-to-face communications are involved. Yet, organizations and functional subsystems also operate on the base of a self-produced culture, or non-questioned semantic forms that act as presuppositions in the realms of communication and self-observation. More generally, all social systems operatively (re-)produce what they need for their (re-)production, that is, an always particular set of communicatively used typical forms or meaning-identities that bind the participating psychic systems, and eventually also other social systems, in their environment.

I have already pointed out that Luhmann's considerations on condensed-confirmed meaning are in line with the cardinal insights of some of the master-minds of French post-structuralism, that is, with Derrida's notions of *iterability* and *différance* on the one hand and Deleuze's speculations about identity as the unity of the difference between difference and repetition on the other. They can be taken up in a more detailed way in a social systems theory that basically remains within the framework outlined by Luhmann but does not underwrite his theoretical skepticism about the notion of culture (cf., Baecker, 2000). Moreover, promising theoretical links seems possible with those branches of cybernetics that try to re-articulate the intellectual heritage of semiotics and semiology in general and the work of C. S. Peirce in particular (cf., Rustemeyer, 2006; Brier, 2007). From the point of medium theory, the proposed notion of culture may also be combined in a fruitful way with the considerations on the same topic by Anthony Giddens in his theory of structuration (see Giddens, 1986). Indeed, Giddens conceptualizes culture as the medium of (condensed and confirmed) meaning that is at once the outcome and the condition of possibility of social relation. Yet, it should be noted that the proposed re-articulation of the concept of culture does not at all imply a culture-oriented overall theoretical framework. Or, as Luhmann himself remarks in one of the lines which directly follow the quotation of *Die Gesellschaft der Gesellschaft* that was the starting-point for my re-interpretation of culture in terms of the medium of condensed forms or meanings:

> These considerations entail a certain skepticism in view of the possibilities of a theory of culture. The surplus of references and particularly the concreteness of the ... condensations which are actualized in all meaning only allow for a selective processing. Something must be said – and this means: nothing else. (Luhmann, 1997, p. 410)

Bibliography

Baecker, D. (2000). *Wozu Kultur?* Berlin: Kadmos.
Brauns, J. (Ed.) (2002). *Form und Medium*. Weimar: VDG.
Brier, S. (2007). *Cybersemiotics: Why information is not enough*. Toronto: Toronto University Press.
Burkart, G. (2004). Niklas Luhmann: Ein Theoretiker der Kultur? In G. Burkart and G. Runkel (eds.), *Luhmann und die Kulturtheorie* (11-39). Frankfurt: Suhrkamp.
Deleuze, G. (1967). *Différence et répétition*. Paris: Presses Universitaires de France.
Derrida, J. (1967). *De la grammatologie*. Paris: Minuit.
Derrida, J. (1972). *La dissemination*. Paris: Seuil.
Derrida, J. (1972a). *Marges de la philosophie*. Paris: Minuit.
Derrida, J. (1988). *Limited Inc*. Evanston: Northwestern University Press.
Esposito, E. (2002). *Soziales Vergessen. Formen und Medien des Gedàchtnisses der Gesellschaft*. Frankfurt: Suhrkamp.
Fuchs, P. (2003). *Der Eigen-Sinn des Bewusstseins. Die Person, die Psyche, die Signatur*. Bielefeld: Transcript.
Garfinkel, H. (1984). *Studies in ethnomethodology*. Cambridge: Polity.
Geertz, C. (1973). Thick description: Toward an interpretative theory of culture. In C. Geertz, *The Interpretation of Cultures* (3-32). New York: Basic Books.
Habermas, J. (1984). *Theorie des kommunikativen Handelns* (Vols. 1-2). Frankfurt: Suhrkamp.
Giddens, A. (1986). *The constitution of society. Outline of the theory of structuration*. Oxford: Polity Press.
Hahn, A. (2004). Ist Kultur ein Medium? In G. Burkart and G. Runkel (Eds.), *Luhmann und die Kulturtheorie* (40-57). Frankfurt: Suhrkamp.
Hall, S. (1997). *Representation: Cultural representations and signifying practices*. London: Sage.
Heider, F. (1993). Ding und Medium. In C. Pias, J. Vogl, & L. Engell (Eds.), *Kursbuch Medienkultur* (319-333). Stuttgart: DVA.
Holl, M.K. (2003). *Semantik und Soziales Gedàchtnis. Die Systemtheorie Niklas Luhmanns und die Gedàchtnistheorie von Aleida und Jan Assman*. Würzburg: Köningshausen & Neumann.
Kneer, G, (2003). Reflexive Beobachtung zweiter Ordnung. Zur Modernisierung gesellschaftlibher Selbstbechreibungen. In H. J. Giegel and U. Schimank (Eds.), *Beobachter der Moderne. Beitràge zu Niklas Luhmanns "Die Gesellschaft der Gesellschaft"* (301-332). Frankfurt: Suhrkamp.
Koselleck, R. (1979). *Vergangene Zukunft. Zur Semantik geschichtlicher Zeiten*. Frankfurt: Suhrkamp.
Laermans, R. (1999). *Communicatie zonder mensen* [Communication without people]. Amsterdam: Boom.

Laermans, R. (2005). Mass media in contemporary society: A critical appraisal of Niklas Luhmann's systems view. *Cybernetics & Human Knowing*, *12*(4), 51-70.

Luhmann, N. (1972). *Rechtssoziologie 1*. Hamburg: Rowohlt.

Luhmann, N. (1980). Gesellschaftliche Struktur und semantische Tradition. In *Gesellschaftsstruktur und Semantik. Studien zur Wissenssoziologie der modernen Gesellschaft* (Band 1, pp. 9-71). Frankfurt: Suhrkamp.

Luhmann, N. (1984). *Soziale Systeme. Grundriss einer allgemeinen Theorie*. Frankfurt: Suhrkamp.

Luhmann, N. (1986). Die Lebenswelt – nach Rücksprache mit Phànomenologen. *Archiv für Rechts- und Sozialphilosophie*, *72* (3), 176-194.

Luhmann, N. (1990). Meaning as Sociology's Basic Concept. In *Essays on Self-Reference* (pp. 21-79). New York: Columbia University Press.

Luhmann, N. (1990a). Identitàt – was oder wie? In *Soziologische Aufklàrung 5. Konstruktivistische Perspektiven* (14-30). Opladen: Westdeutscher Verlag.

Luhmann, N. (1992). *Beobachtungen der Moderne*. Opladen: Westdeutscher Verlag.

Luhmann, N. (1993). Zeichen als Form. In D. Baecker (Ed.), *Probleme der Form* (pp. 45-69). Frankfurt: Suhrkamp.

Luhmann, N. (1995). *Social systems*. Stanford: Stanford California Press.

Luhmann, N. (1995a). *Die Kunst der Gesellschaft*. Frankfurt: Suhrkamp.

Luhmann, N. (1995b). Kultur als historischer Begriff. In *Gesellschaftsstruktur und Semantik. Studien zur Wissenssoziologie der modernen Gesellschaft* (Band 4, pp. 31-54). Frankfurt: Suhrkamp.

Luhmann, N. (1995c). Dekonstruktion als Beobachtung zweiter Ordnung. In H. de Berg and M. Prangel (Eds.), *Differenzen. Systemtheorie zwischen Dekonstruktion und Konstruktivismus* (pp. 9-36). Tübingen/Basel: Francke.

Luhmann, N. (1995d). Wie ist Bewusstsein an Kommunikation beteiligt? In *Soziologische Aufklàrung 6. Die Soziologie und der Mensch* (pp. 37-34). Opladen: Westdeutscher Verlag.

Luhmann, N. (1996). *Die Realitàt der Massenmedien*. Opladen: Westdeutscher Verlag.

Luhmann, N. (1996a). Zeit und Gedàchtnis. In *Soziale Systeme*, 2 (2), 307-330.

Luhmann, N. (1997). *Die Gesellschaft der Gesellschaft* (2 vols.). Frankfurt: Suhrkamp.

Luhmann, N. (2000). *Einführung in die Systemtheorie*. Heidelberg: Carl-Auer-Systeme Verlag.

Luhmann, N. (2000a). *Organisation und Entscheidung*. Opladen/Wiesbaden: Westdeutscher Verlag.

Martens, W. (1999). Die kulturelle und soziale Ordnung des Handelns. Eine analyze der Beitràge Parsons und Luhmanns. In R. Greshoff and G. Kneer (Eds.). *Struktur und Ereignis in theorievergleichender Perspektive* (pp. 70-118). Opladen: Westdeutscher Verlag.

Martens, W. (2004). Struktur, Semantik und Gedàchtnis. Vorbemerkungen zur Evolutionstheorie. In H. J. Giegel and U. Schimank (Eds.), *Beobachter der Moderne. Beitràge zu Niklas Luhmanns "Die Gesellschaft der Gesellschaft.* (pp. 167-203). Frankfurt: Suhrkamp.

Nassehi, A., & Nollman, G. (Eds.)(2004). *Bourdieu und Luhmann. Ein Theorienvergleich*. Frankfurt: Suhrkamp.

Parsons, T. (1951). *The social system*. Glencoe, IL: The Free Press.

Parsons, T. (1978). A paradigm of the human condition. In *Action Theory and the human condition* (pp. 352-433). New York: Free Press.

Reckwitz, A. (2000). *Die Transformation der Kulturtheorie. Zur Entwicklung eines Theorieprogramms*. Weilerswist: Velbrück Wissenschaft.

Rustemeyer, D. (2006). *Oszillationen. Kultursemiotische Perspektiven*. Würzburg: Köningshausen & Neumann.

Schiltz, M. (2003). Form and medium: A mathematical reconstruction. In *Image and Narrative*, 6 (electronic journal: http://www.imageandnarrative.be/).

Schmidt, S. J. (1996). *Kognitive Autonomie und soziale Orientierung. Konstruktivistische Bemerkungen zum Zusammenhang von Kognitionen, Kommunikation, Medien und Kultur*. Frankfurt: Suhrkamp.

Spencer-Brown, G. (1969). *Laws of form*. London: Allen & Unwin.

Stàheli, U. (2000). *Sinnzusammenbrüche. Eine dekonstruktive Lektüre von Niklas Luhmanns Systemtheorie*. Weilerswist: Velbrück Wissenschaft.

Staten, H. (1985). *Wittgenstein and Derrida*. Oxford: Blackwell.

Von Foerster, H. (1981). *Observing systems*. Seaside, CA: Intersystems Publications.

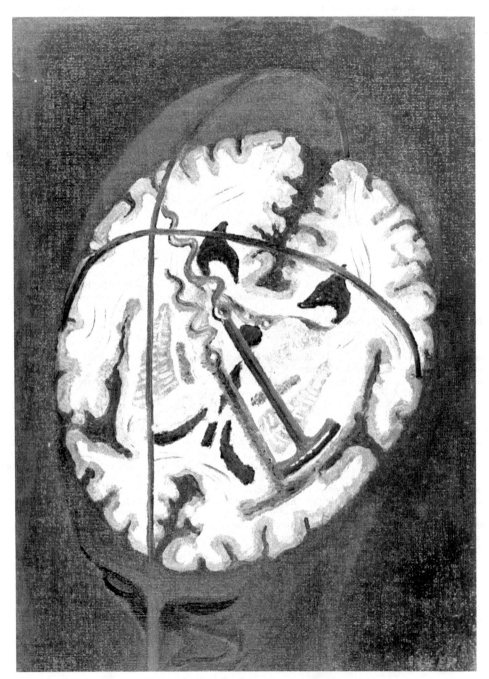

Beer, S. (n.d.). *The Inextinguishable*

Cybernetics And Human Knowing. Vol. 14, nos. 2-3, pp. 85-110

Luhmann and Globalization
The Interplay between nation, state and world society

By Ole Thyssen[1]

In Luhmann's scheme of social systems, *society* is not, as in colloquial talk, the nation. As Luhmann defines social systems in only one dimension, communication, and as communications can easily connect to other communications across geographical borderlines, it is no wonder that the spatially defined nation is not occupying an important position in his theory. Society is world society, the system of all communication. This inclusive system with no social counter-concept is differentiated in functional subsystems such as economy, politics and science which also are global in scope. Globalization is, by the choice of basic concepts, built into Luhmann's theory of social systems.

The concept of a nation, however, is ambiguous. It can, in a neutral sense, refer to a population inhabiting a delimited territory and subjected to a central power. And it can, in a normative sense, refer to a special kind of political self-description, nationalism, developing and flourishing in the period between 1789 and 1914. According to Luhmann, nationalism is a phase in the evolution of political self-descriptions. He considers nationalistic semantics as outdated and unable to describe modern society.

It can be discussed whether Luhmann is correct in arguing that nationalist semantics has lost its power. After 1989, it seems to be strengthening. Still, Luhmann's predilection for temporal as opposed to spatial descriptions makes him describe nations as mere geographical subdivisions of world society. They may exploit irregularities in the functional subsystems but are theoretically unimportant.

Claiming the obsolescence of nationalist semantics does not, however, imply a denial of the significance of the nation or its political representative, the state. Luhmann accepts that nations fulfill important political functions.

So a tension can be seen in Luhmann's theory of social systems. On one side, the world is globalized due to the dynamics of functional subsystems. On the other hand, nations are still the most important political actors. When Luhmann defines the state as "the self-description of the political system," he implicitly takes the point of view of the nation and, as a consequence, accepts a plurality of political systems. Following his theory design there should be only one global political system. Even if that may be analytically true, as all political actors connect to all political actors on the global scene, still there is no effective world state and no global political self-description.

Such irregularities call for a renewed systems theoretical analysis of the relation between nation, state and world society, showing that the dilemma between the global and the national perspective is not a real one. Functional subsystems, organizations and states are structurally coupled and together account for the dynamics of world society. In the end of the paper it is argued that the problems of globalization may be analyzed as consequences of this coupling of three different kinds of social system having different goals, number of stakeholders, relations to time and space and responsibility for stakeholders, namely functional subsystems, private organizations and states. As no political agent is representing the tangled and hyper-complex political system as a whole, it is not possible to harmonize the problems arising from the anarchic interplay of the three systems. Creating second-order super nations such as the EU would not solve the problems, but only rearrange them. This rather pessimistic perspective on the possibility of handling the problems of globalization is inherent in Luhmann's acrid statement in Social Systems: Survival depends on evolution, that is, chance.

1. Department for Management, Politics and Philosophy, Copenhagen Business School. E-mail thyssen@cbs.dk. I want to thank Dirk Baecker and Gorm Harste who read an earlier draft of this paper and by their both critical and constructive comments forced me to rethink, revise and rewrite.

Introduction

According to Luhmann, globalization is not a problem, but a fact (Luhmann, 1997b, p. 67). The conflict between the national and the global point of view is dismissed with a few remarks on the obsolescence of the idea of the nation as "a bunch of transitory semantics" (Luhmann, 1997a, p. 1055) blocking necessary insight. There are, he maintains, "clear and theoretically consistent arguments for a single world society" (Luhmann, 1997b, p. 73). But even if the description of nations as historical, cultural and ethnic unities is outdated, the nation is still alive. Semantics change, nations persist, even if geographical borderlines may change, empires disintegrate, former colonies fight for independence, and smaller groups inside a nation may claim a right to autonomy, invoking a nationalist semantics.

We will define a *nation* as a social system covering a delimited geographical area and with both a geographical and a social boundary distinguishing an inside from an outside and members from non-members. For a nation to subsist, a central power must be able to defend the boundary externally and to enforce collectively binding decisions internally. If any one of these tasks is not fulfilled, the nation ceases to exist; conversely, a nation proves its right to exist by successfully fulfilling them over time. The central power we will call the *state*, so that a state is the political representative of a nation, having the power to describe, reflect and act on behalf of it and making it a unitary system not only to an outside observer, but also to itself. Increasing differentiation means increasing complexity which again creates a need for "self-simplifying devices that makes it possible for the system to use itself as a premise for its own operations" (Luhmann, 1990, p. 167). As the state represents the nation as a political unity, the two words are often used interchangeably and even are combined in the expression *nation state*. State and nation are, however, not identical: A nation is more than just a political unity and may be called a multiple systems concept. Just as a human being can be described in physical, biological, psychic and social terms, descriptions of different types may include the word *nation*. The nation Italy covers 301.302 km2, has 57.5 million inhabitants, is a republic and a member of EU, has a celebrated cuisine, and a flag with three colors.

How the nation describes itself is, however, an empirical question. The Greek *polis* had a different self-description than the Roman Empire and the Medieval Vassal State, so that nation is a medium allowing different forms, which again defines different forms of government or state. Nationalist semantics is a phase in the evolution of national self-descriptions flourishing from The French Revolution to the end of The First World War. Talking about a nation entails, as a minimum, either the ambition or the realization of some kind of political unity.

Currently two different paradigms are fighting each other (see among many Habermas, 2001; Beck, 2004; Held, 2004). The national paradigm confronts the global or cosmopolitan paradigm. According to the latter, the nation is losing its importance and sovereignty due to the global dynamics of functional subsystems, external integration in alliances and internal disintegration in regions. According to the former, the nation is still the most important political actor on the global scene, and the important question is not national vs. global, but successful vs. failed nation (Fukuyama, 2004). The image of a stable and prosperous nation is for the time being the criteria for political success and the challenges of globalization are not weakening, but strengthening the nation.

Luhmann seems to be on both side of this dichotomy. On the one hand, he is a stern proponent for the global point of view, always describing modern society as a world society (Luhmann, 1995, p. 430) and arguing that the problems of modern society can not be treated as regional or national problems. On the other hand, he also accepts the necessity of the nation, even if pointing out that nations are not important for understanding modern society. Regional boundaries are only political conventions, that is, variables. Still, they may be of major importance (Luhmann, 1997b, p. 72f).

In the following the dichotomy between the national and the global point of view will be analyzed in Luhmanian terms. This will require three moves. First, three social systems will be presented: functional subsystems, organizations and nations.

Secondly, the distinction between nation and state will be elaborated, and via an analysis of the irreplaceable functions of the state it will be concluded that the death certificate of the nation is a bit premature, so that the dilemma "national or global" is a bogus one. This creates a mediating position between the two extremes, as nations are seen as vital actors in the globalization process, alongside with functional subsystems and private organizations. The *division of nations* means pluralism and variation, and as nations use identical criteria in describing their success or failure comparison and competition among nations are possible, promoting the global dynamics.

Thirdly the structural coupling between functional subsystems, organizations and states will be discussed. As they have different goals, numbers of stakeholders, relations to time and space and responsibility for stakeholders, tensions arise which are summarized as problems of globalization.

The general conclusion is that as global dynamics depend on the interplay between three different kinds of system, sharing no common ideas of means and goals and having no formal system unity and no political representative, Luhmann's skeptical thesis is well-founded: survival depends not on rationality, but on evolution. After discussing a small problem of terminology, the *dramatis personae* will be presented.

A problem of terminology

Using the vocabulary of Luhmann raises some terminological problems. As the word *society* in his theory is reserved for world society, and as he dismisses nationalist semantics, it becomes problematic to find a suitable word for what in colloquial talk is called society, a geographical territory represented by a state – even if Luhmann sometimes talks about society in the colloquial sense (e.g., Luhmann, 1990a, p. 166, where societies, in the plural, are introduced as special cases of social systems). Some candidates were tested – *land*, *country*, *empire* (in German: *Reich*) and even neologisms such as *geo state*. In the end, the word *nation* was selected with the precaution that it is used in a strictly neutral manner, carefully separated from any nationalist ideology and not using birth, race, language or religion as criteria for inclusion. This makes it irrelevant that, using other definitions, some nations are not states and vice versa. Whether or not a nation is considered a historical, cultural, religious or ethnic unity is a purely empirical question, and the state may assume different forms – dictatorship, military rule, or democratic government. Even if the word *nation* shares linguistic roots with *nationalism* it is a more general concept, involving the normal, if not universal feeling of belonging to a specific place, to which one is emotionally attached, either because of childhood experiences or because it constitutes a familiar life world. This feeling was not created, but exploited by the nationalist ideology, trying to expand it and make the nation "the place where you belong." By making a nation the collective frame of personal identity and the most important symbolic center of loyalty, the ruling elite could expect citizens to accept sacrifices for the national cause.

Functional subsystems

Long before any talk of a "world society," the world was loosely integrated through the activities of merchants, war lords, scientists, ministers and travelers. Driven by need, greed or curiosity man has always been mobile, so that even hostile parts of the world were populated (Kant, 1891, p. 12). This does not imply that the world was globalized in the modern sense of the word. The world could, in theory, be organized as a global market of local contacts with no knowledge of the scope of the market. Only as a consequence of the invention of the printing press in the 15th century and the great discoveries in the 16th century it was commonly known that the world was globular and limited. Based on this insight the word *globalization* became possible.

According to Luhmann modern, as distinct from feudal society, is differentiated in functional subsystems which standardize communication, gaining an advantage of speed and making large-scale social integration possible.[2] They are autopoietic systems, organizing themselves as attractors for specialized problems and solutions. Even if they are used as premises for decisions, they are not themselves action or decision systems. As their activities may take place everywhere and in fact does take place at many places simultaneously, they are impossible to control centrally. They are prime movers of modern integration and modern fragmentation.

A functional subsystem is both semantic and operative. It includes semantic programs and the communications organized by them (Luhmann, 2002, p. 14). Operating in a generalized medium (Parsons, 1967b, p. 273ff) it orients itself towards

---

2. The theory of functional differentiation and functional subsystems is a development of Talcott Parsons' AGIL scheme (Parsons, 1967a, p. 348). Instead of, like Parsons, arguing that for logical reasons there can be only four subsyssems, Luhmann makes the number of subsystems a purely empirical question. In his own theory he specifies ten, but other candidates have been proposed. For further details see (Luhmann, 1976) and (Luhmann, 1997, p. 316ff).

one and only one *distinction directrice*, a binary code with asymmetric poles. As one side of the distinction is to be preferred, a functional subsystem becomes a value system, which takes over the classical functions of rhetoric: simplifying, motivating and measuring success and failure (Luhmann, 1995, p. 161). On the basis of the extreme simplification of a code, artificially splitting the world in two, complicated semantic programs are developed, making specialized communication possible. By coupling and de-coupling words with hinges of many kinds – cause and effect, logic and experience, similarity and difference, proximity and distance in time and space – functional subsystems become semantic resources for collective experience.

The internal dynamics of functional subsystems such as economy, politics, science, mass media, and technology have been the main vehicle for the making of a world society,[3] and no nation dismisses their contributions since success or failure of a nation is defined in terms of the values of functional subsystems. But as always, words come after facts. Only in the beginning of the 19th century could Goethe talk about *Weltlitteratur,*[4] and only in the mid-19th century did Marx argue for an economic world market (Marx & Engels 1848).

Due to their very nature, functional subsystems are global. Their communications take place everywhere, and their meaning horizon is universal as local and distant achievements and possibilities are compared. Even if their communications occur as events in space, they are not spatial systems and are by nature without geographical borders. It might be anecdotally interesting to know exactly where Caesar crossed the river Rubicon, but this "move" in the Roman political system is not dependent on his exact movements in space.

Being highly selective, functional subsystems allow extreme specialization. This facilitates innovation, which has only to be evaluated in one dimension, independent of its ability to fit into programs of other subsystems. New ideas can diffuse quickly, and new communication centers, focusing on a specific subsystem, can arise from day to day. Functional subsystems are organized as markets,[5] so that world society is vitalized by market principles such as comparison, competition, innovation and growth.

Each functional subsystem has its own criterion for simplification, motivation, and measuring. They are not overlapping and the boundaries between them are morally explosive zones, because it is important to know what kind of communication is taking place. Science is supposed to be purely scientific, not economy or politics in disguise. Still, the achievements of one functional subsystem may be of interest to

---

3. When arguing for world society as a fact, Luhmann refers to functional subsystems such as mass media, economy, politics and science (Luhmann, 1997b, p. 67).
4. Goethe did not coin the word *Weltlitteratur*, which is correctly attributed to the German Christopher Martin Wieland (1733-1813). It is found in a note in his own exemplar of his translation of the letters of Horace from 1790. Goethe was, however, the first to disseminate the word effectively, cf. "Weltlitteratur," *Dictionaire International de Termes Littéraires*, http://ditl.info/art/definition.php?term=4559.
5. Luhmann is very close to making the same point when he states that "even if the market is no longer the specific place of exchange, it is anyway a specific social system, which through its specific function distinguishes itself from other systems" (Luhmann, 1988, p. 91)

another subsystem observing with a different distinction, so that different subsystems can be structurally coupled. Religious conflicts may be of economic interest, because trade is affected, and political negotiations may be of scientific interest, because the political system channels resources into the scientific community in the hope of making scientific success a vehicle for political gain. The collaboration of functional subsystems, however, does not mean that they merge. On the contrary, collaboration presupposes meticulous separation.

As each functional subsystem has developed its own internal complexity and at the same time is structurally coupled to other subsystems, modern society has become hyper-complex, accepting the co-existence of stability and change (Luhmann, 1988, p. 74). Cornerstones in modern theories of globalization such as internally stimulated excitement, fluid states and loss of center and control are integrated in Luhmann's theory (Bauman, 2000; Sloterdijk, 2005; Beck, 2004), not in a polemical manner confronting an *ante* with a *post*, but as a simple consequence of his choice of theory model. Luhmann also makes Ulrich Beck's thesis on First and Second Modernity irrelevant (Beck, 2004, pp. 32, 58). A stage of nationalism and internationalism is not followed by a cosmopolitan stage, as modern society is from its very beginning globalized. Luhmann expected functional differentiation to reduce the importance of segmentary and stratificatory differentiations and to undermine national, religious and ethnic conflicts (Kiss, 1990, p. 116). Today it seems highly improbable that these hopes will be fulfilled. After 1989, nationalist semantics seems to be invigorating all over the world.

Even if a functional subsystem both conditions communication and consists of communication (Luhmann, 1995, p. 161), it is not an action system[6] and *does* nothing as a system. It makes it possible to present, ascribe, reject, or simulate communication of a special type (Luhmann, 1986, p. 20). Science and economy are not containers for knowledge or wealth, but "languages in language" with their own history, structures and methods of selection and motivation (Luhmann, 1995, p. 161). It takes action systems such as persons or organizations to act, even when action takes place in the artificial and specialized setting of a functional subsystem. "Collective ability to communicate," argues Luhmann, "can only be ensured by organization" (Luhmann, 2000a, p. 226), so that organizations are indispensable: without their competence of action society would really be lost (Luhmann, 1992, p. 186). They are not enemies, but vehicles of functional subsystems.

---

6. Luhmann reduces *action* to simplified and ascribed communication (Luhmann, 1995, p. 165) in order to maintain the thesis that social systems can be described in only one dimension. This gives rise to serious problems. A declaration of war is communication, whereas actual warfare seems to be more than just communication – and still a social phenomenon. Even if "everything is a sign of itself" (Roland Barthes), so that a battle is a symbolic activity, designating the glory of a nation or an emperor, the consequences of a declaration of war encompasses more than just communication.

Organizations

Prominent users of functional subsystems are organizations. They are autopoietic systems of communication, distinguishing between members and non-members and directing their communication flow towards decisions (Luhmann, 2000b, p. 63) and producing decisions with the help of decisions (Luhmann, 1990b, p. 223).

Whereas a functional subsystem installs a one-dimensional point of view, an organization necessarily combines and balances codes of several subsystems which serve as premises in its decision making process (Luhmann, 1990b, p. 82)—even if Luhmann sometimes argues as if an organization could be part of a functional subsystem (Luhmann, 2000b, p. 387). Since a decision presupposes the co-existence of several possible solutions, and since the values of functional subsystems are incommensurable, decision making has to absorb self-created uncertainty in a non-technical or even illogical manner, introducing the decision-maker as a responsible person who has the official role of reflecting and acting on behalf of his or her organization. Management is an important political function in organizations, in contrast to functional subsystems which have no management, no organizational unity and, therefore, no proper names.[7]

According to Luhmann, organizations have five important functions: 1. they are collective actors, which interaction systems, world society and functional subsystems are unable to be, 2. they regulate inclusion and exclusion, which functional subsystems are unable to do, 3. they transform history, as habits, to decisions, 4. they condense structural couplings between functional systems, which are closed and do not overlap, and 5. they compensate for the loss of authority in modern society (Luhmann, 1994a, pp. 191-196).

Organizations can be divided in public and private organizations. While *private organizations* define their success or failure in monetary terms, *public organizations* have a political agenda and are state-dependent in regard to purpose, rules and budget. As a consequence they are strictly confined to a nation and, consequently, to a geographical area, whereas private organizations are mobile: they are only loyal to themselves and can move abroad, if economic conditions in terms of salaries, taxes and infrastructure are more favorable elsewhere. This possibility does not exist for the community of New York or the Ministry of Taxation in China.

Public organizations describe themselves inside a national and a functional frame, whereas private organizations describe themselves in terms of one or more functional subsystem(s) – as a part of economy, science or art. By doing this, they become fluid and assume a global perspective. Their employees may follow and become what Ulrich Beck calls cosmopolitans (Beck, 2004) and Zygmunt Bauman calls nomads of the wealthy kind, the favored travelers having the whole world as their work place and play ground (Bauman, 1998, p. 94).

---

7. Or, to be more precise: only by being affiliated with an organization, that is, by distinction, can functional subsystems get a name such as "the American economy" or "German post-war politics."

Even if Luhmann, as we shall see, subsumes the state under the category *organization*, an important distinction must be made between organizations proper and states. A *state* is a second order organization operating inside a geographical borderline, defining a legal space for normal organizations and solving social problems which normal organizations can refuse. A legal system makes long-term expectations possible — exactly the reason Hobbes gave for the necessity of a state (Hobbes, 1963, p. 96, 128). By maintaining the distinction between legal and illegal a state creates an "enlarging limitation" (Kierkegaard, 1989, p. 211)[8] for organizations,[9] the latter of which are normally oriented towards a specific functional subsystem, even if other subsystems serve as support systems. A court defines its vital tasks in legal terms, but also needs money, political backing, legal science and technology. These support systems are not part of its purpose, but make it possible to act as a court. In the same way high tech companies which are oriented towards money have to be on the cutting edge of science or technology in order to survive.

The nation in Luhmann's typology of social systems

Why are functional subsystems absent in Luhmann's typology of social systems, as they are not only programs for communication, but also communication proper? A plausible answer is that Luhmann considers them to be elements in world society, evolving by functional differentiation. In a similar manner, nations are not mentioned, because nations have evolved by internal differentiation.[10] In both cases, the important concept is world society. But why is society defined so all-inclusively that it seems to fuse with what may be called the social *tout court*? Where do we find society as normally referred to as Turkish or Vietnamese society (Stichweh, 2000, p. 27)?

Part of the answer has to do with Luhmann's predilection for time as opposed to space. As all social systems are composed of vanishing communications, their major problem is to make sure that communications are continuously being connected to new communications. This is a problem of time, not of space. Among sociologists, Luhmann is the theorist of time *par excellence*. All his basic concepts are saturated with time, whereas the location of communication – space – is less unimportant, even if he admits that a nation requires a territory (Luhmann, 2000a, p. 190: "Furthermore a territorial relation is indispensable"). All space-related centralisms are transcended and space is "belittled due to information technology" (Luhmann, 2000a, p. 220). Instead of an international system of nations defining their territory and being dependent on each other we get a "polycentric, polycontextual society" (Luhmann, 1997b, p. 75), organized by "heterachical, connectionist and network relations" (Luhmann, 2000a, p. 221). This is exactly the *modus operandi* of functional subsystems. In discussing the decline of the nation, Luhmann is in accord with Jürgen

---

8. The English translation uses the expression *enlarging boundary* which I think is incorrect.
9. In the following, *organization* will refer to organization proper in contrast to state.
10. In (Luhmann, 2000a, p. 222) a distinction is made between functional and internal differentiation, the latter referring to a division of territories (cf. also Luhmann, 1981, p. 208).

Habermas, who argues that "rulers of territory" are replaced by "masters of speed" (Habermas 2001, p. 67) and Rudolf Stichweh, who talks about "the destruction of space" (Stichweh 2000, p. 32). Global agents, whether in business, science or criminal gangs, are operating too fast, too flexibly and in too diffuse a way to allow state control.

It is, according to Luhmann, misleading and superfluous to talk of an international system. *International* is a concept *von unten*, combining elements already existing, while Luhmann prefers to talk about world society, which is a concept *von oben*, a system integrating all communication and allowing suitable differentiations of function and territory.

Luhmann's typology of social systems comprises world society, interaction and organization. Even if the nation is part of world society, it is not a mechanical subdivision in the manner of a meter being subdivided in centimeters, nor is it a functional part in the manner of a liver or heart being a part of an organism. If in a thought experiment a single nation was removed, world society would persist. So the question arises of how to categorize the nation.

Contrary to normal usage, society in Luhmann's theory is not the nation, but world society. That the word *society* is used for nations is due to a traditional semantics with no theoretical underpinning (Luhmann, 2000a, p. 220). The internal differentiation is due to the need of dividing world society in smaller units (Luhmann, 1997a, p. 1045; Luhmann, 2000a, p. 190f, 220ff.) Theoretically it is as unimportant as the differentiation of schools or hospitals (Luhmann, 1981, p. 209).

Nations create contingent points of view (Luhmann, 1997a, p. 1088), which reduce complexity by arbitrarily selecting a geographical area as point of departure for system/environment observations. In a similar manner "theories of primacy" (Luhmann, 1997a, p. 571) may arbitrarily give priority to a functional subsystem. In this manner Hobbes made the political system and Adam Smith and Marx the economic system the foundation for understanding society.

As world society gets its dynamics from functional subsystems, the nation is not relevant to understanding modern society. In Luhmann (1997a, p. 1045) nations are peripheral and mentioned only in quotation marks. Centers for world society are "naturally" the big financial markets (Luhmann, 1997a, p. 808), a point of view shared by cosmopolitans such as Ulrich Beck, who identifies globalization with economic and financial markets (Beck 2004, p. 18). Nations, on the contrary, have only a parasitic role: they exploit fluctuations of the world markets, compare and compete with each other, and serve as *Interdependenzunderbrecher* (Luhmann, 1997a, p. 845), preventing causal chains from going wild. Administering boundaries is, however, an important task which deserves more theoretical focus.

Even if a nation is not an autonomous center, still the question remains: what kind of social system is it? As part of world society a nation has other properties than world society itself, for example the ability to interrupt causal chains and to balance the dynamics of functional subsystems. In world society such balances are just happening, governed by the learning processes of an invisible hand. In the nation the attempt to balance is, even if not successful, the outcome of a social will – a visible hand. The national attempts to accelerate and control the functional subsystems are not external to them, but form part of their dynamics so that Castells can argue that the global economy is politically created (Castells 2000, chap. 2). In the same vein Stichweh claims that the institutionalization of nation states is the decisive achievement of world politics (Stichweh, 1995, p. 41).

World society and nation must therefore be distinguished as different kinds of system, not only as a whole and its parts. The same applies to nation and interaction. Interaction systems are informal and have an advantage of speed: they emerge and dissolve quickly as they are not inhibited by demands of formal roles or expectations of binding decisions. Their speed, however, makes it uncertain which *Eigenvalues* will stabilize, so that interaction systems do not allow prognoses (Luhmann, 1997a, p. 1096). Descriptions of problems and solutions are unreliable. Consequently, interaction systems are not stable enough to allow for important national functions such as collectively binding decisions, long-term expectations and large-scale social integration. As a result "the gap between interaction and society has become unbridgeably wide and deep" (Luhmann, 1995, p. 430).

Dismissing world society and interaction, the nation has to be an organization. But this seems to be empirically false. A nation comprises economical, scientific, and religious activities, which belong to functional subsystems with their own trans-national dynamics, not formally organized in one system.

Even if the nation is no organization, it needs a name, a territory, a people and a central power (Luhmann, 2000a, p. 189ff), which leads us to the political system and to the state. Luhmann talks about "the creation of a sovereign territorial system, which was later to be called a state" (Luhmann, 1988, p. 336). Only due to the state is it possible to describe a nation as a unity, so that the state represents the nation, reflects and acts on its behalf and uses the code legal/illegal to frame all activities in a nation, including the communication of functional subsystems. Even if global, on each specific area their public communications are organized and restricted by state-defined laws.

This does not mean that the state is able to control the functional subsystems. Due to the plurality of states, that is, the absence of a world state and of uniform restrictions, they find their ways by finding the spots of minimal resistance.

Nationally, the political subsystem becomes *primus inter pares* among the functional subsystems.[11] Even if the nation is no organization, the state, as the representative of the nation, can be described as an organization. This is also the view of Luhmann. He mentions economic and public organizations side by side (Luhmann, 1997a, p. 841), normally with reference to their primary function, and the state is explicitly called an organization (Luhmann, 1997a, p. 845)—even if modern society "renounces to be an organization (corporation)" (Luhmann, 1997a, p. 836). One may well ask what the expression *modern society* means in this sentence. But leaving this question aside, states must be distinguished from organizations. By maintaining a legal frame for all activities in a nation, the state becomes a second-order organization, integrating other organizations, including itself, without destroying the autopoiesis of organizations or functional subsystems.

Central to Luhmann's definition of an organization is membership and decision making. Here the parallel between organizations and states is convincing. A state distinguishes between members and non-members, and its constitution is decided and at the same time the basis of further decisions. Decisions on behalf of a nation are made by the state, irrespective of which form it takes.

Finally, both states and organizations are limited, not only by physical borderlines, but also by a limited range of decision making power. The boundaries of a state may be defined both geographically and organizationally. As states and organizations are systems maintaining a boundary, they are both in the plural. A state is necessarily one among others, that is, inter-national. States are relational systems and cannot be treated as singular states as "units *per se*" (Luhmann, 1997a, p. 808). Even if a state is not autonomous, as it does not control other functional subsystems, other states or even itself, and even if, for that reason, it is not able to represent society as a whole (Luhmann, 1988, p. 336), it still has a relative autonomy. Global fluctuations of functional subsystems present a state with disturbances which it can or cannot integrate according to its own principles of self-organization defined in its constitution, its tradition and its actual condition.

First detour: State semantics

Luhmann accepts the importance of the state. But accepting states, nations follow. It is not possible to maintain the significance of the state and the insignificance of the nation. To understand the aggressive devaluation of the nation, we will make two detours, *first* discussing the semantics of the state and *secondly* the irreplaceable functions of the state. This done, we will come back to the nation.

In discussing the state Luhmann is mainly focusing on semantic and historical issues.[12] Even if his book on organizations could be expected to deal with the state as a specific kind of organization, one looks in vain in the index for entries of "nation" or "state" (Luhmann, 2000b).

The reason is, of course, that a state is an organization of a very peculiar kind, differing in important respects from normal organizations. First, even if states have

---

11. Even if all functional subsystems are operating on a systems level, only the political system gives formal unity to the nation. In the *oeuvre* of Luhmann it is possible to find expressions which seem to make the economic subsystem the basic one, as all organizations need money. In (Luhmann, 1994b, p. 322) he asks whether it is possible to observe "a latent dominance of economy in modern society." Economy, religion and education are, however, unable to create a formal national unity. This is achieved in a constitution which is a political and legal document, not an economic, religious or pedagogical one. It should be noted, however, that Luhmann uses the expression *the political system* in a technical manner. The political uses the distinction between itself and its environment, society, within itself. "The difference between state and society became part of their constitutional law and a premise for its interpretation" (Luhmann, 1990a, p. 170). In this way, it operates simultaneously on two levels and becomes a paradoxical system. In this context, the interesting point is that the political system comprises and gives national unity to state and society, legal power and property being the two "great codes" (Luhmann, 1987, p. 69).

borderlines and are in the plural, on its own area it must be in the singular. There might be competing corporations, scientific institutions and religious sects. But if there are several competing states, we have civil war and a failed nation. Secondly, even if a state maintains activities of different kinds – security, infrastructure, welfare, education, health, and so forth – these activities must find their place in a legal hierarchy having a common power base whether supported by military or by democratic means. The state is the unity of "uncountable operations" (Luhmann, 1987, p. 96) and protects a vast bureaucracy which gets legitimacy by being part of the state apparatus. Thirdly, a state is restricted by territory and therefore immobile.

Functions of a state are *order, security and wealth*. As seen in the writings of cosmopolitan theorists such as Ulrich Beck, David Held and Zygmunt Bauman, a series of insistent problems – poverty, epidemics, pollution, migration, terrorism and organized crime – are today without national solutions. But instead of becoming cosmopolitans, a significant proportion of citizens react to the all inclusive and spaceless world of functional subsystems by withdrawing into the fictive, but simple citadel of a nation, making the important distinction between "them and us" a national one. Instead of withering away, the nation becomes more opaque, defending itself like a fortress.

State is a medium allowing different forms. In the Middle Ages, the Christian *sacerdotium* was distinguished from the secular *imperium*, and from the Renaissance on, different descriptions can be traced – the power state of Machiavelli, the law-and-order state of Hobbes, the equilibrium state of Spinoza, the property protecting state of Locke and Adam Smith, the absolute state of Kant and Hegel, and later on the democratic state and the welfare state.

In the late 18th century, Rousseau replaced the political idea of the state as the King's Body with the civil idea of the nation as united by a "general will" and a national assembly, giving the nation a new reference of legitimation. Only in the mid-18th century was the state defined as a political concept (Luhmann, 1987, p. 79). After Rousseau, and inspired by him, The French Revolution made the nation into a "necessary concept" (Luhmann, 1997a, p. 1047), which was later given historical and popular depth by Schlegel.[13] Even if a nation, in this strong sense, according to its own self-understanding was not constructed, but had evolved blindly over centuries,[14] it was a political construction, created by a political and cultural elite, traced back in pre-history and strengthened by enemy images, folklore, art and public celebration. In

12. In Luhmann (1995) a single page is used to discuss the problem of the state (p. 462f), and the analysis is only exemplary. In Luhmann (2000b) the state is not even mentioned. In Luhmann (2000a) chap. 6 is devoted to the state, "The state of the political system," but the subject is discussed mainly as "word history" (Luhmann, 1989, p. 80). Elsewhere, Luhmann discusses the state in methodological terms, defining the state as "the self-description of the political system" (Luhmann, 1990, p. chap. 3 and Luhmann 1990a). As we shall see, this is a rather peculiar definition, conflicting with the general line of Luhmann's theory, because it implicitly takes the point of view of the nation. Also, arguing that the state is "the political system reintroduced in the political system (Luhmann, 1990, p. 166) the conclusion seems to follow that the state is representing the totality of the political system – a thesis which is not true, as many actors (mass media, NGO's and even private citizens) are participating in the political system without being part of the state.

13. These sparse statements will not be elaborated further in this context.

art history we learn how specific landscapes in the 19th century were defined and refined as national landscapes.

Not only the evolution of functional subsystems, but also colonial and imperial endeavors demanding a loyal army[15] and loyal civil servants favored national centralization, converging from different paths in the 19th century and vitalized by an overestimation of proper names and the symbolism of art: "A name must be" (Luhmann, 2000a, p. 200). The nation became an imaginary or symbolic unit with the ambition of furnishing an all-inclusive collective frame for personal identity in the style of pre-modern rank and class (Habermas, 2001, p. 58ff). After The French Revolution, in a period of enormous changes in norms and classes, the nation was able to demand a stronger loyalty than functional subsystems. While a functional subsystem is only organizing a role, a segment of the *Vollmensch* (Luhmann, 2000b, p. 148), the nation offers a concept of inclusion independent of functional subsystems and forces the political system to treat all members as equal (Luhmann, 1997a, p. 1052). The democratic nation became the accepted manner of large-scale organizing. By moralizing the idea of representative democracy nations not complying with this model were treated as wrong or backward cases.

The modern nation, based on the idea of *the people,* emerges in a process of regional and cultural differentiation, finding its identity *via negationis* by exhausting military possibilities of expansion, successful self-defense and experimentations with state building, including membership of alliances (Luhmann, 1997a, p. 1046).[16] That this process took place simultaneously with the functional differentiation of society becoming irreversible is no coincidence, since modern nations define their success or failure in the language of functional subsystems. Functional and internal differentiations go hand in hand. Even if functional subsystems are global and nations are regional, the organizations which give social reality to the functional subsystems demand the stability of a state in order to evolve by instability—with the extra twist that the state itself is one of these organizations.

The varieties of loyalty

Even in the golden age of nationalism, however, another type of political self-description emerged, making world society the frame of identity for cosmopolitans and constructing a vision of universal democracy, rule of law, free trade and human rights (Beck, 2004; Held, 2004). The state governed by law was replaced by world

---

14. 18th century British political writers such as David Hume, Adam Smith and Adam Ferguson replaced Hobbesian contract theory with a theory of the autopoiesis of civil society, creating order of noise by the learning processes of the invisible hand. With the distinction between the autonomous civil society and the state, modern society for the first time observed the shift from stratificatory to functional differentiation (Luhmann, 1987, p. 68).

15. According to Charles Tilly the military advantages of a national, as opposed to a mercenary army was an important evolutional factor in the making of nation states as the dominant political system (Tilly, 1992). The national appeal was exploited most effectively by Napoleon.

16. European states emerged in an ongoing process of war making. Only today "the world as whole has stabilized itself in a total map of stable, mutually exclusive state territories" (Tilly, 1992, p. 202).

society sharing uniform institutions. Also Habermas' idea of *constitutional patriotism* is an attempt to define a frame of identity beyond the nation (Habermas, 1999, p. 425ff).

Global identity, however, is an option only for the global elite of politicians, managers, academics and artists, who define their identity in terms of a career path inside a functional subsystem and, following the logic of such systems, transgress national borderlines. For the losers in the rich world national identity is still interesting, because only the nation offers a high level of state-financed welfare without any *quid pro quo*, a privilege they do not want to share with strangers. Even if excluded from the labor market, they are included as citizens in rich nations.[17]

Even for the elite, loyalty to world society is only one loyalty among others and perhaps not a strong one. "We, the mankind" is a weak "we" as compared to "we, the Germans," "we, the doctors" or "we, the family" (Rorty, 1989).

System/environment observations may take different systems as their point of departure. Modern man has many self-descriptions and, consequently, many loyalties. What is the most important environment for an observer is a purely empirical matter. For the sociologist, trying to understand modern society, world society is the most important frame, if not for his personal loyalty, then for his professional interest. For the scientist or business man, their functional subsystem may be the basis for their self-description, making them cosmopolitans. For the politician the vision is divided. Even if he has a global perspective, he must nurse his local constituency in order to be re-elected. And for the common citizen the relevant environment is the life world of his home, working place, school, mall and hospital.

Different levels of loyalty co-exist side by side, so that a person may be loyal to himself, his family, trade, religion, moral principles, nation or world society, allowing context-sensitive loyalty balances and creating insolvable moral conflicts. Facing a policeman in a foreign nation, it might be important to know his most weighty loyalty. The important point is not whether such loyalty is calculated or genuine, but whether is has social effects. Even if the nation is dismissed as outdated, it is real if it has real effects and forms part of the self-description of its members, so that the nation, as a symbolic unity, is a center of interests, even if not worth dying for. For the cosmopolitan, traveling all over the world, the nation has a low position in the hierarchy of loyalty. But for the unskilled worker or welfare receiver, whose income is threatened by immigrants, the nation becomes important.

The decline and rise of the nation

In the late 20th century, national semantics seemed to be weakening, and cosmopolitans both predicted and promoted a New World Order of global governance under the rule of international law, enforceable human rights and democratic

---

17. For Luhmann the "worst imaginable scenario" for the 21st century is that society will use the "metacode of inclusion/exclusion," making some human beings persons with citizenship and career, while others are only "bodies that try to survive the next day" (Luhmann, 1997b, p. 76).

institutions (Held, 2004).[18] These predictions have been challenged by a New Nationalism, supported by the search for national identity in former colonies, the break-down of the Soviet empire in 1989, the demand for ethnic, cultural and religious rights, the critique of globalization and welfare receivers defending their high level of welfare benefits against immigrants.

Following his theoretical strategy of making globalization a fact, not a project, Luhmann minimizes the importance of the nation, stating that the end of the era of nations coincides with the end of the First World War, even if the declaration of peace ironically emphasized national sovereignty in the "Fourteen Points" of Woodrow Wilson (Luhmann, 1997a, p. 1054). From that time, the nation deconstructs itself externally, for example by transferring authority to transnational institutions such as EU or by being forced to make decisions without being able to accept the consequences. In order to attract international investments, nations must offer low taxes, but are unwilling to reduce the welfare benefits so precious for the voters.

Also an internal deconstruction takes place, when sub-national groups fight for autonomy and strengthen their identity by constructing a contrast to the national identity, being a Basque, not a Spaniard. A demand for democracy re-enters in democratic nations. Conflicts arise when suddenly a state comprises several nations, in the emphatic sense, or a nation finds itself divided in several states. In fact, few if any nations are pure in the sense of being immune to separatist claims.

Even if Luhmann claims that the nation is loosing its importance, the same analysis does not hold for the state, which is the political representative of the nation. Downgrading the nation and upgrading the state causes some schizophrenia. It might be argued that what Luhmann dismisses is not the nation, but the nationalist ideology. But this seems not to be the case. In common with many other theorists he states that in a global world the nation is no longer an important unit. But how can the nation be unimportant if its representative, the state, is important? By making a second detour – an analysis of the state and its irreplaceable functions – we may be able to come back to a sober evaluation of the importance of the nation.

Second detour: Irreplaceable functions of the state

The state is a structure in the political system (Luhmann, 1997a, p. 714) – a reflexive concept used in the internal self-description of a nation, but not identical with the function of making collectively binding decisions (Luhmann, 1997a, p. 758).[19] It tries to balance the dynamics of functional subsystems in its own area and serves "the re-stabilization of political centralizations" (Luhmann, 1997a, p. 489). Consequently the state must observe itself in non-political dimensions and limit itself for non-political

---

18. This combination of sociological description and political agitation can be found in Beck (2004).
19. Luhmann, however, admits that the function of politics is to provide "the continuing possibility of collectively binding decision making," and in a footnote he adds that he "sees no serious alternative to this definition" (Luhmann, 1990a, p. 171). In this text he also argues that the state is not a "subsystem in the political system," so that *structure* and *subsystem* must be distinguished.

reasons. Non-political communication must be translated – simplified and distorted – to political communication in order to be suitable for political decision-making and control. Education or art are not only described in their own vocabulary, but also in political terms, so that everything in a nation may assume a political significance. This is the meaning of Luhmann's thesis, discussed earlier, that the political system comprises itself and its environment, society (Luhmann, 1990a, p. 170).

As a consequence of the very size of the state – a *Riesenorganisation im politischen System* (Luhmann, 1997a, p. 841) – state-oriented activities take place outside the state, for example in families or business communities. The whole system of society, Luhmann states laconically, must register that this is so. What is the meaning of society in this sentence? Obviously it is not world society. Also by defining the state as "the self-description of the political system of society" (Luhmann, 1990b, p. 123) Luhmann tacitly makes a change in his frame of reference. society is no longer world society, as no world state exists and as there is no self-description of the global political system except for vague and biased appeals to world society in case of genocide or hunger catastrophe. Luhmann jumps from the technical to the colloquial meaning of the word *society*.[20]

In colloquial talk, the political system is the system of political agents, including governments, mass media, interest groups and private citizens with political ambitions. In Luhmann's theory, the political system is a functional subsystem facilitating communication of power. It is a semantic device and communication defining itself as political is automatically political.[21] This system is global in scope, although in specific contexts it may be understood in a limited, often national sense. Observing with the distinction state/society, the political system identifies itself as state (Luhmann, 1987, p. 71).

As a consequence of the global dynamics of functional subsystems and multinational organizations a series of problems have emerged which can neither be handled by interaction systems, organizations or world society in Luhmann's sense. The only political actor able to handle if not solve them is the state and, consequently, the nation. We will select four. *Firstly* the problem of social order, *secondly* the problem of democracy, *thirdly* the so-called social problem identified in the 19th century by G. W. F Hegel (Hegel, 1991, §244-245), and *fourthly* the problem of global risks, often used as an argument against the significance of the nation. Without going into details a few comments will be made on each theme with the aim of showing that the message of the death of the nation is a bit premature.

---

20. In Luhmann's grandiose re-description of social systems many words get a technical meaning. When sophisticated and theory-laden descriptions run into trouble, however, Luhmann often resorts to the normal meaning of words. Here the example is the word *society*. Other examples can be found in Thyssen (2004).
21. We use the same generous manner of identifying "political communication" as Luhmann himself uses in arguing that "teaching/education ('Erziehung') are all those communications which in interactions are actualized as teaching/education" (Luhmann, 2002, p. 54). As Luhmann explicitly states, such a definition is quasi tautological.

1. *Social order.* A functional subsystem can pose no limit to itself, as it is observing in only one dimension and having no means of limitation. It has an anarchic tendency, even if persons using the code to condition their communication accept self-restrictions as they realize that not anything goes. From its own point of view nothing is more important than itself. It views society as an environment which ought to favor its growth by yielding unlimited resources, preferably in a liquid and non-binding form as money. How the infrastructure necessary for a subsystem to function is created and maintained and how conflicting demands from different subsystems are balanced is not the business of a functional subsystem—even if, as a matter of prudence, it may learn to exploit structural couplings with other subsystems.

The problem for the state is not to inhibit or compete with the functional subsystems, but to attract and integrate them by curbing their single-minded ambitions and directing them for the benefit of what in colloquial talk is called society. As control is impossible, this demands an on-going effort, a day-to-day calibration as second-order cybernetics (Luhmann, 1992, p. 206). This effort is outside the scope of not only functional subsystems, but also of private organizations.[22] The state has an integrative task, as functional subsystems and private organizations are elements in a division of functions, but unable to define and handle the unity of their differences. This integration cannot be done and must be done. It is left to society as a whole – and society, in this context, is not world society, but the state. So even if the state is not in control of its own fate, and never has been, still its contribution is necessary. Luhmann admits this in his argument that organization is necessary for society (Luhmann, 1992, p. 186).

The global dynamics of functional subsystems is the background for what Manuel Castells has baptized the new medievalism (Castells, 2000). The argument is that as states have lost control over the economic market, the information process, education and so forth, they are atrophying. Not even the welfare system can be controlled.

There are several flaws in this argument. In the first place, states were never in control and were never autonomous in a strong sense. Their dependency on functional subsystems and on each other prevented this. They ride the tiger and try to be winners in a world where not everybody can win. Social order, security and wealth have always been scarce resources. Secondly, even if functional subsystems are global, they are operating in local contexts, demanding a legal system and organizations which again demand a state. Thirdly, there is no inherent conflict between functional subsystems and states. Luhmann argues that competition between nation states is an important feature of the dynamics of functional subsystems (Luhmann, 2000a, p. 224). Globalization is promoted because the plurality of states makes sure that functional subsystems are not universally restricted or politicized, so that innovations can take place somewhere and quickly be distributed.

As functional subsystems and organizations are only organizing fragments of human beings and as people, consequently, can walk in and out of their functionally or

---

22. even if private organizations inside their own boundaries face similar tasks.

organizationally defined roles, the nation is indispensable in offering a concept of inclusion not dependent on any specific subsystem (Luhmann, 1997a, p. 1052). It supplies a collective frame of personal identity more stable than the liquid identity granted by functional subsystems and organizations, and it takes over the function of finding solutions to problems of unbalance on both macro- and micro-level. As the state is allowed and even summoned to regulate all aspects of everyday life,[23] we witness contradictory lamentations of the obsolescence of the nation on the one hand, and of the unrestrained growth of the state on the other.

So even if functional subsystems and private organizations may be highly innovative, they need a stable world for their operations, as stability is a precondition for innovation. This cannot be achieved by private organizations, because money is too limited a criterion for observing the success or failure of a nation. Both functional subsystems and organizations call for a second-order organization, the state, which is committed to social order on a national scale.

2. *The problem of democracy*. Luhmann is aware that the nation cannot be totally dismissed. Even if it in many ways is left behind, it is indispensable for democracy (Luhmann, 1997a, p. 1096). Without a constitution and a public sphere, no democracy can exist, and the nation furnishes exactly this. As Western nations have moralized the concept of democracy, political legitimacy demands a constitution and popular support, demonstrated in free elections. If the nation is indispensable for democracy, it is not obsolete. That a world state should become attractive seems for the present rather unlikely.

To this is added another argument. As the world population is living under very different conditions, defined in terms of climate, economy, culture and religion, no single government is able to represent all these differences. Simple majority rule would meet heavy resistance, as "the Dutch would always be voted down by the Chinese, the Portuguese by the Indians" (Luhmann, 2000a, p. 223). Consequently, to optimize the political function, defined in terms of democracy, internal differentiation is indispensable, having the additional bonus of allowing political experiments and impeding universal politicization of functional subsystems.

So we find two not wholly harmonized currents in Luhmann's theory – a main current stressing globalization and a subordinate current accepting the nation as more than just a simple geographical element in world society.

3. *The social problem*. As functional subsystems are constructed in a binary fashion, they create differences between more and less, that is, winners and losers.[24] In the very attempt to maximize the positive side, the negative side is accentuated, not only

---

23. The modern state, claims Luhmann, "has the aim of making sure that everybody is happy" (Luhmann, 2000a, p. 206). This task, of course, has no natural limits, so that the modern welfare state continuously creates those crises which forces it to expand the scope of its activities, so that every solution creates new problems in an autocatalytical manner (Luhmann, 1990a, p. 171), which has no logical end, only exhaustion.

24. Also Hegel remarks that in a market society equality is impossible (Hegel 1991, p. ß 200).

as a logical necessity, a reflection form, but as an unintended social reality. When all people try to get rich, some get poor. Even if most people are law-abiding, some are criminals – not only because, logically, law makes crime possible, but also, empirically, because the reason to make laws is that illegal tracks are tempting.

The normative critique of globalization, put forward by Zygmunt Bauman, Pierre Bourdieu, and Manuel Castells, is anticipated by Luhmann. The global dynamics of functional subsystems strengthen the so-called social problem of people unable to make a living. Luhmann refrains, however, from any moral critique. As differences between more and less are built into the functional subsystems, they can only be eliminated by eliminating the subsystems. Luhmann uses his so-called functional argument, focusing not on perfection, but on available alternatives. As stability depends on absence of better alternatives and as alternatives to functional differentiation, for example religious or political fundamentalism, are unacceptable, functional subsystems are stable even if not perfect.

In this context, the interesting point is that the social problem cannot be handled by interaction systems, by functional subsystems, by private organizations or by world society. Interaction systems are too unstable to handle structural problems. From the point of view of economy or science, the fate of losers is irrelevant unless, of course, money can be made on nursing the losers or scientific theories can be made by describing and explaining their behavior. Also for private organizations losers are uninteresting. When an employee is fired, the organization has no longer any responsibility for him. Its aim is to earn money, not to create social balance. Finally, world society in Luhmann's sense is irrelevant, because it is not an action system and cannot solve transverse problems. Losers are not helped just by talking or being talked to, even if this makes them part of world society.

Still, the losers must somehow be integrated in society. They must be included as excluded. The state is the only organization which can, if not solve, then at least handle what Bauman calls the "wasted lives" of persons made superfluous by modernization and globalization (Bauman, 2004).

In a democratic state, the interest of the state cannot be distinguished from the interests of the population, which are not defined in the language of one single subsystem. A private organization only appoints persons competent to fulfill a specific job, whereas the state cannot deny membership to its members,[25] only to foreigners. The state not only has to stimulate the wealth of the nation, but also to organize the welfare of the nation, caring for the persons who are unattractive for private—and public—organizations.

As millions of people are dependent on welfare benefits, and as they make up a significant part of the electorate, in a democratic nation they have considerably political influence. Politicians cannot just dismiss their claims as absurd or parasitic. The focus on growth both in private wealth and public welfare makes national democracy a threat to the survival of world society. But if elected politicians did not

25. although it may carry out ethnic cleaning or degrade specific groups as second class citizens.

promote wealth and welfare they would violate established expectations and minimize their chances for re-election.

4. *Global risks.* A normal argument for the irrelevance of the nation is global risks such as pollution, terrorism, epidemics and crime (see among many Beck, 1992 and Held, 2004). No single nation can handle global problems in an effective manner, as its frame of reference is too narrow. When costs and benefits are seen in a national perspective, it is argued, no overall solution or even relevant effort is possible.

Also this argument has several flaws. Even if it is possible, in theory, to transfer global problems to global agents, as a matter of empirical fact only states are able to handle them. The consequence is that global problems are balanced with local problems such as national security, employment and natural resources. Global agents such as United Nations can collect and process information, organize global treaties and call for practical action. But as the UN is financed by nations and has no independent system of justice and no monopoly of violence, it cannot run faster into the future than allowed by the nations or solve problems against the will of the nations.

Structural couplings

Accepting that the state fulfills irreplaceable functions and that the state is acting on behalf of the nation, the conclusion must be that the nation is not obsolete. The state, says Luhmann, "is important and, until today, is an irreplaceable evolutionary universal (Luhmann, 1990a, p. 172) – where the content if the precaution "until today" is not specified. That the nation is not sovereign in the strong sense of the word is no counter argument. The nation was never sovereign and was never in control. Or to put it differently: The nation is only sovereign in the weak autopoietic sense: It can only be externally controlled via its internal structures.

So there is no need of choosing between the national and the global perspective, as nations are vehicles for world society. The same holds good for organizations and functional subsystems. The three kinds of system are structurally coupled in the sense that each system is dependent on the complexity of the others and each system is making its complexity available for the others in a simplified form (Luhmann, 1995, p. 213). A functional subsystem is unable to realize itself and to limit itself. It takes organizations to do so, because organizations have to balance the conflicting demands of functional subsystems in their ongoing decision making, as when a person is wondering whether he should use the code of love or the code of money in choosing a spouse. Rich and unattractive, or poor and attractive? Furthermore, it takes nations to create a stable environment for highly specialized private organizations. So, even if states are unable to control organizations and even if organizations are unable to grasp the sophistication of the functional subsystems, still states can use organizations and organization use functional subsystems for their own purposes. So systems with conflicting goals are able to cooperate.

Even if it is accepted that the nation is alive and kicking, it might be argued that the modern nation is only an administrative unit, not a nation in the strong 19th century sense of the word. That might be true. But each nation creates a public sphere of its own, and even if pervaded by global information, it also creates a specific if arbitrary point of view, as when an Irish newspaper announced the Titanic catastrophe under the headline: "Irishman drowned in shipwreck." In mass media, global, national and local news compete. Also in this respect nations serve as *Interdependenzunterbrecher*, reducing complexity and satisfying the human need for identity and belonging. Different loyalties are not necessarily in conflict, as persons are located in what Hegel calls "a system of mutual dependency," making egoistic goals dependent on the universal fulfillment of the goals of others (Hegel, 1991, §183).

The Three Tempi of Globalization

The problems of globalization can be traced back to structural differences between functional subsystems, private organizations and states.

Functional subsystems, organizations and states are dependent on each other and in conflict with each other. Functional subsystems have only one goal, growth, but need organizations and states to exist and expand. This dependency goes both ways. Both organizations and states use the values of functional subsystems to define their success or failure. Their self-descriptions include references to all subsystems, making it possible for them to compare their achievements and compete with each other. Also organizations and states are interdependent. As production of wealth, irrespective of what kind,[26] is transferred to private organizations, states must create an environment attractive for private investments. Just like organizations compete on the economic market, states compete on the political market to attract private organizations to produce wealth, jobs, and taxes.

Functional subsystems, organizations and states are different kinds of social system. Functional subsystems serve as frames of specialized communication, whereas organizations and states are decision making systems and, consequently, action systems. They have different goals, different scope and different criteria for success and failure.

A functional subsystem has no inherent limit to growth, whereas private organizations have no interest in the unlimited unfolding of the potentialities of one single subsystem. Their basic interest is money, not science or technology as such. At the same time, an organization can see no reason for curbing its own growth and has no inherent solidarity with a national purpose. Even if the systems are dependent on each other, they are in no spontaneous harmony. On the contrary, all conflicts of globalization can be seen as conflicts between the inherent dynamics of these three kinds of social system.

---

26. - as each functional subsystem is oriented towards wealth of its own making. We disregard that states may exert political control over functional subsystems.

To make the differences between functional subsystems, organizations and states more precise, five parameters will be used, namely: 1. Goal; 2. Number of stakeholders; 3. Space; 4. Time; and 5. Responsibility for members. This can be shown in a diagram.

	Goal	Stake-holders	Space	Time	Responsi-bility for Members
Functional Subsystems	one	one	– (global)	super fast	none
Organiza-tions	one/many	one/many	+/– (local/global)	fast	few
States	many/many	many/many	+ (local)	slow	many

A. *Functional subsystems* have, according to their nature, only one goal, defined by their code. Therefore they have only one stakeholder, namely organizations and persons who program their communication in the language of the subsystem. Isolating a functional subsystem requires an analytical operation, distinguishing between communication of a specific kind and the organizations furnishing the social frame for such communication. In this way it becomes possible to talk about "science" as a system of publications independent of scientific organizations. Scientifically it is irrelevant whether a breakthrough takes place in Japan or Brazil, or which university or theorist is the originator. But for a state or for a private organization it is of vital importance to be the center of innovation and reap its political and economic benefits. In the same manner it is of minor importance for the world economy whether a private organization or even a state goes bankrupt. The economy may flourish, even if Africa perishes and irrespective of whether the US or China dominates the economic game. But as autopoietic systems both organizations and states have their own survival and prosperity as top priority.

A functional subsystem has no specific position in time and space and no center, as cutting edge activities may change place from one season to the next. Innovations are diffused super fast, although private organizations may try to conceal or patent scientific or technological innovation in order to get a competitive advantage. But the very moment a new product enters the market, competitors tear it apart to see whether it contains innovations worth imitating.

Functional subsystems constitute what Hegel calls an "external" social system (Hegel, 1991, §183). Communicating inside such a system, sender and receiver need not know each other. They can presuppose a shared language, shared communication channels and shared motivation. And just using the language of a functional subsystem creates no responsibilities towards other actors.

B. *Organizations* have normally one goal, supported by subordinated goals. They have one main stakeholder, whether it is the state (in the case of a public organization) or the shareholders (in the case of a private organization). But to fulfill expectations and get a license to operate other stakeholders must be served as well. If customers, employees or environmentalists are highly and loudly dissatisfied with the products or working conditions of a private organization, it is improbable that the shareholders will be satisfied in the long term.

Public organizations are not mobile, whereas private ones are. Even if private organizations do not have the speed of functional subsystems, and even if their offices and plants must be placed somewhere—there are limits to how virtual an organization can be—they can move according to opportunities and consider the whole world as their space of activity.

A private organization is able to exploit global possibilities relatively fast. Innovation presents chances and risks, but also enforces the organization to react. It is committed to profit and must get lean, grow, move—whatever it takes. But organizations may also put pressure on a state, threatening with moving abroad. As states have a vivid interest in employment and taxation they will struggle to create acceptable economic conditions for business. So organizations may exploit political differences and turn states against each other. Between organizations and states a recurring ambivalence can be observed.

Private organizations have a responsibility to their shareholders: they must create a surplus. Towards other stakeholders their responsibility is indirect and limited. Employees are only relevant because of their competencies, and customers only because of their money. What happens outside the meeting area of the market place for man power and purchase power is not the business of a private organization. It has no responsibility to what happens elsewhere in society or to employees and customers in general, and it is not obliged to balance social considerations.

C. *States* have many goals, and each goal has subordinate goals. They must make sure that functional subsystems and organizations thrive, because a state is doing exactly as well as the functional subsystems and the corresponding organizations inside its area. But unlike organizations states must balance many considerations: economic growth, political security, scientific dynamics, education, health and so forth.

A state is exclusively related to a geographical area and is according to its nature immobile. Even if it can expand, it cannot move abroad. Guatemala or Malaysia cannot threaten anybody with moving, and the same applies to public organizations. Also, a state cannot fire its members, if they show incompetent. To a certain degree, varying from state to state, it has full responsibility to its members, including health, education and mental state, accepting what Anthony Giddens has called "life politics" (Giddens, 1994, p. 91).

To avoid radical losers creating social disorder, the state must—for political if not for moral reasons—meet the demands of welfare and support members unable to take care of themselves, irrespective of whether the problems they suffer are unemployment, incompetence, illness or age. Due to this plurality of considerations and the need to balance responsibilities, the speed of a state is slow.

So, whereas the semantics and communications of functional subsystems are diffused all over the world in no time, and whereas the products of private organizations are quickly distributed, there is no similar political mechanism able to define and solve global problems. The political system of world society is a system without a representative being able to reflect and act on its behalf. Actors are states, which must balance not only a plurality of parameters, defined by functional subsystems, but also the relation between wealth and welfare. By doing so the state contributes to and finds its place in world society. Globalization is the name both for the dynamics of world society and for the ongoing redefinition of the place of nations in their global environment.

Conclusion

Luhmann presents a large-scale analysis of modern society as a system of functional subsystems, creating global, hyper complex and heterarchical networks of communication. As a consequence, the idea of autonomous nations is dismissed as obsolete. He enters the group of sociologists and philosophers who choose the global paradigm as opposed to the national one.

This line of thought, however, meets another line. Even if the nation is dismissed as theoretically unimportant, the state, as the political representative of the nation, is not. As a consequence the political system is not only the functional subsystem of politics, which is not represented by a world state, but also includes the national state, which is not just a mechanical part of world society, but has specific and irreplaceable functions.[27] It is a second-order organization, creating a legal frame for normal organizations, including itself. Accepting the importance of the state, the importance of the nation has to be accepted too.

Functional subsystems, private organizations and states are structurally coupled to each other. They are necessary for each other and at the same time have conflicting goals. The problems of globalization can be analyzed as the consequence of differences in goals, speed, time-and space-relations and stakeholder responsibilities of these three kind of social systems.

Going beyond the perspective of the present paper, it may be asked how the conflict between the national and global perspective might be handled in the future. As no world state and no legally competent global institutions exist, there are no political mechanisms able to solve the problems arising from the anarchic dynamics of functional subsystems, organizations and states. Two lines of argument can be traced. In the first place, the national point of view may be transgressed by second-order nations such as the EU. On the basis of an EU constitution, European nations might

---

27. As a functional subsystem, the political system is unable to act and therefore needs actors, which are not only organizations such as states, communities, interest groups and mass media, but also "a variety of interactions which understand themselves as political" (Luhmann, 1994a, p. 191).

find their place as constituent states in a federation or a super-nation, just as the US is considered a nation, because its constituent states from the very beginning were part of an over-arching unity. At present "we, Americans" is a stronger *we* than "we, Europeans." Whether the EU can be a center for loyalty depends not only on the existence of European values, but on purely empirical factors such as charismatic leaders, worthy causes and, perhaps, a common language. But even a United Europe would not solve the conflict between the national and the global point of view, as it would still be a nation, even if a big one. Driving the argument to its end and considering the possibility of a world state is at present either a utopian dream or a dystopian nightmare.

Secondly, it can be argued that the heterachical, connectionist, and network relations of world society have their own learning processes. Even if not formally organized as a political unity they inevitably converge towards universal institutions, both inside functional subsystems such as economy, politics and law and in institutions combining different subsystems. Step by step, along many lines and in a process with many backlashes, world society is being integrated. Many theorists with a global vein combine a scientific and a propagandist point of view, and even Luhmann at a time thought that the evolution of functional subsystems might overcome national and religious conflicts. His last word was, however, skeptical. Against the hope of rational progress he claimed that what is needed for survival is evolution (Luhmann, 1995, p. 477). But, as is well known, evolution depends on chance.

References

Beck, U. (1992). *Risk society: Towards a new modernity*. London: Sage.
Beck, U. (2004). *Dear kosmopolitische Blick oder: Krieg ist Frieden*. Frankfurt am Main: Suhrkamp.
Bauman, Z. (1998). *Globalisation: The human consequences*. Cambridge: Polity Press.
Bauman, Z. (2000). *Liquid Modernity*. Cambridge: Polity Press.
Bauman, Z.(2004). *Wasted Lives: Modernity and its outcasts*. Cambridge: Polity Press.
Castells, M. (2000). *The rise of the network society*. Oxford: Blackwell.
Fukuyama, F. (2004). *State building. Governance and world order in the twenty-first century*. London: Profile Books.
Giddens, A. (1994). *Beyond left and right*. Cambridge: Polity Press.
Habermas, J. (1999). Der europäische Nationalstaat unter dem Druck der Globalisierung. *Blätter für deutsche und internationale Politik, 4*, 425-436.
Habermas, J. (2001). *The postnational constellation: Political essays*. Cambridge, MA: The MIT Press.
Hegel, G. W. F. (1991). *Elements of the philosophy of right*. Cambridge: Cambridge University Press.
Held, D. (2004). *Global covenant*. Cambridge: Polity Press.
Hobbes, T. (1963). *Leviathan*. Oxford: Oxford University Press.
Kant, I. (1891). Perpetual peace: A contribution to political science. In *Kant's principles of politics* (pp. 31-48). Edinburgh: Clark.
Kierkegaard, S. (1989). *The concept of irony*. Princeton, NJ: Princeton University Press.
Kiss, G. (1990). *Grundzüge und Entwicklung der Luhmannschen Systemtheorie*. Stuttgart: Enke.
Luhmann, N. (1976). Generalized media and the problem of contingency. In J. J Loubser, R. C. Baum, A. Effrat, & V. M. Lisz (Eds.), *Explorations in General Theory in Social Science, 1-2*, (pp. 507-532). New York: The Free Press.
Luhmann, N. (1981). Identitetsgebrauch in selbstsubstitutiven Ordnungen, besonders Gesellschaften. In *Soziologische Aufklärung, vol. 3*(pp. 198-227). Opladen: Westdeutscher Verlag.
Luhmann, N. (1986). *Love as passion*. Cambridge: Polity Press.
Luhmann, N. (1987). Die Unterscheidung von Staat und Gesellschaft. In *Soziologische Aufklärung 4* (pp. 67-73). Opladen: Westdeutscher Verlag.
Luhmann, N. (1988). *Die Wirtschaft der Gesellschaft*. Frankfurt am Main: Suhrkamp.

Ole Thyssen

Luhmann, N. (1989). Staat und Staatsräson im Übergang von traditionaler Herrschaft zu moderner Politik. *Gesellschaftstruktur und Semantik, vol. 3* (pp. 65-148). Frankfurt am Main: Suhrkamp.
Luhmann, N. (1990a). The "state" of the political system. In *Essays on Self-Reference* (pp. 165-174). New York: Columbia University Press.
Luhmann, N. (1990b). *Political theory in the welfare state.* Berlin: De Gruyter.
Luhmann, N. (1992). *Beobachtungen der Moderne.* Opladen: Westdeutscher Verlag.
Luhmann, N. (1994a). Die Gesellschaft und ihre Organisationen. In H.-U. Derlien, U. Gerhardt, & F. W. Scharpf (Eds.), *Systemrationalität und Partialinteresse: Ferstschrift für Renate Mayntz* (pp. 189-201). Baden-Baden: Nomos.
Luhmann, N. (1994b). *Die Wirtschaft der Gesellschaft.* Frankfurt am Main: Suhrkamp.
Luhmann, N. (1995). *Social systems.* Stanford: Stanford University Press.
Luhmann, N. (1997a). *Die Gesellschaft der Gesellschaft,* Frankfurt am Main: Suhrkamp.
Luhmann, N. (1997b). Globalization or World Society: How to Conceive of Modern Society. *International Review of Sociology, 7* (1), 67-79.
Luhmann, N. (2000a). *Die Politik der Gesellschaft.* Frankfurt am Main: Suhrkamp.
Luhmann, N. (2000b). *Organisation und Entscheidung.* Opladen: Westdeutscher Verlag.
Luhmann, N. (2002). *Das Erziehungssystem der Gesellschaft.* Frankfurt am Main: Suhrkamp.
Marx, K. & Engels, F. (2000). *Communist Manifesto.* (originally published in 1848) Retrieved November 9, 2007 from http://www.marxists.org/archive/marx/works/1848/communist-manifesto/ch01.htm
Parsons, T. (1967a). On the Concept of Political power. In *Sociological theory and modern society* (pp. 297-354). New York: The Free Press.
Parsons, T. (1967b). Some reflections on the place of force in social process. In *Sociological theory and modern society* (pp. 264-296). New York: The Free Press.
Rorty, R. (1989). *Contingency, irony, and solidarity.* Cambridge: Harvard University Press.
Sloterdijk, P. (2005). *Im Weltinnenraum des Kapitals.* Frankfurt am Main: Suhrkamp.
Stichweh, R. (1995). Zur Theorie der Weltgesellschaft. *Soziale Systeme, 1*(95), 29-46.
Stichweh, R. (2000). On the genesis of world society: innovations and mechanisms. *Distinktion, 1,* 27-38.
Thyssen, O. (2003). Luhmann and management. In T. Bakken & T. Heines (Eds.), *Autopoietic organization theory* (pp. 213-234). Oslo: Liber.
Thyssen, O. (2004). Luhmann and epistemology. *Cybernetics and Human Knowing, 11* (1), 7-22.
Tilly, C. (1992). *Coercion, capital, and european states AD 990-1992.* London: Blackwell.

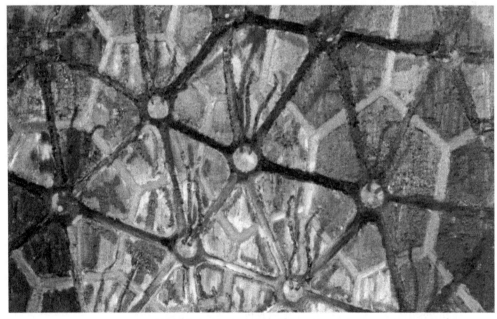

Beer, S. (n.d.). *Computer Volvox* (detail)

Cybernetics And Human Knowing. Vol. 14, nos. 2-3, pp. 111-131

Structural Couplings Between Organizations and Function Systems
Looking at Standards in Health Care

Morten Knudsen[1]

The paper is concerned with the relationship between organization and society. It reinterprets Luhmann's conceptualization of the relation between decision-making organizational systems and code-based function systems in order to enable the theory to observe (historical and current) changes. The relations between organizations and function systems are described in terms of structural couplings and the couplings are set in relation to the deparadoxizations of organizations. The thesis of the paper is that the organization makes itself irritable to function systems through its deparadoxization strategies. This idea is first treated theoretically and then the paper demonstrates its productivity through an analysis of how standards in health care form structural couplings between decisions in health care organizations and function systems as they deparadoxify decisions. The analysis shows how the health care organizations seem to become irritable (and thus coupled) towards a plurality of function systems when they deparadoxify their decisions by means of standards.

Introduction

In Niklas Luhmann's theoretical architecture difference comes before identity. This basic theoretical decision finds many expressions with the most fundamental one being the definition of a system as the difference between the system and its environment. And it is a theoretical decision which makes relations in need of explanation, as they cannot be taken for granted. This paper is about the relation between decision making organizational systems and code-based function systems. The point of departure is the contention that Luhmann's conceptualization of this relation not only is theoretically inconsistent but also makes it difficult to observe new developments in the relation between organizations and function systems. The purpose of the paper is to reinterpret the conceptualization of the relation between organizational and function system in a way that makes the theory able to observe historical and current changes in this relation.

The paper has two parts. It starts from a short critique of Luhmann's idea that organizations are *within* function systems. Instead it is suggested that organizations are coupled to function systems in a way which is closely related to how the organizations deparadoxify their decisions (section I). This idea I try to make plausible in an analysis of the way different kinds of standards in health care form structural couplings between decisions in health care organizations and function

---

1. Department of Organization, Copenhagen Business School, Kilevej 14 A, 2000 Frederiksberg, Denmark. Email: mk.ioa@cbs.dk

systems as they deparadoxify decisions, and as the standards are themselves deparadoxified. The purpose is to demonstrate the analytical fruitfulness of the proposed concept of structural coupling vis-à-vis contemporary developments (section II).

I) Deparadoxizations as Vehicles of Structural Couplings

According to Luhmann we have primarily three different kinds of social systems: *interaction systems* structuring communication on the presence of communicative partners; *organizational systems* structuring communication (which have the special character of decisions) on decision premises and membership; and *function systems* structuring their communication on binary codes and specific programs. The question of this paper is how to understand the relation between organizational systems and function systems.

Luhmann has dealt with this question both in more general terms (Luhmann, 1994a, 1997, 2000a) and in relation to specific function systems (for instance Luhmann, 1994b, p. 302ff; 2000b, p. 226ff; 2000c, p. 228ff; 2002, p. 142 ff.). To Luhmann the biggest and most important organizations are formed within the function systems (Luhmann, 1997, p. 840). The organizations are assigned (zugeordnet) to specific function systems (Luhmann, 1997, p. 841f), they assign there own operations to function systems and thus they are assigned to society through functional differentiation (Luhmann, 2000a, p. 405). Schools are assigned to the educational system, courts to the legal system, banks to the economic system, churches to the religious system, and so forth The assignment relates to the fact that the organizations take over the primary function (Funktionsprimat) and the binary code of the different function systems (Luhmann, 1997, p. 841). If the organizations did not do this, they would not be recognizable as schools, banks, hospitals, and so forth.

According to Georg Kneer's interpretation organizations are in Luhmann's perspective subunits of societal function systems, they are subsystems of politics, law, science, economy, and so forth (Kneer, 2001, p. 411). It is not difficult to find quotations supporting Kneer's interpretation. Luhmann often uses the genitive form when speaking about organizations *of* specific function systems. He also speaks about organizations *within* or *in* the function systems. For instance he asks "wie es überhaupt möglich ist *innerhalb* des Gesellschaftssystem und sogar innerhalb *seiner* Funktionssysteme Organisationen zu bilden" (Luhmann, 2000a, p. 387, my emphasis). He also talks about the role of the construction of organizations *in* the function systems (Luhmann, 1994a, p. 190). Related to the legal system he talks about the organized decision-making system *of* the legal system (Luhmann, 1993, p. 145). He even talks about organizations as centers of function systems (Luhmann, 1994a, p. 190). And the idea of organizations as subsystems is expressed explicitly in the following quotation: "Auch können Familien nicht Teilsysteme anderer Funktionssysteme sein, was für Organisationen möglich, ja typisch ist" (Luhmann, 2000a, p. 436). And even though Luhmann describes the relation between function system and organization as a complementary one, he also claims that "innerhalb des so konstituierten Systems für zweitrangige Möglichkeiten der Exklusion gesorgt werden, und genau das geschieht durch Einrichtung von Organisationen" (Luhmann, 2000b, p. 234f, my emphasis).

If we follow Kneer's interpretation, and this paper does, then we must also follow his critique. According to Kneer it leads to theoretical inconsistencies to locate organizations within function systems. Against the assignment of organization systems to specific function systems speaks the observation of organizations taking part in several function systems (Kneer, 2001, p. 412). Organizations orient themselves towards several function systems. Universities for instance both have to deal with research (related to the scientific system) and teaching (related to the educational system) (Luhmann, 1997, p. 784). Private companies may also have research departments, legal departments and sometimes they also take part in political communication. According to Luhmann almost all organizations need money. And all payments with money are internal operations of the economic system, including funding of governments and churches. Thus Luhmann states that all organizations also operate in the economic function system (Luhmann, 2000a, p. 405); for instance schools both operate in the educational and the economic system.[2]

The premise that organizations are assigned to one specific function system is not compatible with the observation that organizations operate in several function systems. The idea of the organization being within two different function systems is inconsistent with the system theoretical premise of a sharp distinction between system and environment (Kneer, 2001, p. 412).[3] A system is the difference between system and environment. According to this premise something is either part of the system or part of the environment, it cannot be both. It cannot both be part of the economic system and part of its environment. If the school is a subsystem of the educational system it cannot at the same time operate in the economic system which is in the environment of the education system. This is also expressed with the term operative closure. Communicative elements are only elements of the system in which they are produced. The elements cannot at the same time be in the system and in the environment of the system. If the school is a subsystem of the educational system it cannot at the same time operate in the economic system.

We may relate this to health care organizations, which will later form the system reference for the empirical analyses. Probably Jost Bauch is the one who has made the most ambitious analysis of disease treatment as a function system (Bauch, 1996). And in his study Bauch does not discuss how the hospital as an organization is coupled to

---

2. Luhmann even gets close to Althussers famous expression about the "economic determination in the last instance," when he writes "Man muss sich natürlich fragen, ob über diese Kette: Geldabhängigkeit der Organisationen→Organisationsabhängigkeit *der meisten Funktionssysteme* nicht eine latente Dominanz der Wirtschaft in der modernen gesellschaft sich durchsetzt"(Luhmann, 1994b, p. 322).

3. Kneer has a double critique of Luhmann. He criticizes the idea that organizations are subsystems of function systems and he criticizes the idea, that organizations can communicate with each other. Taken together these two theses lead to an idea of an inter-organizational intermediation between function systems, an idea Kneer sees as too close to mainstream sociological diagnoses of the cooperative state.

health care as a function system with a specific code. Instead he states that "Wie Wolff konstatiert, ist das Krankenhaus selbstverständlich Teil des Gesundheitssystems" (Bauch, 2006, p. 16). Now, my point is that this is not that evident. In a hospital we find not only communication drawing on the code of the health care function system (whether it is ill/healthy [Luhmann, 1990b] or life-promoting/life-preventing [Bauch, 1996]). We also find decisions related to a legal code, an economic code, a scientific code, and so forth. Thus it is not that evident that the hospital is a part of the health care system. As Dirk Baecker puts it: "Vor allem im Rückblick erstaunt, wie sehr es dem Krankenhaus gelungen ist, sich zum Schnittpunkt der Ansprüche hochgradig untershiedlicher Funktionssysteme zu machen" (Baecker, 2007). It seems hard to combine the idea of the hospital as a touch point of different function systems with the idea of the hospital as a subsystem of one specific function system.

On the one hand it seems evident that many organizations have a close relation to one specific function. On the other hand Kneer has a point when claiming that Luhmann's way of conceptualizing this relation is inconsistent with basic premises of his own systems theory. The above mentioned thesis about organizations as being *within* function systems is not only problematic because it is theoretically inconsistent with basic theoretical premises of systems theory but also because it blocks out insights in changes in the ways specific organizations are related to function systems. As Luhmann claimed that organizations are within function systems he did not have to analyze historical changes in the relations between organizations and function systems. But if one concedes this theoretical decision we need a theoretical functional equivalent to describe the relations between an organization and function systems. In continuation of his critique of Luhmann, Georg Kneer suggests analyzing organizations and function systems as environments of each other. I follow Kneer's suggestion and use the concept of structural coupling as a central concept in the description of the relations between the two types of system.

The concept of structural coupling is an answer to the question of how autopoietic and thus operatively closed systems are related to their environment when they have no direct contact to it (Luhmann, 1997, p. 100; 1993, p. 440f). Even though autopoietic systems are operatively closed they are not independent of their environment. Social systems can be influenced by psychic systems, which can be influenced by organic systems - but the economic system can for instance also be influenced by the legal system. Forms of structural coupling facilitate influences of the environment on the system. But not the environment as such: a structural coupling stands for chosen system-to-system relations (Luhmann, 1990a, p. 41). It designates relations between system and environment, which in the long run[4] influences the self-produced structures of the system without overruling the autopoiesis of the system.

---

4. For event-like couplings Luhmann has developed the concept of operational coupling designating the situation when the "same" event is used as element in two different systems (which of course determines the event differently, the same event does not have the same meaning in the different systems) – see Luhmann 1993, p. 440f.

Structural couplings may enhance the influence of environment on the system, but they do not make a direct determination possible. Luhmann talks about the couplings triggering irritations in the system - irritations to which the system reacts in its own way. And it is the system itself which determines what might irritate it and what might not. Only a system can be irritated, not the environment. Structural coupling describes the situation in which one system cannot remain indifferent to another system (la Cour, 2006, p. 50). The concept directs attention to the question of how systems are "able to make themselves sensitive to operations in their environment." (la Cour, 2006, p. 51). In itself the concept of structural coupling is to be understood as a heading of different solutions to the same abstract problem: how are different and operatively closed systems related? How do they influence each other? How do they co-emerge? As the concept is an answer to a very general problem it remains itself abstract. The structural couplings depend on the kind of systems involved, and with functional differentiation it is not possible to mention just one kind of coupling. Language is a structural coupling between social and psychic systems; the constitution, property and contract couples the legal system with the political and the economic system (Luhmann, 1993, p. 443 ff.), and so forth. When Luhmann discusses structural couplings in relation to organizations it is a discussion of how organizations may couple between function systems (Luhmann, 2000a, p. 397f). He does not discuss what structural couplings relate organizations and function systems, a topic he has made superfluous because he has placed the organizations within function systems (and with the ability to communicate with other organization systems).

But the criticism of Luhmann's ideas both of communication between organizational systems and of the organizations being inside function systems brings back the problem to which structural coupling is an answer: how to describe and understand relations between a system and systems in its environment.[5] As mentioned, there are, according to Luhmann, many different kinds of structural couplings. It is therefore also to be suspected that organizational systems are coupled to function systems in different, changing and historically different ways. My suggestion is to follow Luhmann in his basic idea of the paradoxical nature of decisions and to use this idea as a guide for observing and analyzing structural

---

5. Niels Åkerstrøm Andersen has developed an alternative interpretation of the relation between organization and function systems (Andersen, 2003a). He suggests that the relation lies in every decision which must be made in a function system specific symbolically generalized medium. This idea seems to have some problems. For example, the decision to hospitalize a patient: which medium is it made within? There may be medical reasons for it, there may be a legal aspect (it is made in order to prevent possible legal problems following non-admittance), and it may have economic reasons. And probably all considerations play a role. Of course, different function systems can observe and connect to the decision in their specific ways, but at an organization level the medium is not a generalized symbolic medium but decision premises.

In his theory of the firm Dirk Baecker has also developed a kind of system theoretical network description of the relation between organization and function system (Baecker, 2006). His theory draws on Spencer Brown's notation of observation. His model shows there is a relation between the different kinds of systems. But when it comes to analyzing specific relations between specific systems I have found the model too general to serve as the analytical point of departure.

couplings between organizational systems and function systems. In order to clarify this idea I shall briefly describe Luhmann's concept of organization and decision.

The concept of organization and the paradoxical nature of decisions
According to Luhmann an organization is a network of recursively connected decisions (Luhmann, 2000a). Organizational systems are like other social systems operatively closed: They cannot operate (i.e., make decisions) in the environment and the environment cannot operate in the system. Decisions should be understood as communicated decisions, not individual choices. Luhmann develops his organization theory out of the idea of the paradoxicality[6] of decisions (Luhmann, 2000a, p. 123ff, 2005). It is this idea which generates Luhmann's theory and observations of organized communication. It is thus a logical place to start when generating theses about organizational systems' structural couplings with function systems. In the following I shall give a short presentation of Luhmann's concept of the paradoxicality of decisions.

The communication of which organizational systems consist has the form of decisions (and decision-related communication). A decision is an indication in the frames of a distinction which has the form of an alternative. This means that the other side of the distinction could have been indicated — or could have been decided in the frames of a different distinction — otherwise it would not be a decision but the result of a calculation. The decision fixes contingency and absorbs uncertainty as it indicates one side of the alternative: this and not that. But communicating itself as a decision it cannot help co-communicating that it could also have been made differently: the other side of the alternative could have been indicated or could have been indicated in the frames of another distinction (Luhmann, 2000a, p. 147). This clash between message and information, form and content is a central reason why Luhmann characterizes the decision as paradoxical. The problem (and what makes the concept of the paradoxical decision a generator of observations and organizational theory) in this paradoxical nature of decisions has to do with connectivity and contingency.

Connectivity (Anschlussfähigkeit) is essential in Luhmann's concept of decision (and in his concept of communication in general), since it is only the connections of further decisions which can turn a decision into a real decision and not just noise. A decision which no further decisions connect to, turns out not to be a decision, but noise (Knudsen, 2006). The term *paradox* has a rather broad sense in Luhmann's oeuvre. In my interpretation, it is very close to contingency. What is paradoxical about the decision is that it is contingent (neither necessary nor impossible), and it cannot avoid communicating this. And this contingency makes the connectivity less likely: Why connect to a decision which itself says that it could also have been made otherwise?

---

6. Luhmann uses the concept of paradox in a rather loose way, sometimes it denotes a more classical logical paradox, and sometimes it is used more rhetorically as a way to increase attention. When it comes to decisions the inherent paradox has much to do with contingency in the Aristotelian sense — as will be further developed below.

At the core of Luhmann's way of doing organizational theory is the question: How do organizations manage the paradoxicalness, the lack of necessity, the contingency of their decisions? As the organizations exist they must have managed the paradoxes. And as the paradox cannot be solved, but only handled or managed, this leads to the question of how organizations deparadoxify their decisions. To deparadoxify means to handle the contingency of the decision so it is less likely to paralyze further connections. The general answer is that this is done by making the contingency invisible or by displacing it to a less disturbing place (Luhmann, 2005). To deparadoxify means to place the contingency of a decision at a less disturbing (paralyzing) place. Classical rhetoric had a well-developed teaching of such places (for instance they can either be common [loci proprii] or specific [loci communes] where arguments are found [and thus where contingency can be displaced to]). The places were understood as a storehouse, as subjects and categories useful for argumentation (Curtius, 1973, p. 89ff). Especially when this reservoir of arguments belongs to tradition its contingency is hidden and thus efficient for deparadoxization.

An organization can deparadoxify itself in several different ways – it is an empirical question *how* it is done, but a theoretical premise *that* it is done. It can displace the paradox of a decision to its decision premises,[7] it can displace it to a decision maker (and thus ascribe intentions), by means of hearings it can displace it to the hearing partners. It can also deparadoxify the decision by interpreting it as a necessary answer to environmental development, thus displacing the paradox to developments in the environment (see Luhmann, 2000a; Andersen, 2003c; Knudsen, 2005).

Here the idea is to combine deparadoxization and structural coupling. If the displacements shall work, if it shall place the paradox at a less disturbing place, then the displacement cannot be completely random. It must be plausible that the place to which the paradox has been displaced has some kind of importance, that is, makes some kind of difference. If the place shall be less disturbing the organization must make itself sensitive to this place. If the organization displaces the contingency of its decisions to the consensus of the employees, the organization must in some way or the other make it plausible that it is sensitive to the opinions of its members; otherwise the displacement might only work for a short while. It must be plausible that the organization can be irritated by the members opinion. The displacements will be more persuasive if they are not completely random. The displacement is a way of rendering the contingency of the decision less visible and disturbing. And if the displacement itself seems too contingent not much has been obtained.

In order to avoid the randomness of displacements the organization must make itself irritable to the place to which it displaces the contingency. Luhmann relates the term *Resonansfähigkeit* (the ability to be resonant) to structural coupling. There is no coupling if the system is not resonant. And here the idea is that the organization can

---

7. The decision premises have more functions: they structure the communication as they establish expectations which can be expected. But they also deparadoxify decisions as they establish a possibility for displacement.

develop more stable displacements if it develops resonance towards the places to where it displaces its paradoxicalness. The movement goes in two directions: a) from the decision to the less disturbing place as the paradox is being displaced;and, b) from the less disturbing place back to the decision (and the organization). If the organization displaces the paradox of a decision to political development the paradox becomes less disturbing if the organization can make it credible that it is somehow sensitive to the political system. It can be seen as a deal: the price the organization must pay for displacing the contingency to the environment is increased sensitivity to this specific place of the environment.

In the next part I shall show and analyze an example of how the structural couplings of organizations to function systems emerge from the deparadoxizations of the organization.[8] I shall also demonstrate how the suggested approach to organizational systems' structural coupling to function systems opens up the analysis to historical changes in the form of the couplings. History has not stopped; the relations between organizations and function systems still changes. And the suggested approach may be a way of keeping the analysis open to these changes.

II) Standards in Health Care

I shall demonstrate the analytical potential in the above suggestions using standards in health care as an example. The point of departure for the empirical analysis is the hypothesis that standardization is an increasingly important element in the deparadoxization of decisions in health care organizations. My ambition is not to explore the totality of couplings between health care organizations and different function systems. Instead I limit the analysis to one kind of coupling: standards. In this analysis the function system of disease treatment (Luhmann, 1990b, Bauch, 1996) has not become very visible. This does not, of course, mean that there are no couplings between health care organizations and the function system of disease treatment. But it indicates that the couplings have other forms than standards.[9]

I start by observing how standards offer themselves as decision premises for decisions in health care. In other words: how they offer themselves as places to which decisions in health care may displace their paradoxicalness. As the standards themselves may be seen as decisions, this raises the question of where their paradoxicalness is placed. The organization itself does not communicate about the relation between decision and decision premises as a question of displacement. Rather it is treated as if it were a causal relation (even though experiences show this is not the case). In the following I shall use the terms *coupling* and *to couple* as terms for how observers relate decisions to decision premises or how they relate decisions to a less

---

8. Organizations have, of course, couplings to other kinds of systems as well: to other organizations; to interaction systems; and to psychic systems. The couplings to these different systems must be analyzed in their own right.
9. This paper explores only one kind of coupling (namely standards) between organizational systems and function systems. Health care organizations and the health care function system are probably also coupled by education, professions, the high level of job-change, the daily conferences, common purposes, and so forth

disturbing place. The analysis is based on different standards and discussions of standards as found on central web-sites and in scientific journals nationally (with Denmark as the point of focus) and internationally.

Standards in the Health Care Sector

Since the 1990s there has been a remarkable growth in the amount of standards in the health care sector—nationally and internationally. We find standards concerning communication (terminology, information-practices), service, evaluation-practices, organizational routines, treatments, outcomes, and so forth. Especially with regard to quality we find a considerable growth in the amount of standards. The remainder of this section will focus on two of the more comprehensive kinds of internationally spread standards, namely accreditation and clinical practice guidelines.

A short terminological remark: In this paper, I define a standard as a possible premise for a decision. Brunsson and Jacobsson (2000) discuss the relation between rules, norms and standards. Even though they tend to define standards as something voluntary they choose to keep the exact definition open. I find this a reasonable strategy. Even though it may seem somewhat unsatisfactory to have such an open definition, it is precisely this liminal status (placed in the continuum between the rule and the voluntary good advice) which characterizes a standard. One may visualize the relation between decision and standard (decision-premise) as follows:

Figure 1

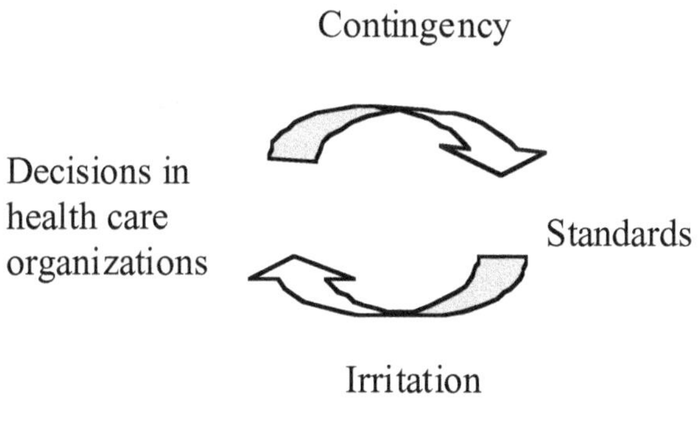

Contingency

Decisions in health care organizations   Standards

Irritation

The figure indicates that contingency is displaced from decisions made in health care organizations to standards. When the question "why this decision?" is answered with "because the standard says so" then the contingency is moved from decision to standard. It is a movement and not an eradication of contingency because one could of course follow up and ask why this standard? At the same time the figure indicates that the standard influences the decision. The argument is that in so far as the displacement is to convince, the decisions must somehow be irritated by the standards. The term irritation means that the organizations have resonance towards the standards, which thus have some influence. But the term irritation also indicates that it is not a causal relation; it is the organization itself which determines how it can be irritated, influenced and how it should react to the irritation.

Inspired by Luhmann, one can distinguish between two different kinds of standards: end-standards establishing ends (which ends the decisions are to aim at), and conditional-standards (which use if/then structures: if this disease then this treatment) (Luhmann, 2000a, p. 260f). In the following, clinical practice guidelines will serve as an example of mainly conditional standards, whereas accreditation will exemplify mainly end-standards.

Clinical practice guidelines
There are different kinds of standards directed towards clinical decisions. The individual wards traditionally have "instruction-books." But in recent years there has been a huge growth in clinical practice guidelines (CPG) which are not tied to a single ward or organization. Instead specific diagnoses are the core of the CPG's. The size of a CPG may vary from a few to several hundred pages. The standard definition (see www.openclinical.org/guideline) is the following: "Clinical practice guidelines are systematically developed statements to assist practitioner and patient decisions about appropriate health care for specific clinical circumstances" (Field & Lohr, 1990, p. 38). The CPG offers instructions on sorting diagnostics, treatment, documentation, information and sometimes economic aspects. In 2002 it was estimated that 1000 new guidelines were produced every year in the US (Berg & Timmermans, 2002). According to Grol "The number of clinical practice guidelines included in Medline increased from one (in the period 1975-1980, MK) to more than 450 per year (at the end of the 1990s MK)" (Grol, 2000, p. 455). The guidelines are normally produced by medical societies, groups within such societies or (groups of) individual physicians.

In Denmark an office for guidelines was established in August 2000. The head of office defines a guideline this way:

> A clinical guideline combines the available scientific evidence about a disease with clinical experiences in order to give recommendations, which can support the clinical personnel in the planning of the treatment of the patient – as they give due consideration to aspects of health economics and have the overall purpose of increasing the quality of the health services." (Jørgensen, 2003, my translation)

The quotation points to an important difference between earlier local books of instruction and clinical practice guidelines. The ambition of the latter is to couple clinical decisions with scientific evidence. Since the 1990s the guidelines have been an important part of what has been entitled "Evidence-Based Medicine" (EBM). Kravitz defines EBM in the following way: "Evidence-based medicine is the application of scientific evidence to clinical practice" (Kravitz, Duan,& Braslow, 2004, p. 661). It has become a strong movement with its own journals, campaign centers (centers for EBM), EBM-societies, and websites. Books about EBM have been published, there has been a vigorous debate about it. It is now being taught at different health care education facilities, and a host of instruments facilitating the practice of EBM has been developed (among others, methods of evaluating the quality of evidence).[10] One of the fundamental problems in EBM is, of course, the translation from medical science to clinical practice. And here the clinical guidelines play a central role. A widespread understanding of clinical guidelines is, that they establish couplings between scientific evidence (preferably in the shape of randomized clinical trials) and clinical practice (Berg & Timmermans, 2002). This understanding is built into the guidelines, the central elements of which are recommendations of specific practices and references to scientific evidence. We may draw it like this

Figure 2

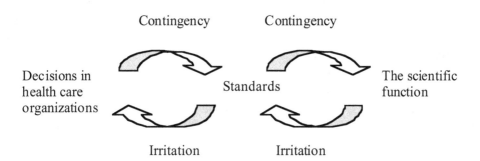

The drawing illustrates the following relations: Decisions in health care are being deparadoxified as the contingency inherent in the decisions is moved (by observers) to a less disturbing place, that is, the clinical practice guidelines. Clinical practice guidelines are also being deparadoxified as the contingency inherent in the guidelines is moved to research evidence (the scientific function system). The movements described can be reversed: if the decisions in health care are deparadoxified by means of clinical practice guidelines they must make themselves sensitive to the guidelines. And if the guidelines are being deparadoxified by means of research evidence they must be made sensitive to research evidence.

Observed like this the standards can be seen as a structural coupling between decisions in health care and the scientific function system.[11] Now we shall make a similar analysis of another type of standard: end-standards.

---

10. And the term has proven so successful that we currently witness a push for evidence-based education, evidence-based politics (Pawson, 2006), evidence-based management and even evidence-based research.
11. Vogd has developed a similar idea on the level of function systems and related to "evidence based medicine" (Vogd, 2002).

Accreditation

Accreditation in health care has been taking place since 1919, when the Joint Commission on Health Care (JCHA) was founded in USA (Roberts, 1987). The idea behind accreditation is that an independent accreditation organization formulates a line of standards (and the necessary measurable indicators) which is then used to evaluate organizations. The organizations may take account of the accreditation in advance and use the standards, against which they will be compared, when they make decisions. Accreditation means a) formulation of standards b) (external) control of the adherence to these standards. The accreditational-standards are thus both decision premises and visualizations of obtained results. The accreditational-standards typically concern the existence of internal standards and politics within the accredited health care systems. The experience from the accreditations in Denmark is that it leads to a major growth in the amount of standards produced within the system as it tries to meet the accreditational standards. This gives accreditation some similarity to Michael Power's concept of audit (Power, 2003). Central to Power's concept of audit is its mechanism of control of control. What is accredited is thus, and not least, the hospitals' ability to control their own activities (e.g. to determine that members of the staff actually have the education they claim to have).

The practice of accreditation has become much more common in recent years. Internationally the amount of accreditation programs has doubled every five years since 1990 (Shaw, 2003, p. 455). In Denmark the Association of the Counties[12] and the Danish Government have agreed to make accreditation compulsory for all Danish hospitals by 2008.

Whereas the clinical guidelines ascribe to themselves the function of coupling decisions in clinical practice with results from medical science, the standards in accreditation are ascribed the function of giving decisions in health care more quality. Quality has become a widespread – and positive – word. Similar to the EBM movement, a quality movement has risen with new publications, journals (e.g., *International Journal for Quality in Health Care*), quality societies (Danish, European, and International Society for Quality in Health Care), and websites. Accreditation is discursively and institutionally closely connected to quality. For instance, The International Society for Quality in Health Care (ISQua) has—as we shall see—developed standards for accreditations.

Even though quality has another, more diffuse status than research evidence, we illustrate with Figure 3 how standards are ascribed the function of coupling decisions in health care with quality. As accreditation to a large extent consists of standards aimed at establishing whether the hospitals have standards concerning their own decisions, the figure shows:

---

12. In Denmark the Hospitals were owned by the counties until January 2007, where ownership was transferred to five newly established Regions.

Figure 3

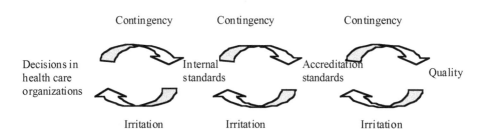

The movements are: the contingency of the decisions is moved to the internal standards, the contingency of the internal standards is moved to the accreditational standards and the contingency of the accreditational standards is moved to "quality." It is, of course, questionable what quality is, but if we follow Lindeberg, quality can be understood as a function system with a specific code and programs (Lindeberg, 2006). If we follow the movements the other way we can see how accreditation and the involved standards constitute a way of coupling decisions in health care to the quality function system.

To sum up: Seen from an organizational point of view the standards form new decision premises and seen from the viewpoint of the proponents of the standards it is a way to couple decisions in health care with research evidence and quality. Seen from a system theoretical point of view standardization is an increasingly important way of deparadoxifying decisions in health care organizations, the effect of which is new types of structural couplings between health care organizations and function systems.

In the next section, I will review the most common criticism of both types of ascribing couplings.

Critics of the ascription of couplings

Above I have only interpreted the couplings, which the proponents of the standards connect with standards. In this part we shall see how critical observers question the couplings established by standards. The criticism calls for alternative couplings (if the coupling to quality is not really the function - then what is?); this will be discussed later. But the criticism also shows that even though there is a relation between deparadoxization and structural coupling the coupling is not necessarily as tight as the above mentioned analyses may indicate.

Difficulties in the translation from science to practice

The clinical practice guidelines are, if possible, based on randomized clinical trials, which use averages of large groups. However, the actual patient is never average. Actual patients react individually to the same treatment, both physically and mentally. EBM has its point of departure in probabilities in research groups, but for several reasons this does not allow for conclusions regarding the treatment of individual patients with hyper-complex, genetically differently biological systems (Behrens, 2003, p. 263; Færgeman, 2002). It is highly problematic to apply global evidence (averages) to local problems—individual patients never fit an average (Kravitz et al., 2004; Breinholdt, 2005; Feinstein & Horwitz, 1997, p. 529).[13]

It has also been stated that for the clinician an important part of the problem regards the insecurity about the dynamics of the situation – an insecurity that cannot be overcome by means of standards. The situation is always more complex than the standards allow for. Insecurity and complexity demand subjective answers like the faculty of judgement, a willingness to take both risks and responsibilities and the like (Vogd, 2004, p. 195).

Loose coupling between the guidelines and the scientific basis
Since the clinical guidelines are to function as a coupling between research evidence and clinical practice, naturally they ought to be closely linked to the research evidence. However, the closeness of the link has been questioned. For instance, in an investigation of whether clinical guidelines for the testing of cholesterol mirror research evidence Savoie, Kazanjian, & Bassett (2000) conclude, that four out of five guidelines investigated had a problematic link to research evidence: "The groups [which developed the investigated guidelines, MK] with the exception of the EHCRT, did not develop recommendations that were linked to research evidence. In some cases, the recommendations contradicted the groups' own conclusions on the research evidence."(Savoie et al., 2000, p. 80). According to Feinstein & Horwitz (1997) it is not an easy task to evaluate the quality of the meta-analyses behind guidelines. Variations among the different randomized clinical trials under comparison can make it difficult to assess the basis for the guideline.

A review of approaches employed to rate the quality of the evidence reported in individual studies showed 121 different approaches to rate the quality of an individual study (Steinberg & Luce, 2005, p. 82). There are thus many different definitions of what good evidence actually is—the line between opinion and evidence is not at all clear. A German study of the relation between guidelines and the supporting evidence showed that physicians, even within the same specialty, estimated the relation differently. Some thought the literature supported the guidelines, others that it did not (Porzsolt, 1998, p. 579).

Regarding the evidence behind the standards used in accreditations Mainz, Krog, Fog, and Bartels note that the level of evidence is not stated in the publications from the international accreditation organizations. Thus it is not possible to estimate whether the standards are well founded.

---

13. A problem related to the mismatched scientific results regarding an average patient vis-à-vis an actual and individual patient is currently sought overcome by means of genetic tests, which may give more information regarding how individual patients may react to a given treatment.

Lack of evaluation of accreditation.

In the literature it is generally acknowledged that there is no solid scientific proof of the ability of accreditation to improve quality or to ensure a more efficient use of resources (Shaw, 2003, Mainz et al., 2002). Or as Øvretveit states: "Considering the amount of time and money spent on organizational assessment, and the significance of the issue to governments, it is surprising that there is no research into the cost-effectiveness of these schemes." (Øvretveit, 2001, p. 233). It has also been marked that accreditation has not been evaluated with comparable methods to permit synthesis (Shaw, 2003, p. 455), thus Frølich and Christensen state "It is a weakness of accreditation that a connection between accreditation and improvement of the patient treatment cannot be shown." (Frølich & Christensen, 2002, p. 4416, my translation). A typical argument against accreditation is that the resources used could have been used better in a more direct way.

To sum up we may say 1) Standards like accreditation and clinical guidelines are ascribed the function of coupling decisions in health care with research evidence and quality. 2) This ascription is questioned in different ways by other observers, as demonstrated above. It may be diagrammed like this:

Figure 4

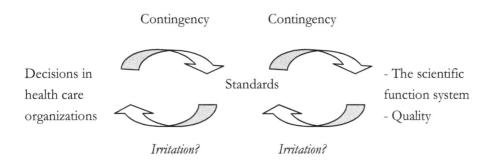

The Ascription of Alternative Functions to the Standards

The criticisms mentioned above raise the following question: if the standards to which the contingency of health care decisions are displaced do not necessarily couple decisions with science and quality, what then do they couple? In this section we will review some of the most common ascriptions. We will see how observers link standards to different functions.

Some ascribe the clinical guideline the function of coupling decisions in health care to economic considerations. Thus it is still more common to incorporate or to refer to cost analyses in the guidelines. A study conducted by the Tufts Center for Study of Drug Development shows that nearly 30 percent of current clinical practice guidelines incorporate or refer to cost analyses (www. Csdd.tufts.edu/newsevents/ NewsArticle.asp?newsid=46). One of the 23 checkpoints in the AGREE-instrument, which is developed in order to evaluate the quality of guidelines, is: "The potential cost implications of applying the recommendations have been considered." Thus the function of guidelines is potentially to couple decisions in health care to cost considerations - only those treatments that have a documented and economically efficient effect ought to be offered at hospitals.

In Denmark Holger Højlund has analyzed how central governmental players see the introduction of accreditation and other kinds of quality standards as a condition for creating a market for welfare-products (Højlund, 2004). The products must be made visible in order to facilitate the customers' "free choice" - and the establishment of standards and the matching control mechanisms is one way of visualizing "the product" (see also Callon et al., 2002). This would imply that the standards couple decisions in health care with the economic function system.

Another ascribed function is to create transparency. With reference to Max Weber and his idea of *Entzauberung* (disenchantment), Behrens claims that the EBM is about

> einen Schritt im Prozess der Entzauberung ärztlichen Handelns vom magischen Heilen zum professionellen handeln, das wissenschaftlich kontrollierte Erfahrung für den einzigartigen Fall des individuellen Patienten in Respekt vor der Autonomie der Lebenspraxis des Patienten nutzt. (Behrens, 2003, p. 262).

In the Danish debates on quality the creation of transparency is also a central argument, for instance the Government has issued a discussion paper named "An Open and Transparent Health Care System" (Indenrigsministeriet, 2003) in which the quality measures (based on standards) are given a central position in the creation of transparency. This transparency is, from a political point of view, a way of enhancing the political control of health care. In this perspective the standardization is a way of establishing possibilities for further couplings between decisions in health care and the political system.

A central topic, not least in the USA, is whether "courts will treat CPGs [clinical practice guidelines, MK] as setting the legally required standard of care." (Rosoff, 2001, p. 332). Thus the function of the guidelines could be seen as coupling decisions in health care to the legal system. In the debate on guidelines further functions are ascribed, for instance Færgeman ascribes a whole host of functions, of which the main function is the administrative control of physicians (Færgeman, 2001). Systems theoretically this could be interpreted as a way to couple the "health function system" (Luhmann, 1990b; Bauch, 1996) closer to organizational systems (like hospitals).

The documentation of the multiplicity of functions ascribed to standards could be expanded, but the general point has been illustrated: Neither the clinical guidelines nor accreditational standards (or other quality-standards in health care) can be said only to make one coupling. If the courts use the standards and if the organizations let themselves be irritated by this use then the standards have coupled not decisions and science, but decisions and law. The standards may establish a multitude of new couplings. This observation indicates that we have to see the relation between deparadoxization and structural coupling as a variable relation. The deparadoxization triggers a coupling, but the function system to which the contingency is displaced by the standards is not necessarily the only place from which the deparadoxization opens the organization to irritation. We may draw it like this:

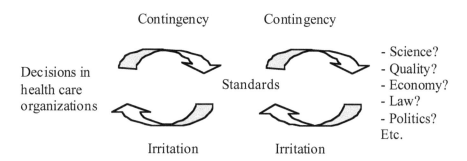

Meta-standards

One of the reactions to the multi-coupling ascribable to standards is the development of meta-standards. In this section I will show some central examples of standards with the explicit function to strengthen the coupling between standards and quality and/or research evidence.

The "International Society for Quality in Health Care" (ISQua) raises a troubling question regarding the standards meant to secure quality: "How can each organization know if its standards are on track?" (http://www.isqua.org/isquaPages/ Accreditation.html). The standards are meant to connect the decisions in health care to quality, but how do we know if the standards themselves possess quality—a prerequisite for their ability to connect decisions and quality. Thus the problem of quality is repeated (now not the quality of the decisions, but of the standards), but, as we shall see, so is the solution. ISQua offers to measure the quality of the standards, and this is - of course - would be done by the use of standards:

> Standards are assessed by an international expert panel against ISQua's International Principles for Healthcare Standards. This is an internationally tested and approved framework of requirements i.e. principles and their criteria (= standards and indicators, MK), which should underpin health care delivery standards. (http://www.isqua.org/isquaPages/Accreditation.html)

ISQua talks about "Accrediting the accreditors…" If the accredited accreditors fulfill the standards (called ALPHA) they get an ALPHA-certificate.

One can find many similar doublings related to clinical guidelines, and many guides to the development of clinical practice guidelines have been published. Some of them can be seen at the Guidelines International Network (http://www.g-i-n.net/ - look under resources). A widespread tool to estimate the quality of the guidelines is the AGREE-instrument developed by the AGREE-collaboration. The AGREE-instrument, which has been translated into 13 different languages, is comprised of 23 questions (standards) on which one can base the evaluation of the quality of a guideline. Both the Alpha and the AGREE-instruments are instruments which are to strengthen the coupling of standards to quality / research evidence by means of standards.

The introduction of meta-standards offers new possibilities of deparadoxization. The contingency in the standards may now be displaced to the meta-standards. This displacement can be problematized as we can ask what is the quality of the standards securing the quality of the standards securing the quality of decisions. Or what is the quality of the meta-standards? This question seems even more pressing, since the meta-standards obviously do not live up to their own standards. The "International Principles for Healthcare Standards" published by ISQua demonstrates the problem neatly. The first principle goes like this: "All processes for the external evaluation of healthcare services should be based on a well-established and tested set of standards" (ISQua, 2004a). This standard has itself not been tested (at least it does not document that it has), so according to its own criteria it is a bad standard! The problem is logically insoluble since one can question the quality of the meta-meta-meta.... standard ad infinitum. Instead, we see different kinds of deparadoxification or displacement, where the paradoxes and holes are made more or less invisible, or placed at less disturbing places. One of the methods is to introduce consensus conferences, where an expert answers the open question—after which we are all supposed to imagine that she bases her answers on solid arguments, even though they are invisible. The consensus conferences displace the paradox to the diffuse "consensus."

To sum up, the standards are ascribed the function of connecting decisions in health care to quality and research evidence. This connection is questioned and alternative functions are ascribed. The original ascriptions are sought to be strengthened by means of the introduction of meta-standards. This reflexive movement is a well-known mechanism for stabilization (i.e., stabilizing standards with standards, Luhmann, 1972). Time will show whether this strategy is successful or whether it merely creates ever more communication.

III. Conclusion

The purpose of the paper has been to suggest a way of describing the relation between decision-based organizational systems and function systems, which is both conceptually consistent and sensitive to historical changes at a less basic level than societal differentiation. The basic form of societal differentiation may remain unchanged while the relations between organization and function system change. The suggested approach might make the analyses sensitive at a less general level, forcing the researchers to make more historically and spatially specific analyses.

The idea was to describe the relations between organizations and function systems in terms of structural couplings and to relate the couplings to the deparadoxizations of organizations. The thesis was that the organization makes itself irritable through its way of deparadoxifying itself. I have tried to demonstrate the applicability of this idea through an analysis of the role of standards in health care organizations. The analysis shows how the health care organizations seem to become irritable (and thus coupled) towards a plurality of function systems when they deparadoxify their decisions by means of standards. This way the environment of the organization becomes more complex (as the environment is dependent on the systems observing it). And the organizations must themselves increase their complexity in order to meet the complexity of their environment. The organizations must become able to navigate in a world not only of disease but also of law, science, economics, politics, and so forth. As such, the standards can be seen as an important element in the emergence of more *polyphonic* (Andersen, 2003a) organizations.

If we developed the analysis further and included structural couplings between organizations we would probably also observe how the standards are active in the creation of a new type of inter-organizational steering regime. Standards are developed by a variety of actors, government institutions, NGOs (like many of the accreditation organizations), different kinds of societies (quality societies, associations of physicians and the like), campaign organizations, different kinds of network organizations with members from the industry, doctors, journals and the like. In so far as standards have an impact in the health care organization, they are part of the emergence of a steering regime which is less based on national regulation than on a variety of boundary-crossing, polycentric types of regulation (see also Teubner, 2002, and related to the medical profession:. Vogd, 2005, p. 252). Today there is no well-defined administration and no clearly demarcated physical boundaries, but rather international, polycentric networks developing standards coupling health care organizations both to function systems and to different kinds of (inter)national organizations in new and important ways.

The analyses above should, though, only be seen as a demonstration of some of the analytical perspectives in the basic idea of this paper: to observe structural couplings as a result of the deparadoxizations used by an organization. The analyses can only be indicative, as I have been observing ascriptions of couplings, not how the systems are actually irritated. An analysis of how the standards actually couple the systems would require much more detailed analyses of how the standards are used in decision making, how the legal system uses standards, how health organizations observe the legal use of standards and so forth. It would have to see standards in relation to other kinds of deparadoxizations and the related structural couplings. Some paradoxes are displaced to standards, others to tradition, to the chief physicians as a decision-maker, to legislation, and so forth. The different deparadoxizations establish different couplings. And more couplings do not necessarily mean less autonomy, to establish new couplings may be a way to loosen older couplings. Future studies must analyze further aspects of the problematic.

I have suggested understanding the relation between organization systems and function systems in terms of structural couplings emerging from the way in which the organization deparadoxifies its decisions. Now, if this suggestion is accepted further research might go back to the phenomenon which has led to the idea that organizations are part of function systems: the observation that organizations often seem to be closely related to one particular function system. It is, for instance, evident that the hospital is more closely coupled to the health care function system than to the art system. Both empirical and theoretical research might try to describe this phenomenon without turning organizations into parts of function systems, without giving up the theoretical premise of operative closure. Instead of taking it for granted we may now ask why so many organizations seem to have a preference for one function system—a state of affairs in need of explanation, no longer an unquestioned fact.

References

Andersen, N. Å. (2003a). Polyphonic organisations. In Bakken, Tore & Tor Hernes (Eds.), *Autopoietic organization theory* (pp. 151-182). Oslo: Abstrakt.

Andersen, N. Å. (2003b). *Discursive analytical strategies: Understanding Foucault, Koselleck, Laclau, Luhmann.* Bristol: The Policy Press.

Andersen, N. Å. (2003c). The Undecidability of Decision. In Bakken, Tore and Tor Hernes (Eds.), *Autopoietic organization theory* (pp. 235-259). Oslo: Abstrakt.

Baecker, D. (2006). Theory of the Firm. *Organization, 13*, (1), 109-142.

Baecker, D. (2007). Zur Krankenbehandlung ins Krankenhaus. In I. Saake & W. Vogd (Eds.), *Moderne Mythen der Medizin: Studien zu Problemen der organisierten Medizin.* www.uni-wh.de/baecker/

Bauch, J. (1996). *Gesundheit als sozialer Code. Von der Vergesellschaftung des Gesundheitswesens zur Medikalisierung der Gesellschaft.* München: Juventa Verlag.

Bauch, J. (Ed.) (2006). *Gesundheit als System. Systemtheoretische Beobachtungen des Gesundheitswesen.* Konstanz: Hartung-Gorre Verlag.

Behrens, J. (2003). Vertrauensbildende Entzauberung: Evidence- und Eminenz-basierte professionelle Praxis. *Zeitschrift für Soziologie, 32,* (3), 262-269.

Berg, M., & Timmermans, S. (2003). *The gold standard. The challenge of evidence-based medicine and standardization in health care.* Philadelphia: Temple University Press.

Breinholdt, M. (2005). Evidensbaseret medicin får modspil. *Ugeskrift for Læger, 167*(5), 546-547.

Brunsson, N. & Jacobsson, B. (2000). *A world of standards.* Oxford: Oxford University Press.

Callon, M., Méadel, C., & Rabeharisoa, V. (2002). The economy of qualities. *Economy and Society , 31* (2), 194-217.

la Cour, A. (2006).The Concept of Environment in Systems Theory. *Cybernetics and Human Knowing, 13* (2), 41-55.

Feinstein, A. R. & Horwitz, R. I.(1997). Problems in the "Evidence" of Evidence-based medicine. *The American Journal of Medicine, 103,* 529-535.

Field, M. J. & Lohr, K. N. (Eds.). (1990). *Clinical practice guidelines: Directions for a new program.* Institute of Medicine. Washington, DC: National Academy Press, 1990.

Frølich, A. & Christensen, M. (2002). Akkreditering af hospitaler. En gennemgang af internationale erfaringer. *Ugeskrift for læger, 164* (38), 4412-4416.

Færgeman, O. (2002). Evidensbaseret medicin, sundhedspolitik og administrativ kontrol med lægers arbejde. *Ugeskrift for læger, 164* (11), 1538-1543.

Grol, R. (2000). Imlementation of evidence and guidelines in clinical practice: A new field of research? *Int J for Quality in Health Care, 12* (6), 455-456.

Højlund, H. (2004). *Markedets politiske fornuft: Et studie af velfærdens organisering i perioden 1990-2003.* København: Samfundslitteratur.

Indenrigsministeriet. (2003). *Et åbent og gennemsigtigt sundhedsvæsen.* Copenhagen: Indenrigs- og Sundhedsministeriet (Ministery of health and internal affairs).

ISQua. (2004). *International Accreditation standards for healthcare external evaluation bodies* (2nd ed.). London: ISQua.

ISQua. (2004a). *International Principles for Healthcare Standards.* Melbourne: ISQua.

Jørgensen, H. (2003, June). Sekretariatet for Referenceprogrammer, *SfR. Nyhedsbrev fra Dansk Selskab for Kvalitet i Sundhedsvæsenet.*

Kneer, G. (2001). Organisation und Gesellschaft. Zum ungeklärten Verhältnis von Organisations und Funktionssystemen in Luhmanns Theorie sozialer systeme. *Zeitschrift für Soziologie, 30* (6), 407-428.

Knudsen, M. (2005). Displacing the paradox of decision making: The management of contingency in the modernization of a Danish county. In D. Seidl, & K. H. Becker (Eds.), *Niklas Luhmann and organization studies* (pp. 107-126). Copenhagen: Liber and Copenhagen Business School Press.

Knudsen, M. (2006). Autolysis: An operation-analytical observation of noise out of order. *Soziale Systeme 12* (1), 79-99.

Kravitz, R. L., Duan, N. ,& Braslow, J. (2004). Evidence-based medicine, heterogeneity of treatment effects, and the trouble with averages. *Milbank Quarterly , 82* (4), 661-687.

Lindeberg, T. (2006). *Evaluative technologies. Quality and the multiplicity of performance.* Unpublished Ph.D. dissertation, Copenhagen Business School.

Luhmann, N. (1972). Reflexive Mechanismen. In *Soziologische Aufklärung 1*(pp. 92-112). Opladen: Westdeutscher Verlag.

Luhmann, N. (1990a). *Die Wissenschaft der Gesellschaft.* Frankfur am Main: Suhrkamp.

Luhmann, N. (1990b). Der medizinische Code. In *Soziologische Aufklärung 5*(pp. 183-195). Opladen: Westdeutscher Verlag.

Luhmann, N. (1993). *Das Recht der Gesellschaft.* Frankfur am Main: Suhrkamp.

Luhmann, N. (1994a). Die gesellschaft und ihre Organisationen. In H.-U. Derlien, U. Gerhardt, & F. W. Scharpf (Eds.). *Systemrationalität und Partialinteresse* (pp. 189- 201). Baden- Baden: Nomos.

Luhmann, N. (1994b). *Die Wirtschaft der Gesellschaft.* Frankfurt am Main: Suhrkamp.

Luhmann, N. (1997). *Die Gesellschaft der Gesellschaft.* Frankfurt am Main:Suhrkamp.

Luhmann, N. (1998). *Die Wissenschaft der Gesellschaft.* Frankfurt am Main: Suhrkamp.

Luhmann, N. (2000a). *Organisation und Entscheidung.* Opladen/Wiesbaden: Westdeutscher Verlag.

Luhmann, N. (2000b). *Die Religion der Gesellschaft.* Frankfurt am Main: Suhrkamp.

Luhmann, N. (2000c). *Die Politik der Gesellschaft.* Frankfurt am Main: Suhrkamp.

Luhmann, N. (2002). *Das Erziehungssystem der Gesellschaft.* Frankfurt am Main: Suhrkamp.

Luhmann, N. (2005). The paradoxy of Decision. In D.Seidl, & K. H. Becker (Eds.), *Niklas Luhmann and organization studies* (pp. 85-106). Copenhagen: Liber and Copenhagen Business School Press.

Mainz, J., Krog, B. R., Fog, K. , & Bartels, P. D. (2002). Sundhedsfaglige standarder i akkreditering. *Ugeskrift for læger, 164* (38), 4408-4411.

Øvretveit, J. (2001). Quality evaluation and indicator comparison in health care. *International Journal of Health Planning and Management. 16* (3), 229-241.

Pawson, R. (2006). *Evidence-based Policy. A realist Perspective.* London: Sage Publications.

Porzsolt, F. (1998). Wann nutzen Leitlinien dem Arzt, dem Patienten, dem System? In K. Merke (Ed.), *Umbau oder Abbau im Gesundheitswesen? Finanzierung, Versorgunsstrukturen, Selbstverwaltung* (pp. 579-584). Berlin: Quintessenz-Verlag.

Power, M. (1997). *The Audit society: rituals of verification.* Oxford: Oxford University Press

Roberts, J. S, Coale, J. G., Redman, R. R. (1987). A history of the joint commission on accreditation of hospitals. *JAMA, 258,* (7), 936-940.

Rosoff, A. J. (2001). Evidence-based medicine and the law: The courts confront clinical practice guidelines. *Journal of Health Politics, Policy and Law, 26* (2), 327-368.

Savoie, I., Kazanjian, A., & Bassett. K. (2000). Do clinical practice guidelines reflect research evidence? *Journal of Health Services Research and Policy, 5* (2), 76-82.

Shaw, C. D (2003). Evaluation accreditation. *International Journal for Quality in Health Care, 15* (6), 455-456.

Steinberg, E. P. , & Luce, B. R. (2005). Evidence Based? Caveat Emptor! *Health Affairs, 24,* (1), 80-92.

Teubner, G. (2002). Idiosyncratic production regimes: Co-evolution of economic and legal institutions in the varieties of capitalism. In J. Ziman (Ed.), *The evolution of cultural entities: Proceedings of the British Academy* (pp. 161-181). Oxford: Oxford University Press.

Vogd, W. (2002). Professionalisierungsschub oder Auflösung ärztlicher Autonomie? *Zeitschrift für Soziologie, 31* (4), 294-315.

Vogd, W. (2005). Medizinsystem und Gesundheitswissenschaften - Rekonstruktion einer schwierigen Beziehung. *Soziale Systeme, 11* (2), 236-270.

Beer, S. (n.d.). *Travelling*.

Cybernetics And Human Knowing. Vol. 14, nos. 2-3, pp. 133-150

Steering as Paradox
The Ambiguous Role of the Political System in Modern Society[1]

Werner Schirmer[2] and Claus Hadamek[3]

Generally it is taken for granted that social problems such as unemployment, demographic aging and uncontrolled immigration can be effectively met by counter-steering. The usual question, then, is *how* to do this, but not *who* should do it? It is assumed that the agency to perform this task is the state. In this article the authors put this into question and ask how the need for steering can be explained with theory of society. They discover an inherent paradox in the approach to steering society: Steering is necessary because it is impossible.

Structurally, modern society lacks a place from which the momentums of the self-referential subsystems (and their complex effects) can be steered. It has neither a center nor a top. Notwithstanding, the problems are observed as "problems" which call for a solution. Because steering is structurally impossible, the vacuum must be filled semantically. The explanation has to be found here why this task can only be fulfilled by the political system and neither by science nor by economy. Politics' societal function addresses the problem of collectivity: to bind a collectivity and, at the same time, to be made responsible for it. That is why the political system is considered to be the steering agency of society, and has to fail.

1. Introduction

We probably all agree in that mass unemployment, demographic aging or uncontrolled immigration pose major problems for society. They seem to be due to complex social processes that require countermeasures. The usual question, then, is *how* to do this, but not: *who* should do it? Accordingly, we probably (automatically) agree on the political system's responsibility to solve these problems. Isn't it the task of politics to steer? However, since the track records of most governments are not the best, this attitude could astonish. In a strikingly constant way, great expectations are followed by equally great disappointments. Some react with disenchantment with politics, resignation or gallows humor. Others stay to their unshakable confidence in politics' capability of steering and continue keeping up the illusive promises—from election to election. Though these strategies are different or might even point in opposite directions they do agree in one crucial point: They all trust in an at least *potentially* given political capacity to act. Even if social problems continue and cannot be solved, whom do we ask? The political system!

---

1. This article is based on a conference paper presented at the 37th World Congress of Sociology in Stockholm 2005 in a session on systems theory. We would like to thank Vessela Misheva for the organization.
2. Department for Sociology, Uppsala University, Sweden. E-mail: werner.schirmer@soc.uu.se.
3. Department for Sociology, University of Tromsø, Norway. E-mail: claush@sv.uit.no.

As we think, this needs to be explained from a theory of society perspective. The central research questions of our article—which largely follow up the premises of Luhmann's systems theory of society—are the subsequent: How can the need of steering be explained sociologically? Why is it politics standing in the focus of attention and not for example economy or science?

In the following, we will argue that due to the *primary structure* of society – functional differentiation – steering has to be an illusion. Although it is often intended, direct intervention into subsystems is not possible.[4] Society is nothing more than the differentiated (and hardly integrated) unity of its self-referentially closed subsystems. Since the subsystems are autonomous and coequal, there is no central instance for inter-systemic coordination somewhere "above." Not even the political subsystem can fill this position. It can neither be an integrative center nor the top of the society. Against this background, we will argue that the strong need for societal steering has to be explained exactly by this structural lack: Because it is structurally impossible to steer, there is a strong need for steering *as semantics* (section 2). In the next step, we attend the question why it is nevertheless politics which is expected to steer. It is as well a question of the term of society being used as it is a question of the specific functions the subsystems fulfil for society. Besides the political system, we take a look at both the scientific system and the economic system. The most promising candidate, however, will finally be politics. It is a part of politics' function to represent society as a whole and that is exactly the reason why politics is forced to compensate the lack of structural steering semantically (section 3). Politics stands ready to shoulder the burden to steer with best intentions. But, at the same time, it gets into the ungrateful position of having to take on responsibility for all kinds of unpredictable outcomes of its attempts at steering. And it is because of this general responsibility that politics suffers from permanent self-overloading. Thus, it is no wonder that most of the citizens are frustrated or disenchanted about the performance of politics.[5] Thereby the utopia of an integrated and steered political society is reproduced. But even this attitude presupposes the utopia of an integrable and steerable society. Steering, thus, is the semantic answer to the society's structural lack of steering. One could bring it to the paradox formula: *Steering is needed because it is impossible* (section 4).

2. Steering and the structure of society

Obviously, a lot of processes in society do not run as they should. Obviously, these processes cause some side effects that are observed as major social problems. We do not deny that there are a lot of things to do—simply look at the examples of social problems mentioned at the beginning of this article. Once a large number of people is

---

4. We understand the term *intervention* in the meaning of a predictable and clear cause-effect-logic (input-output). It is the nations' constitutional and basic laws which assure the autonomy of the subsystems. The subsystems are protected against direct political intervention, for example by the institutions of freedom of opinion/speech, freedom of ownership, freedom of scientific research, sanctities of private sphere, etc.
5. In saying this we do not want to be understood as proponents of neo-liberal convictions as to a 'better' market/ politics relationship. Our critique is based on sociological assumptions and not ideological presuppositions.

concerned, one is in search for an address equipped with the power and resources to "solve" those problems and to avoid them in the future. In other words: to intervene into the causes of the problems and steer their outcomes. We want to examine what the phenomenon of steering and intervention actually is about. How does it function? Why are there so many attempts of intervention, and why do most of them fail, that is, do not show the wished outcomes? We try to give answer to these questions from a systems-theoretical perspective. When Luhmann, in his theory of society (see Luhmann, 1989, 1997b), speaks of functional differentiation, he means a society that consists of different functional subsystems (e.g., law, economy, religion, education, science, politics, family). These systems are autonomous and dependent at the same time. The relation between subsystems is characterized by coequality concerning rank; thus, no subsystem can claim to be on whatever hierarchical top of society (Luhmann, 1995, 1997b). In this respect one cannot easily say that economy is more important than science or that religion is more important than education. Nevertheless, politics is likely to be observed as more important than the other systems: as an authority being able to integrate society (Luhmann, 1997b, p. 630).[6] Luhmann's general theory of social systems is associated with the terms operative closure, self-reference, system/environment and, as the core element of social systems, communication.[7] Social systems reproduce the elements they consist of by elements they consist of. This formula is inevitably tautological. To put it into other words: Social systems construct both a description of their own as well as of the rest, that is, their environment. Since they are meaning-processing systems, it is only up to them how and what they observe. They observe their environment, and by observation they generate information from noise. According to their structure and their available modes of observation, they can distinguish between information regarded as relevant and information regarded as irrelevant. To give an example: Does information that is gathered by observation with the distinctions capital/labour or equality/inequality really matter? Can it be regarded as relevant information or not? Both observation and further meaning processing are a system's internal operations, that is, self-referential operations. Due to their operative closure, no system can communicate *with* the environment any more than it can communicate *with* any other system (as if they were ontological entities) but only *about* it, and this is a main reason why intervention into social systems from the outside is impossible (Luhmann, 1997a, pp. 47-48; Luhmann, 1997b, p. 753). Applied to the political system, this means:

> The political system is thus only able to steer itself by a specific political construction of the difference between system and environment. That this happens and how it happens has without any doubt tremendous effects on the society because the other functional systems must orient themselves along the differences thus produced. But this effect is certainly not steering and it is not possible to steer it because it depends on the construction of differences in the context of other systems and because it falls under the steering programmes operating in these systems (Luhmann, 1997a, pp. 47-48).

---

6. As we will see later, this self-overestimation is both functional and problematic at the same time.
7. For a more detailed description of the terms see Luhmann, 1995.

So, first and foremost, the political system steers itself. Nevertheless, political measures can indeed have consequences for systems in its environment.. When a state's president advises against new terrorist threats, then, the state's government may spend more money on arms and security measures. When, afterwards, parts of the population buy respirators or have bunkers built in their gardens, it is not a causal effect from politicians' actions and statements but the citizens' attribution of certain relevant information that then prompted them to act economically. Luhmann speaks in this manner of initial causality (Auslösekausalität) in contrast to the reach-through causality (Durchgriffskausalität) (Luhmann, 2000b, p. 419). Of course, one can attribute the (good) intention of an attempt to steering: One can say that it was the president who made his people buy respirators. But one cannot logically state that this was a successful steering. It is only a routine of attribution and, therefore, an unavoidable simplification. Against this background, research on steering options and practical implementations rather sticks to empirical probabilities than to some "fundamental" theoretical knowledge or wisdom.

Not least because of these attribution problems, there has been a long debate about the meaning of steering. According to Renate Mayntz, there has not even been a real (and useful) definition of what steering actually is (Mayntz, 1996). Both Renate Mayntz and Fritz Scharpf have contributed to the steering and implementation debate on large scale. Interestingly, both authors hold on to the conviction of action theoretical steering capacities on the side of the state while they, at the same time, describe network and negotiation systems as a third form of steering besides the classical dualism between the market and the state. In other words: The action-theoretical perspective still prevails while the number of actors rises a lot, and also non-state actors gain more and more importance especially in the light of the "new social movements" (see Mayntz, 1996; Mayntz, 2004; Scharpf, 1992). Luhmann defines the term steering (or regulation) in a rather abstract way. He mentions three main characteristics.[8] At first, steering is the *minimizing of differences* in a given distinction. Examples are the decrease of unemployment rates, an adjustment of wage gaps between women and men or the reduction of the pollutant emission, to name but a few. Secondly, steering is always *self-steering of acting systems*. Since social systems are self-referentially closed systems, the difference which causes an action is drawn by the system itself. If, for example, the Norwegian unemployment-rate decreases after the introduction of the labour-market initiative "et mer inkluderende arbeidsliv," most politicians in charge of the implementation of that program would surely accredit this to their personal effort. Apart from the fact that it is very complex to trace success factors such as labour promoting factors,[9] it is the intervened systems'[10] own reactions to certain distinctions that were constructed by the corresponding systems themselves. Thus, it is not the political initiatives as such which function; it is rather the intervened systems' potential of irritation and their mode of operation that decide whether or not and—even more important—*how* the

---

8. See for further information Luhmann (1997, p. 48ff)

political motives are met.[11] A third characteristic of steering is that the difference-minimizing programs aim at preferring one (better) direction. This is no (big) problem if the system to be steered is a trivial machine (von Foerster, 2003). Trivial machines (like vending machines, computers, or cars) can be steered/controlled very easily once one is familiar with their user interface because they have a mechanical and/or programmed mode of operation. Therefore, trivial machines either function, that is, they do what they are supposed to do or not. In the latter case, they are defective. There is no other possibility. However, for self-referential systems, being non-trivial machines, it is more puzzling to find criteria whether they function or not. They often do unexpected things (even unexpected for themselves) that other observers dislike. For example may the economic system under normal operations produce unemployment from time to time – possibly even as a market effect which can be functional for economic means. Nonetheless, the political system will observe unemployment as a problem. Politicians do not talk about a sane mean of unemployment rate. Rather, they construct illusive visions of how to reduce unemployment to a more pleasant level. A specific asymmetric notion of what is better is already underlying: Low unemployment is regarded as better than high unemployment.[12] Concerned people and the government of a political system would certainly subscribe to this view but at least for opposition parties and economic corporations high unemployment can be very profitable.

At this point, we have to add a few characteristics of steering and intervention that are not explicitly mentioned by Luhmann but which can be derived from the societal and general social aspects of his systems theory. At first, the simple fact that attempts at steering automatically are observable[13] leads to new constructions of new differences which in turn can be observed. For example: The leading parties of the current German big coalition of chancellor Angela Merkel deal with amending and adjusting single factors of the labour market reforms passed under the former Schröder government. These attempts at steering are mostly based on figures and statistical material (such as reduction of the administration costs or raise of unemployment benefits). However, not all observers share the advantages of these

---

9. Not without reason there is a whole academic discipline with the name *evaluation research*. It scrutinizes possible factors and measures to reduce existing unemployment. Its instruments – classical quantitative methods – developed from simple formulas of correlation to more complex multi-factorial instruments of analysis and they are constantly improved and criticized. The field of evaluation research would disabuse us if it, all of a sudden, found *the* solution to the problem of unemployment. Even a sociologist like Ulrich Beck, who is not very susceptible to systems theoretical thoughts claims in a definite way: "Everybody who promises to have a cure to the unemployment problem does not tell the truth!" (Beck, 2000, p. 7).

10. The grammatical plural does not only refer to the fact that several functional systems can be the aim of an intervention but also to organizational systems and non-social systems with their own self-reference (such as psychic or or biological systems).

11. in the sense that the desired outcomes are achieved, attempts of amendments and improvements of initiative programs (as they are in heaps observable in any steering process) would not be necessary. It is obvious that the desired outcomes appear differently for each observer/actor.

12. Exactly for this reason politics and political theory are eager to normative and moral statements. Mass media, as a functional system of its own, takes up these valuing differentiations.

13. Formulated precisely, steering is attributed by observers.

difference-minimizing programs. Rather there are enough "experts" trying to give evidence for their "better" point of view. Thus, one can say, attempts at steering provoke other attempts at steering—a process that in most cases can only be stopped by time-restriction.

A second point is the relation between difference-minimizing programs on the one hand and difference-prevailing operations as a structural necessity of social systems. If one thinks of the social-theoretical premise that social systems have to delimit from one another in order to prevail, it is just a short step to the consequence that construction of differences is an infinite as well as a necessary process. As a result, masses of inequalities become visible (Reich & Michailakis, 2005)—these inequalities derive from the fact that social systems continuously produce asymmetries. They increasingly center the question of inclusion and exclusion on the back of the individuals and make them responsible for their own individual fate. With their operations, functional systems create differences between individuals: The economic system produces people with lots of money and people without money, the religious system produces believers and infidels, the legal system produces victims and villains. And then it is, of course, organizations which have to decide whether people become members or not and promote the simple inequality between members and non-members (often with far reaching consequences). Interaction systems "discriminate" those people not being present and those people not being able to contribute to certain topics. In summary, social systems have been and keep on producing inequalities, wherever you look at. Last but not least it is sociology as an academic discipline that for a long time had its self-understanding based on detecting inequalities. We are sure that the sociology of social inequalities is far from ending in a blind alley, since there will always be inequalities to be detected. Inequality is not the exception but the rule!

Thirdly, acts of steering project (or try to achieve) a future that is better than the present – otherwise it would be nonsensical. But, while politicians decide on the proper strategy of steering, society's autopoiesis and dynamics do not stop. The present future as condition for present decisions looks differently compared to the future the present steering is meant for. Already short time after the decision, the decision itself can be criticized because 'very important additional variables' had not been taken into account. And indeed, it is never wrong to criticize decisions, even political decisions. Mind: There is no center perspective in modern functionally differentiated society. In principle, every perspective claims to be right; it is then up to the systems' programs to decide under which condition decisions are regarded as being right or wrong. There are (only) coequal subsystems in an everlasting competition for the best perspectives that none can win. Every perspective can (and does) provide new information about new problems that call for new attempts at steering. This temporary aspect of steering is exactly the reason why there will always be steering, more than ever before, just because there is no central unit in society that could provide an obliging perspective and say a final stop. That is why steering is the *semantic* answer to the structural lack of steering! In this regard, steering is a phenomenon happening every day. Social systems steer all the time, sometimes even without knowing it. With their operations, they produce a high potential of irritation for many other observing systems,[14] and those other systems themselves react in one or another way. It is a matter of definition, whether one calls this steering or not. This depends on whether you prefer an agent who steers or whether you prefer to judge by success/failure. In a systems-theoretical perspective, however, it is not a question of who steers whom and what; rather it is a question of which scheme of differences is regarded as relevant for one's own self-referential procedure. We will see later on that it is the political system's special set of functions that makes it the most popular candidate for steering. Last but not least, the political system's cutting edge on societal self-descriptions has to be seen in conjunction with other semantics like the postulate of equality and human rights. As mentioned before, difference-minimizing programs aim at reduction of inequalities, inequalities that no longer are regarded as legitimate.

> The difference-minimizing programmes are directed towards the diminishing of inequalities. Inequalities are no longer seen as a description of the perfection of the world (as *multitudio et distinctio* in the sense of medieval cosmology) but as a reason for countersteering. … By steering, all functional systems always also create differences and in effect inequalities. (Luhmann 1997a, p. 50)

Moreover, the socially acknowledged postulate of equality is somehow the motor of the "steering mania" (Luhmann 1997a, p. 50). One can wonder about why there still is inequality in a society that calls itself *modern*. Second order observers can see that it is exactly the semantics of modern society that makes the problem of inequality visible in the first place. To put it bluntly: Without a postulate of equality there would be no inequality because it could not be observed. Equipped with modern semantics, one could see its general contingency and criticism the observed inequality as inappropriate. Then it appears as potentially solvable (or at least reducible), or better: it could be steered. A morally charged observer could claim: it *has to* be steered! This demand for steering derives from the fact that indeed everything in society is contingent[15] and therefore enough reasons could be found to regard current conditions in society as unpleasant. In modern society, not only everything is possible; it is even possible in different ways simultaneously. Problems generally could be handled politically, economically, judicially, educationally and of course scientifically; and all at the same time!

3. Steering: by whom?

We have now seen for which structural reference problem steering is the solution. Because of their self-referential closure, the subsystems operate autonomously with an own momentum. They cannot be coordinated from a central location. For this

---

14. Former systemic approaches would describe this as an output.
15. Mind: We use the term contingency in its modal-theoretical meaning: neither necessary nor impossible.

reason, we can observe the emergence of amplifications of deviance [Abweichungsverstärkungen], which let the encompassing system look less integrated. This is the way theory of society would explain why steering is structurally impossible and at the same time needed in the first place. In our article, we assume that (national) political systems step into the breach and try to solve this structural impossibility *semantically* while pretending to be able to steer society.[16] From the perspective of theory of society, however, we have to ask why of all systems it is the political system that is expected to steer. Why for example is it not the economic or the scientific system?

This suspicion is not as unrealistic as it may seem. Economic perspectives (and consequently according eco-political programmes) intensively point out a liberalized market's ability to steering and its positive effects for society. Recently, knowledge has begun to play an important role in societal self-descriptions, shown as well by educational debates as by the growing demand for consultant agencies and think tanks. Sometimes, the prominence of scientists and experts is extrapolated to unsolved questions about the future and then finally on steering. To find some explanations, one has to think of the symbolically generalized media of communication power, money and truth. Long ago, their differentiation from each other and from religious forms in the first place enabled the operative closure of self-referential systems we know today as politics, economics and science. The function of these media of communication is to transform unlikely acceptances of communicative offers into more likely ones (Luhmann, 1997b, pp. 320). To put it into a language more related to theory of action: equipped with such media, one can get another person to do what one wants them to do more easily. The point is to steer other systems/agents/units by forcing them with power, by rewarding them with money or to convince them with knowledge/truth. Instead of media of communication, Helmut Willke therefore speaks of *media of steering* (Willke, 2001).[17]

Willke accepts the systems-theoretical principle of functional differentiation and the self-referential closure of the subsystems. In this regard, he rejects linear-causal concepts of intervention and input/output-models; in accordance with Luhmann he constitutes, that steering only can be successful as adopted self-steering by the addressee systems. So, steering 'degenerates' to a 'decentralized context steering[18,] (Willke, 2001, pp. 130ff). The regulating system provides potential of irritation that is observed by the addressee system; maybe these observations cause a structural change within the latter—maybe not. This is beyond the intervening system's control. Nevertheless, Willke assumes, that it is the task of the political systems to intervene

---

16. Generally, functional systems' (politics, economy, law, religion, families, education, arts and so on) operation modes hold true for society as a whole which, in systems theory means world society. In spite of supra and transnational governance models the nation states are still the 'number one agencies' concerning steering and intervention acts. The nationalization of social problems goes along with the political systems' referential problem and function which is concerned about finding collectively binding decisions. Little wonder that it is the citizens as the largest national collectivity which is focused upon.

17. However, instead of using truth as the media of science, Willke speaks of knowledge (see Willke, 2001, p. 246ff).

18. This and the following translations from German are our own.

into other systems with the help of media of steering (virtually as instruments): be it with the help of power (new laws), with the help of money (subventions or taxes) or with the help of knowledge (education programs).

The central question of *who* shall steer *whom* is already pre-answered. Politics as regulating agent (howsoever informed by systems theory) shall act on other societal subsystems. Although Willke speaks of *decentralized* steering (because steering can only be successful if decentralized, and thus can only be implemented by the addressee systems themselves), the political system nevertheless takes on the role of a center in society. Even if steering takes place decentrally, the (intentional) impulse finally comes from the political system which, in this regard, is re-centralized.

So, Willke finds his place in the long row of a politics-centric understanding of society shared by numerous recent diagnoses of present society [Zeitdiagnosen] and normative political theory like it can be traced in Mayntz's as well as Scharpf's notions of a changed understanding of *political* attempts at steering. This is due to a *term of society* which narrows down social facts to social dimension: society as a gathering/sum of human beings who have something in common that makes them a community, such as common values, shared norms, unitary culture, common interests or common problems.

Following Armin Nassehi, approaches of this kind start from a *unity* of society (Nassehi, 2003a; Nassehi, 2004), that is they already have a picture in mind of what society (as unity) looks like. Functional differentiation in this context mostly means a division of labour in Durkheim's manner. The parts drift apart and have to be integrated by an organic solidarity. Therefore, differentiation appears as a problem of missing or lacking integration. Parsons' AGIL-paradigm can be read quite similarly: It assumes a decomposition of a unity into its parts and explicitly claims a special functional system for integration of society (I-function).

Starting from society's unity, one imagines (whether consciously or unconsciously) society as a *collectivity* which acts and accomplishes its goals with the help of its political system (think of Parsons' G-function, i.e., goal attainment). This term of society is already a *political* term of society (see Nassehi, 2003a, p. 180). Society then is treated as an address one can appeal to and to which one can put all kinds of reproaches and many well-meant claims to: more tolerance, more willingness to risks, and more willingness to reform. However, it mostly remains unclear *who* actually is addressed, and consequently those who had claimed often wonder why nothing has happened afterwards. And even that can be used for a new reproach and for a new claim for more activity. In short: Once we use such a political term of society, we confuse society as a whole with an agent able to collective action. Such a term of society differs hardly from one used in mass-medial communication because it does not always distinguish clearly between functional systems and organizational systems (e.g., Beck, 1993; Willke, 1991). It should be obvious that this kind of term of society is almost inappropriate for sociological analyses.

Luhmann's term of society takes up much more radically since it constitutes a unity only towards non-social environment. Society, in this regard, is a unity only insofar as it delimits from non-communication (psychic and organic systems, physical environment, etc.). This term of society neither requires normative integration nor a common culture nor even shared interests and values. Luhmann's systems theory provides conceptual discriminatory power and is able to keep the different references of systems apart, as there are functional systems, organizations and face-to-face-interactions. Only with this perspective one can see that neither society as encompassing system nor its functional systems have any agential qualities nor have they addresses (see Schirmer, 2007). Society and its functional systems then only appear as horizons (see Nassehi, 2004, p. 102). Each of them appears as not yet actualized possibilities of meaning processing, that is, as a frame of possible future communication. This frame itself, however, can never be reached because every attempt to describe or indicate it only pushes the horizon further forward. It makes sense that claims addressed to a horizon finally must vanish into nothingness.

At this point we may already offer a partial explanation to why it is the political system that is expected to steer. The role one ascribes to politics in modern society is always pre-structured by the used term of society. If one understands society as a community integrated by common norms and values, it stands to reason that one may regard it as a political collectivity capable of acting. A theory of self-referential systems that treats society as communication cannot be convinced by such a notion. On the level of observation of observations, however, one can see that the political self-descriptions of society are more persuasive and collectively effective than others—for example, sociological ones. Political self-descriptions have gained "air superiority" (Nassehi, 2002, p. 45). Political self-descriptions, starting with steering by politics, normally take on the view of a theory of action. They assume an intentionally acting agent who recognizes problems and rationally looks for possible solutions.[19] The attractiveness and collective range of such a way of thinking should not be underestimated because it produces both the expectation that societal problems (e.g., mass unemployment, demographic aging, or growing slums in cities) are solvable in principle and the expectation that society is formable and controllable. Earlier in this article, we have shown that this is a (necessary) illusion—though hardly communicable.

The other part of the explanation why politics is the candidate for steering is connected to the principle of functional differentiation, and especially connected to the function of politics for society as a whole. According to Luhmann, the political function is "the provision of capacities to collectively binding decisions" (Luhmann, 2000a, p. 82). It is about the old Hobbesian problem which was the main problem for Parsons, too: How is social order possible? Thus, it is the question of how the parts' degrees of freedom can be contained to the benefit of the whole. Starting at complex self-referential systems, one can see that there is always more communication

---

19. This causality can even be reversed without changing the content of the argument: 'The action theory approach forces the raising of the question about steering of social systems (or even of any system) as 'who' questions. Almost immediately this leads to the assumption that it is the task of politics to steer society and almost as immediately this inevitably leads to the realization of its failure' (Luhmann, 1997a, p. 47).

potentially possible than actualized during one moment. Collectively binding decision-making thus is *one* functional solution to the reference problem of society's complexity. Modern society can no more be coordinated by face-to-face-interaction, and therefore, during socio-cultural evolution, it firstly differentiated decision-making roles and later on an especially appropriate subsystem which has performed quite successfully as measured by the fulfilment of its function. A function, however, is and remains a function; as a system (closed around its function) it remains *part* of society, not society as a whole. Luhmann therefore cautions against the equation of the function "collectively binding decision-making" and steering:

> But this success of organization which allows, supports, maintains and reproduces the differentiation of the political system must not lead to the illusion that politics can represent or even steer society (Luhmann, 1997a, p. 47).

The role of the political system for whole society therefore has to be put in perspective. However, even systems-theoreticians cannot abandon it completely: "The need for collectively binding decisions is still—and maybe even stronger than ever—a central reference problem of society that has to be served functionally" (Lange, 2002, p. 188). Politics, thus, is indispensable for modern society. The theorem of functional differentiation assumes just this: The subsystems each exclusively fulfil an essential function for the whole system. If one of these functions failed permanently, the consequences for the whole system and its primary structure would probably be immense.

The formula of the political function already suggests the inherent reference to order. However, it looks unclear at first sight and therefore needs a more detailed illustration. What is then meant by the formula collectively binding decisions? Decisions of the political system do not always have a positive effect on the concerned. Mostly the concerned have to bear something they would not choose if they had the choice. Think of laws that contain personal freedom or simply think of the fact that you have to pay taxes or contributions to social insurance. Thus, it is a characteristic of political decisions that they are *binding*. Binding means that the concerned either has to comply with the decision (e.g., a law) or else to face negative sanctions (in extreme cases prison or physical force). The binding effect of the decisions is ensured by the symbolically generalized medium *power*.[20] Sure enough, nothing is stated yet about the kinds and contents of the decisions themselves. The function cannot inherently fix how or what is decided. What will be decided, on which problem, first and foremost depends on the system's history, thus on an earlier system status because, as any other social system, the political system is determined by its own structure. Above all, the question of how to decide has to stay open. Decisions are conscious selections in front of the horizon of alternative possibilities from which to

---

20. To be precise, one would have to talk about the attempt to ensure the binding effect: crime (in Western and other industrial states) respectively civil war (in numerous African states) show that bindingness sometimes is far from successful.

chose. Thus, they are inevitably contingent because, given alternatives, one could have decided differently: for example to raise the income tax and not to reduce it in order to boost the economy.

A consequence of this unavoidable contingency of political decisions[21] is that they will even be regarded as contingent by that collectivity the decisions are binding for. The decisions will be attributed to certain agents (politicians) as actions, and consequently they will be evaluated, often with strong moral bias. Since those decisions on a functional level are of importance for the whole society – binding a collectivity – they need a special legitimacy from this collectivity, be it of moral, religious or procedural kind (elections, etc.). Hence, Nassehi emphasizes the component *collectivity* from the function's formula and stresses that one "does not get around the collectivity of politics" (Nassehi, 2003, p. 176). He suggests not only to focus on the production of collectively binding decisions (thus the *decisions*) but also on the *collectivity*, that is, the "production of societal visibility and accountability" (Nassehi, 2002, p. 45). The reference problem of politics is then, though being a part, to represent or to have to represent the whole (Nassehi, 2003b, p. 139). The political system has to be semantically available for something that structurally is impossible (see Schirmer/Kleinschmidt, 2006, p. 74). Collectivity as the central problem is both a blessing and a curse for politics. The political system not only relies on legitimacy for its decisions by the collectivity; the collectivity itself (and thus the political system) is produced by collectively binding decisions in the first place (Bonacker, 2003). Hence, it is a blessing that a lot of degrees of freedom evolve for political actors and organizations: When setting topics on the agenda and canalizing the according opinions, when setting the inside/outside-boundary of collectivities (we patriots, we left-wingers, we democrats, etc.). If steering does not succeed in *factual* dimension, politics can compensate this lack at least semantically in *social* dimension. When, for example, the reduction of ancillary wage costs does not lead to the desired economic boom, the political system reacts with personalization: The political opposition accuses the government or certain politicians of failure and announces to do it much better when it is their turn.

At the same time, collectivity is a curse for politics since political decisions rely on legitimacy by the collectivity and therefore they have to take on the form of legal proceedings. As a consequence, politics becomes downright slow and needs a lot of time. Often, it needs too much time compared to the tempo of evolution in the environment of the system, especially the economy. This is an important difference to other functional systems which do *not* rely on the acceptance by collectivities and which therefore have quite different options at their disposal. That however leads us to

---

21. When we speak of political decisions, we mean those decisions that are supposed to have a binding effect on society as a whole, thus we mean decisions that can be attributed to the state or one of its administrative sub-organizations. The definition of party programs and the filling of party jobs are, in principle, political decisions too. But, in the first place, they concern the parties themselves as organizational systems, and they do not affect society as a whole. Therefore, they are of minor interest for our argument.

the question, why both of the other promising candidates for steering – science and economy – cannot take over the role of politics.

Following the principle of functional differentiation, no functional system can substitute another one. Each functional system fulfils its function exclusively. So far, the argument does not explain politics' responsibility for steering; the argument would be tautological. At this place, we have to be more precise and look at the functions and their relevance for the whole society. The function of *science* is the production of scientific knowledge (Luhmann, 1990, p. 355). Science provides knowledge for its environment. Other systems apply it (or reject it as not suitable) according to their own criteria and programmes. Thus, it is the other systems (more precisely, their organizations) which decide whether, and how scientific knowledge is used or not. It is not science itself!

Scientists, of course, can attempt to influence certain developments with help of their knowledge. They can present the results of their research to a non-scientific public, and they might warn against new pathogens, against climatic change or against social disintegration. Sometimes they demand countermeasures which might be scientifically well reasoned, that is, according to criteria of scientific truth production. However, *whether or not and how* these measures are pushed through, depends on many factors that defy scientific control. To get measures of greater momentousness taken at all, an organization is needed which is capable of collectively binding decisions. It is clear at first sight that this cannot be done by universities or research institutes but only by governmental (thus political) facilities with the authority of legislation and backed up by a power-based infrastructure (Willke, 2001, p. 170).

Scientific warnings often carry along displeasing components that demand a lot from the addressee. Besides the ever-present economic question of how much this will cost, it is foremost unclear how it can be transferred into political decision-making programs and—if successful—pushed through by power. However, even more unclear are the desired and undesired effects of the political decision for society. For a theory of society, it is then especially interesting to distinguish between the consequences within the political system (attribution of responsibility) and in the environment of politics, both the social one and the non-social one. For the scientific system it could have the effect of more provided funds for research; it could raise the call for tenders of new research projects; it could initiate a multitude of new publications; it could support the reputation of some researchers and possibly even the development of new scientific disciplines. From a normative perspective, one could subsequently ask how all of this should help society in regard of those problems preceding and initiating the whole process. Unfortunately, we cannot answer this question here. But one thing is clear: Steering of society by science drops out. Knowledge is obviously not enough.

What about the *economic* system, then? Its reference problem is to manage "future stable precaution with present allocation" (Luhmann, 1988, p. 64) under conditions of scarcity. With this formula, neither is anything said about the kind of allocations, nor whether economic operations generate problems of allocation that cannot be solved economically. Accordingly, social justice is no *economic* term, nor is the distinction of poor/rich. For the autopoiesis of economics, there simply has to be enough spending power among people (and organizations) to enable the medium money to circulate and payments to follow up payments. Earlier in this article, we stated that functional systems only are horizons which one can use in order to reach communicative acceptance; they are not agents/addresses capable of acting.

The potentially increasing difference between poor and rich is, therefore, an unavoidable effect of economic operations. The economic system has no central organization that could attend to this, analogous to the state within political system.[22] This would not benefit the autonomy of economy, anyway, as the experiments with planned economy in real socialism have shown. It is part of the logic of the economic system to put forth something like rationally acting, profit-maximizing agents who are more interested in their individual welfare than in common welfare. If Adam Smith's famous picture of the invisible hand were true, the question of common welfare would not emerge at all because everybody would strive to his own advantage and the outcome would be good for everybody, so, where is the problem? Obviously—and not only pointed out by Marx-inspired literature—there is no invisible hand and only because of this fact can individual and common welfare be distinguished at all since they cannot always conform. One can assume that Smith's invisible hand actually takes on the function of a semantics of unity between the economic system and its inner-societal environment rather than the role of a realistic description of modern economy, although it is often used in public debates as a substitute for otherwise lacking evidence to prove the regulating capabilities of a free market.

From the viewpoint of a theory of society, it seems to be more fruitful to distinguish symbolically generalized media of communication. Agents in the economic system (e.g., corporations, households, public organizations[23]) operate within the medium money (and not power). Whether a multinational corporation will invest in country A or country B is first and foremost an economical and not a political decision. The decision depends more on expected profits and less on expected chances at elections, thus it depends more on a possible gain of money and less on a possible gain of political power. In this regard, corporations are not political but economic agents. Therewith it is by no means denied that decisions made by corporations could have effects on society. Quite the reverse: Corporations may play off two competing states against each other. So they might even have "stronger effects on the shape of regions than politics" (Nassehi, 2003a, p. 181). Investments announce the provision of new jobs, and it is obvious why states want them to invest on their territory. States (and their governments), being political organizations, depend on new jobs within their territory because they depend on a collectivity that legitimizes them. The medium money is much more flexible than the medium power. It can be transferred from one region to the other, according to market conditions; power, by contrast, is

---

22. Central banks cannot take on this role.
23. The latter only in the case that they perform as payers or receiver of payments. A payment *is not a* collectively binding decision but rather its product.

strictly bound to one territory and to one collectivity. Corporations are responsible only towards themselves while states are responsible for their collectivity.

Due to the autopoietic logic of the economic system – the recursive network of payments enabling payments – there is neither a teleological system status nor a stopping mechanism that instructs agents to stop bargaining. Therefore, economic transactions tend to concentration of capital (as Marxists point out) and to several severe regional imbalances (as dependency theory and Wallerstein's world systems theory point out).

The consequences for steering are evident. The autonomous economic system (the market) does not solve the referential problems of steering—*it is one important cause for steering itself.* Steering does not mean to have effects on other systems. Nearly every system's operations have effects on the operations of other systems, and in most cases one would not speak of steering. Steering means to *steer against* the effects of each system's operations, to steer against the autonomy of systems, in other words: to steer against side effects of functional differentiation. Following Luhmann, we called steering the minimizing of differences earlier in this article. The differences are those which are observed as problematic, unjust, dangerous, unequal, against human dignity and so forth.

And so we can attend to the question whether the political system takes on a special role among the functional systems. The answer is—not surprisingly—a paradox: yes and no. On the one hand, there is no other system available to fulfil the societal reference problem equivalently, and in this respect, politics has indeed a special role. In this respect however, every functional system has a special role and among every system being special, *speciality is no speciality.* But there is one "real" speciality of the political system which we can detect anyway. The decisive part of its function to provide collectively binding decisions is to be responsible for the *collectivity it addresses* with its decisions. No other functional system has to generate collectivities it is responsible for. Politics in this regard represents society semantically and stands for visibility and accountability. The mission statement of a politically steered society therefore fulfils a latent function in society that should not be underestimated. With its optimism of steering, the political system conducts a kind of unintended but very useful absorption of uncertainty for society and each of its subsystems (see Lange, 2002, p. 188). In other words: Structurally, it is part of the political function to stand in semantically and take on responsibility for something it actually cannot be responsible for.

4. Consequences for politics

Steering obviously describes a paradox: It has to be done only because it is impossible. Would it be possible, it would not be needed. Would the world consist only of trivial machines running after a master plan,[24] once the master plan is written and the machines programmed, nothing more has to be done—except for maintenance work, of course. Even this fictional situation is impossible because it requires at least one self-referential observing system constructing the master plan. Since we know that there are numerous non-trivial machines, steering becomes necessary and at the same time impossible. Common societal self-descriptions ignore this structural condition and tend to present simplified pictures of problems, their causes and those who rationally solve them by steering—the utopia of a potentially integrated and steered societal community.

Due to its function to represent society as a whole, the political system stands ready to shoulder the burden of steering and it tries so with best intentions. But, at the same time, it gets into the ungrateful position of being accountable for all kinds of unpredictable outcomes of its attempts at steering.

Steering is not possible in the factual dimension (the problems), and so political communication evades by moving from factual dimension into social dimension (persons responsible for the problems). Therefore it needs "charismatic persons, simple messages, simple conflicts and, most notably, addressable collectivities to make capacity to act and accountability *visible*" (Nassehi, 2003a, p. 176). The political system makes its performance roles visible as rational, sensible actors: rightly elected, competent politicians. It is easier for communication to attribute success and failure to concrete persons or organizations (namely parties), and so factual discussions (about how to steer, which programmes to use etc.) transform into personalized conflicts in social dimension (Kleinschmidt & Schirmer, 2006, p. 107), canalized by the code of government/opposition. Whatever one camp says or does is observed by the opposite camp as wrong, either too much or too little, wrong method, wrong goals, no clear concept and so forth. But mostly this is not due to things happening in the systems' environment – for example, economic depression, bad results in PISA-study or terrorist attacks somewhere else in the world – but to the self-reference of political communication: The observation from which side of the code the respective statement comes from (government or opposition). The other-reference is then reduced to abstract truisms like "for the future of our country," "for economic growth," "for the people's sake," "for peace and justice," "for freedom." This list may belengthened arbitrarily.

With the help of this rhetoric, the public can be included into political communication as an audience and a special target group – however not into the process of decision-making, of course. At least for democracies, the public plays an important legitimizing role for political communication as taxpayers and, first and foremost, as electors. Being electors, they have certain expectations, claims and demands they want to be fulfilled. Since democratic states orient themselves on public opinion, they complimentarily regard themselves as responsible for those expectations, claims and demands. "As a consequence, the needs themselves grow, the aspiration levels rise and finally the 'state' is expected to provide services which it technically cannot yield with political measures, with collectively binding decisions,

---

24. One might ask then who should have programmed this master-plan? The traditional answer was God but this does not convince anymore in a functionally differentiated society, since religion has been degraded from the perspective to one among others.

at all" (Luhmann, 1987, p. 98). And it is because of this general responsibility that politics suffers from permanent self-overloading. The range of variation of topics that can be politicized is infinite: more than security and unemployment are political topics. Toad tunnels and hot-air dryers in public toilets become problems of the political system, once they have appeared on the agenda of claims.[25] So it is no wonder that frustration and disenchantment with politics on the part of the citizenry is high. Like all of the other functional systems, politics has no in-built stopping mechanism, so potentially any topic could be politicized and become the object of a claim. No political reason can be found to refuse it: "This escalating mechanism cannot find dosage and limits within itself. It cannot be steered politically. Only its supply of energy can be chopped" (Luhmann, 1987, p. 98).

References:

Beck, U. (1993.) *Die Erfindung des Politischen.* Frankfurt/Main: Suhrkamp.

Beck, U. (2000). Wohin führt der Weg der mit dem Ende der Vollbeschäftigungsgesellschaft beginnt? In U. Beck (Ed.), *Die Zukunft von Arbeit und Demokratie* (pp. 7-66). Frankfurt/Main: Suhrkamp.

Bonacker, T. (2003). Die Gemeinschaft der Entscheider. Zur symbolischen Integration im politischen System' pp. 62-79 in K. Hellmann, K. Fischer and H. Bluhm(Eds.), *Das System der Politik. Niklas Luhmanns politische Theorie.* Opladen: Westdeutscher Verlag.

Foerster, H. von. (2003). Understanding understanding: Essays on cybernetics and cognition. Springer.

Kleinschmidt, J., & Schirmer, W. (2006). Differenz statt Einheit. Zur Ambivalenz der Werte in der politischen Kommunikation. In L. Hofer, J. Schemann, T. Stollen, & C. Wolf (Eds.), *Düsseldorfer Forum Politische Kommunikation. Akteure, Prozesse, Strukturen* (pp. 97-115). Berlin: poli-c-books.

Lange, S. (2002). Die politische Utopie der Gesellschaftssteuerung. In K.-U. Hellmann & R. Schmalz-Bruns (Eds.), *Theorie der Politik. Niklas Luhmanns politische Soziologie* (pp. 171-194). Frankfurt/Main: Suhrkamp.

Luhmann, N. (1981). *Politische Theorie im Wohlfahrtsstaat.* München/Wien: Olzog.

Luhmann, N. (1987). Staat und Politik. Zur Semantik der Selbstbeschreibung politischer Systeme. In N. Luhmann (Ed), *Soziologische Aufklärung 4. Beiträge zur funktionalen Differenzierung der Gesellschaft* (pp.74-103). Opladen: Westdeutscher Verlag.

Luhmann, N. (1988). *Die Wirtschaft der Gesellschaft.* Frankfurt/Main: Suhrkamp.

Luhmann, N. (1989). *Ecological communication.* Chicago: University of Chicago Press.

Luhmann, N. (1990). *Die Wissenschaft der Gesellschaft.* Frankfurt/Main: Suhrkamp.

Luhmann, N. (1995). *Social systems.* Palo Alto: Stanford University Press.

Luhmann, N. (1997a). Limits of Steering. *Theory, Culture & Society, 14* (1), 41-57.

Luhmann, N. (1997b). Die Gesellschaft der Gesellschaft. Frankfurt/Main: Suhrkamp.

Luhmann, N. (2000a). *Die Politik der Gesellschaft.* Frankfurt/Main: Suhrkamp.

Luhmann, N. (2000b). *Organisation und Entscheidung.* Opladen: Westdeutscher Verlag.

Mayntz, R. (1996). Politische Steuerung: Aufstieg, Niedergang und Transformation einer Theorie. In K. von Beyme & C. Offe (Eds.), *Politische Theorien in der fra der Transformation* (pp.148-168). Opladen: Westdeutscher Verlag.

Mayntz, R. (2004). *Governance Theory als fortentwickelte Steuerungstheorie?* Working paper 04/01. Berlin: Max Planck Institut für Gesellschaftsforschung.

Nassehi, A. (2002). Politik des Staates oder Politik der Gesellschaft? Kollektivität als Problemformel des Politischen' In K. Hellmann & R. Schmalz-Bruns (Eds.), *Theorie der Politik. Niklas Luhmanns politische Soziologie* (pp. 38-59). Frankfurt/Main: Suhrkamp.

Nassehi, A. (2003a). *Geschlossenheit und Offenheit. Studien zur Theorie der modernen Gesellschaft.* Frankfurt/Main: Suhrkamp.

Nassehi, A. (2003b). Der Begriff des Politischen und die doppelte Normativität der "soziologischen" Moderne. In A. Nassehi & M. Schroer (Eds.), *Der Begriff des Politischen* (pp. 133-170). Baden-Baden: Nomos.

Nassehi, A. (2004). Die Theorie funktionaler Differenzierung im Horizont ihrer Kritik. *Zeitschrift für Soziologie, 33*(2), 98-118.

Reich, W. & Michailakis, D. (2005). The notion of equal opportunity in political communication – A theoretical analysis. *Revue française des affaires sociales, 59*(1), 49-60.

---

25. With a little irony, Luhmann even speaks of boat wharfs for Sunday sailors as a problem the welfare state has to care for (see Luhmann, 1981).

Scharpf, F. (1992). Die Handlungsfähigkeit des Staates am Ende des 20. Jahrhunderts. In B. Kohler-Koch (Ed.), *Staat und Demokratie in Europa* (pp. 93-115). 18. Wissenschaftlicher Kongress (18th scientific congress) der DVPW. Opladen: Westdeutscher Verlag.

Schirmer, W. & Kleinschmidt, J. (2006). Die Politik und der Arbeitsmarkt. Gesellschaftstheoretische (Un)Möglichkeiten. Berliner Debatte Initial, 17(3), 67-77.

Schirmer, W. (2007). Addresses in world societal conflicts: A systems theoretical contribution to the theory of the state in international relations. In S. Stetter (Ed.), *Territorial conflicts in world society: Modern systems theory, international relations and conflict studies* (pp.125-148). London: Routledge.

Willke, H. (1991). *Systemtheorie.* Stuttgart: Fischer.

Willke, H. (2001). *Systemtheorie III: Steuerungstheorie.* Stuttgart: Lucuis & Lucius.

Beer, S. (n.d.). *Relativity* (detail).

Cybernetics And Human Knowing. Vol. 14, nos. 2-3, pp. 151-172

Steering Technologies as Observation

Niels Thyge Thygesen[1]

The article contributes a program that illustrates how technology can be observed as observation. In its development of this program, the article focuses in particular on the way in which steering technology provides public management with specific forms of observation. The article first installs and develops three fundamental concepts in the program on the basis of Niklas Luhmann's systems theory: 'technology', 'steering', and 'management'. Second, the article points out this program's potential for enunciation through an analysis of goal management in the Danish public sector. Thirdly, the article discusses the insights generated by the program in the light of three alternative approaches to an analysis of technology. By employing such a tripartite structure, the article elucidates the new epistemic potential inherent in the proposed program for observation.

Steering technologies as program for observation

The present article focuses on new steering technologies in large public organizations and shows how these technologies are of vital importance for the management's observation of the organization. One of the most traditional steering tools, economic steering (accountancy), provides a good example of the way in which the manager's horizon is shaped by a technology.[2] This technology installs money as a medium for the decisions that can be made. Thus, from the perspective of technology, it makes sense to conceive of the organization as a set of economic transactions, the user as a cost, and the citizen as a tax base. In general, economic steering defines a horizon for steering that places the steering entity in charge of balancing the budget, and not of achieving any other balances such as the balance between quality standards and fulfillment (quality management) or the balance between competencies and responsibilities (competence control). The point is that steering technologies facilitate a specific management role, condition a particular perspective, and even shape the possibility of the continued existence of management. In the case of economic steering, the activities of management are shaped in particular as reactions to shortcomings and solvency building.

The above example serves to emphasize the very point of departure of the article, that is, the fact that management is conducted through technologies, and the fact that they shape, in different ways, the observations of management. Expanding on the way in which steering technologies can be observed as observation, the proposed program for observation takes nothing less than technologies and their constitutive effect on

---

1. Niels Thyge Thygesen, Associate Professor. Department of Management, Politics and Philosophy Copenhagen Business School, Denmark. E-mail: ntt.lpf@cbs.dk
2. The example that follows is fictitious but draws on and corresponds to the constitutive effects of financial steering (e.g. Munro & Mouritsen, 1996, Chapts. 1,4,and 5; McKinlay & Starkley, 2000, Chapts. 6 and 8; Scheytt, 2005).

management as the subject of analysis, including the possibility of reproduction. With respect to constitution, the program studies the way in which management's observation of the organization, and thus the function of management, emerges in relation to the horizon provided by steering technologies. With respect to reproduction, the issue of constitution is specified as a question of the technology's possibility for feedback, that is, the management's potential for self-influence as opposed to merely having an influence on others. On this basis, the article suggests a program that develops ways in which technology can be studied as observation.

Throughout this article, three concepts play an important role in relation to the suggested program for observation. First of all, the concept of *technology* constitutes the possibility of studying the possibility of observation for management. As illustrated by the above example, economic steering (accounting) allows for the observation of the organization as a bundle of economic transactions, whereas quality management outlines the observation of the organization as a set of standards for quality. Second, *steering* becomes an important characteristic because the organization as a social steering domain cannot be likened to a trivial machine but must be assumed to re-act to, or even counter-act, established decisions, thus raising the possibility of reproduction. The point is that management's registration of such reactions, i.e., the feedback loop, can be observed as a consequence of the observation made available by technology. As an example, economic steering provides a distinction between budget and accounting in which the latter relates deviations from economic calculations. Quality management, on the other hand, provides a perspective by which implicit knowledge can be viewed as deviations from the ideal of explicit standards. Third, *management* is studied as a function whose observation of the organization is made possible in different ways depending on the technology employed.

This article falls into three parts all attempting to demonstrate the insight into management inherent in the proposed program for observation. The article begins by elaborating on the above mentioned concepts: technology, steering, and management, which are all based on Luhmann's systems theory. Subsequently, the article puts the proposed program into use and seeks to demonstrate the possibilities and conditions for management occasioned by the widespread use of *goal management* in public organizations in Denmark. In conclusion, the article expounds on the insight provided by the program in light of three alternative propositions for a technology analysis: subjectivism, structuralism, and structuration theory. This construction of three alternative programs functions solely as a basis for a discussion of how the proposed program has prioritized steering technology as a point of observation and the knowledge that results.

Steering Technology as Observation

Before expounding on the systems-theoretical definition of steering and technology and the way in which these concepts are employed in the study of management, I will give a brief introduction to Luhmann's use of the concept of observation in order to further elucidate how steering technology can be seen as observation. In doing so, it is important to make a distinction between two levels, that is, to point out that what becomes the object of observation is the observation as it becomes available to the management function through steering technologies. Thus, observation appears in two different forms but remains part of the same operation. This distinction forms the background for a definition of the concept of observation: as the difference between observation of the first and second order.

Observation

The reason that technologies are observed as observation is that they supply a particular difference according to which indications can be made. Observation, as it is, consists of the juxtaposition of two operations: a difference and an indication (Spencer-Brown, 1979). The relation between these two consists in the fact that an observation is always tied to a difference so that what is indicated is seen as different from what is not indicated. The case of goal management provides another example since this technology allows for the future to be articulated in a particular way, and when indicated—as future competencies, for example—we often find past experiences on the un-indicated side and hence ignored as a strategic resource. The principle is that ignorance is a precondition of observation because it is impossible to focus on both sides at once in the process of observation.

Observation in a social system is tied not to persons as a cognitive act, but to communication. In the context of goal management, communication often indicates the future, that is, the goals with which the future can be met. The undefined future becomes fixed, in other words, in order to allow for management's continued effort to minimize the difference between the shortcomings of the present and the realization of goals. Thus, we witness the emergence of a management vocabulary that stresses *change* in favor of *stability*, *development* in favor of *routines*, *proactive* in favor of *reactive*, and so forth. On a more general level, this vocabulary is enabled by the particular distinction of observation supplied by technologies and hence represents nothing less than the formation of the communication of management.

What is important when we speak of observation is that observation is unable to observe its own difference. That would be a bit like a circus horse trying to sit in its own saddle. As Von Foerster (1981) might put it, this constitutes the blind spot of observation. This has implications for the analysis of technologies because, contrary to much theory of learning, it uncovers the way in which full reflexive access to one's own possibilities and conditions are rendered impossible. That does not prevent learning from taking place, but it limits the possibility of learning and questions the assumption of sovereignty often associated with technologies in the hands of strong managers.

Moreover, the blind spot of observation leads to the principle of scientific observation as second-order observation. Whereas a first-order observation is unable to observe its own difference, a second order observation observes other observations, that is, focuses on the difference – the blind spot – that shapes the observation. As such, the proposed program represents a second-order program for observation because it specifically observes technology as observation and the difference it makes for management.

Following this introduction to the concept of observation, attention will be directed toward the management-related insight achieved by the systems-theoretical concepts of technology and steering. But first the article will turn to the systems-theoretical concept of management as the frame of reference.

Management

As a sociologist, Luhmann is interested in management as a function and not in the manager as a person (Luhmann, 2000, pp. 84-88, 218-221). Although Luhmann repeatedly criticizes the notion of the manager as embodying "the illusion of control" and contends that complexity is reduced in many other places in the organization, it is still possible to argue that he accepts the idea of a particular management function, perceived as the part that makes decisions on behalf of the whole (Thyssen, 2003). An organization has to conceive of an environment in the same way that it has to conceive of itself and fly its own flag in various programs as an integrated system of action. We know this activity from organizational diagrams, policies, visions, and so forth. Thyssen describes it like this: "It has to describe itself in order to perform the impossible act of being outside itself inside itself" (Thyssen, 2003, p. 225). This is where management comes into play; its function is to symbolize the whole to the outside and to take responsibility for making the organizational self-description matter on the inside. Economic steering (accounting) and value management has already been mentioned. As a further illustration, the technology in scientific management consists in the mapping of minute elements in a process, which enables the manager to observe the whole in the form of sequences. Human resource management represents motivational techniques that enable the manager to relate to the organization as latent resources. Human Relations, on the other hand, is a tradition whose techniques open up for the observation of the organization as synergy as more than what it is. Naturally, the relation between management and organization are far less unambiguous than suggested by classical conceptions. Organizations are fully engaged in the employment of many other technologies, which, independently and in combination, supply the manager with an increasing number of totalizing abstractions of the organization. And this function is in particular related to management, which implies that other specialized functions in the organization are able to work without such compulsion. Although management is criticized as utopian, Luhmann, ultimately, is unable to circumvent management as a function whose decisions and representation of the whole together enhance the organization's absorption of uncertainty (Luhmann, 2000, pp. 218-221). Thus, management is observed as the part that observes and makes decisions about the whole.

Management, as the part that relates to the organization as a whole, constitutes a consideration which by no means only represents a philosophical abstraction or a suggested normative hypothesis. It is a systems function; that is, it is reflected in specific incidents. Most managers carry with them, in the form of business cards, a semantic 'tattoo' of the whole. The municipal director is responsible for the municipality as a whole. The head of the department is responsible for the department. The leader of an institution has the institution as his object and the project manager manages the project. In each case, it is about the relation between part and whole. Management, as the master of the whole, draws upon a traditional notion of control, which invokes the notion of a sovereign management function. However, this notion is shaken by the fact that the controlling function is itself subject to the act of controlling (Luhmann, 1990b, p. 228). This control can take on many forms. Therefore, this is where a specific interest in steering technologies comes into play in order to track and explore the ways in which the management function achieves the ability to observe the whole as premises for other actions, which can be calculated and hence changed. In this respect, management is observed as an authority relating to the whole of the organization as an object. The important thing to note, however, is the way in which this whole emerges according to the distinction of observation provided by different technologies.

Technology
The second concept of the program is the concept of technology, which allows the study of the constitution of management in relation to observation.

 The point of departure for understanding the presence of technologies in organizations extends all the way to the central function of the organization. As explained by Luhmann, the organization operates by means of decisions that develop and establish their own past, present, and future. And in order to avoid arbitrariness, the organization's given responsibilities and roles can be assessed on the basis of the time they take/waste or whether they are in or out of step with the times. One may discuss efficiency as it relates to saving time (e.g., scientific management related technologies); being at the cutting edge of the future (e.g., goal management); or controlling time by means of administrative procedures, standards,, and so forth (e.g., planning) (Luhmann, 1990a, chapter 6). In fact, without such time mastery, which is provided by technologies, the beginning and end of each responsibility could not be defined and would also entail the absence of subsequent calculations, adjustment, and optimization. The point is that in order for an organization to master time, it has to also secure its own technology.[3] On a general level, technology provides such mastery of time by supplying isolated causal relations. We are familiar with this process in the shape of goals, means, regulations, and control, which all represent the effort to secure expectations relating to which causes can be said to result in future effects. For example, goal management hardly leaves any doubt as to goal fulfillment, especially as goals are often broken down into intermediate goals and anticipated means. It is a

---

3. This point refers to Luhmann's own reflections on technology as function system and its presence in organizations (Moe, 2003, chapter 10; Seidel, 2005). A general introduction to Luhmann's concept of organization can be found in Luhmann (2000) and Bakken & Hernes (2002).

question, therefore, of controlling the uncertainty of time by means of causality. The uncertainty that time naturally represents is transformed into certainty when future effects are expected to materialize as a result of specific causes. On the basis of this general definition of technology, we are able to observe technology as the formation and provision of causality. As Luhmann remarks: "Seen from the point of view of second order observation, technology rests on the attribution of causality, on the selection of some out of many causes and some out of many effects" (Luhmann, 1990b, p. 225). Figure 1 illustrates this formation, or attribution, as the selection from among a number of possible causes and a number of possible effects and the juxtaposition of these (Luhmann, 1993; 1990b).

Figure 1

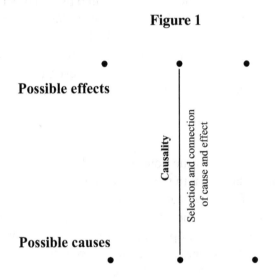

So far, we have referred to technologies on the organizational level, such as economic steering (accounting), goal management, scientific management techniques and so forth; however, it would appear that also more innocent and intimate micro-technologies draw up forms of causality and hence the possibility of control. In the increasingly and more widely used personal development reviews (PDRs), the ambition is often to establish a connection between the employee's inner motivation and the organization's exterior goals whereas the new wage scales offer exterior motivation for the fulfillment of the inner goals of employees. The specific forms of causality that are provided by the technologies do not imply that the manager's intention always results in the anticipated effect. If that were the case, only a minimal level of management would be required and everything else would be rendered superfluous. Instead, the attribution of causality by technologies introduces a number of factors. On the one hand, it opens the observation of how the expectations of the management function develop in calculated form and present themselves as certainty, and, on the other hand, it opens the observation of how uncertainty develops in management as the result of registered deviations from calculations. In other words, the observation of causality is the observation of self-inflicted certainty and hence also the possibility of failure. Therefore, the important characteristic of technology is that it directs the observation toward the way in which management observes and hence relates to the organization in a causal manner.

This isolation of causal relations represents an abstraction that allows for organizations to be embraced as a whole. When the SWOT analysis divides the world into internal chores and external competition and subsequently offers management the possibility of observing the organization as a collection of strengths and weaknesses, it represents a gross simplification. Similarly, goal management represents the art of simplification as it facilitates an observation of the organization as goals and means. However, the benefit is that it causes the whole to emerge and even as the object for mastering both efficiency and the future of the organization. Moreover, this heightened level of abstraction possesses the important quality of extending the manager's latitude into areas that are too complex—perhaps too knowledge-intensive or too remote—for the manager to know in depth. Any form of goal management in a municipality rests fundamentally on the ambition to direct countless unknown institutions, projects, and employees towards a defined goal. Likewise, economic steering seeks to balance an endless number of financial transactions that the financial manager is not in control of or has any chance of knowing in detail. Thus, technologies not only supply the possibility of anticipated causality, they also extend causality by means of heightened abstraction. They make it possible to regulate even in areas where the manager has limited or no insight and hence renders the potentially inaccessible accessible. That is, technology allows us to observe how the construction of causality works.

Without this level of abstraction it is not possible to treat a problem as a matter of routine or outside the place where it occurs. The time mastery inherent in goal management, for example, would quickly become too time-consuming if it could not be repeated. Therefore, management technologies provide universal principles so that one may approach every unique problem with the same formula. It often happens that visions and goals are applied as the solution to more or less any organizational problem. As such, the trait of universality represents one of the key characteristics of technology, which also specifies which kind of causal relations can be observed. The benefit of universality is that management does not become overwhelmed by its own complexity. This also means that to a certain extent management becomes a trivial function because it has to subscribe to repeatable and universal solutions to unique and highly differentiated problems. With a specific perspective on the repeatability of technologies, we can observe that technologies allow us to observe how isolated causal relations are always expected to result in the same effect.

As Luhmann notes, technology does not point to a verifiable relation between cause and effect, nor does it indicate a verifiable repeatability (Luhmann, 1990b, p. 223). However, both elements work to heighten expectations by reducing complexity into forms that are seemingly manageable. This happens when technology narrows down cause and effect to the point that they can be attributed to the function of a person as opposed to, for example, ecological changes, which take place over a longer period of time (Luhmann, 1993). Therefore we often see management celebrate itself as the cause of organizational success, resulting in a self-inflicted sense of indispensability. As Luhmann points out, technology in particular shapes expectations about strong personal vigor. This provides the opportunity to observe management as a function that, by referring to a given technology – goal management, economic steering, SWOT, or various micro technologies – addresses itself as management by ascribing to itself the status of cause of specific effects and in this act disclaims other areas of responsibility. In other words, the technology opens up for the observation of management as a function of a person, which is shaped by expectations about the mastership of causality.

Together, these characteristics of observation – the expectation of repeatable causality –can be employed to inquire into the expectations that generally organize management's systems-internal relations to the organization as its external environment.

Steering

Steering is the third and last concept in the proposed program and is strongly related to the previous concept of technology. As Luhmann notes with reference to his considerations of technology:

> These considerations strongly suggest reformulating the concept of *steering*. It cannot mean to produce the intended state of the system, certainly not in the long run. Instead, it means (in the sense of cybernetic control) to reduce the difference between a real and a preferred state of specific variables (for example, the rate of unemployment [Luhmann, 1989]). But reducing differences also means producing differences. You never get a system which no longer deviates from expected values … In this sense, steering seems to be a *self-sustaining* business. (Luhmann, 1990b, p.228, my italics)

As Luhmann explains it, the connection between steering and technology rests on the fact that whereas technology directs the perspective towards the selection and connection of cause and effect, the steering aspect makes the observation particularly sensitive to the minimization of deviations from this anticipated causality. This process of minimization is never assumed to be complete since the steering produces the very difference that it seeks to minimize. This is why Luhmann stresses steering as a "self-sustaining business." Thus, these two independent perspectives comprise a mutual connection, which directs observation towards management causal relation to its environment (technology) and the possibility of reproduction through the feedback mechanisms that produce deviations from these causal anticipations (steering). Figure 2 illustrates this steering process to which Luhmann also refers as "differenzminderung" (1992, p. 208).

Figure 2

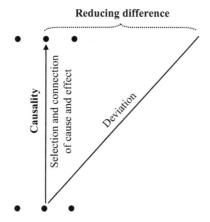

Luhmann's basis for considering steering as a minimization of difference can be found in cybernetics, which supplies a different concept of steering than the one we usually associate with steering; the latter is often employed in much traditional management theory.[4] A frequently used metaphor for the concept of steering in cybernetics is the thermostat, whose function is to eliminate the difference between the registered temperature and the desired temperature. This minimization entails steering. If we translate this principle to municipal economic steering, the minimization is expressed in the difference between the fixed budget and the registered deviations. However, scientific management has developed a well-known arsenal of tools that define a different steering difference, namely, the one between standards for efficiency and action. And in the HRM department, for example, working with equal opportunity policy implies the difference between the wages of men and women to be minimized. The observation of steering is a question of localizing the difference that is sought to be minimized.

Unlike the thermostat, this systems-theoretical definition suggests the observation of the system's self-influence rather than its effect on others, which corresponds to the development in cybernetics towards a second-order cybernetics. The thermostat

---

4. Operations management provides the best example of the concept of steering most commonly used in management theory (e.g., Slack, Chambers & Johnston, 2004). This management tradition defines an operation as equal to the juxtaposition of goals and optimal means. Deviations, e.g. registered through evaluations, represent an important aspect in this tradition, but they are seen as the result of unmanageability. When the present article chooses to instead draw upon the concept of steering as it has been developed in cybernetics, this relation is reversed. This means that steering is seen as equal to the minimization of deviations from the established or intended condition. Cybernetics traditionally makes a distinction between first-order cybernetics and second-order cybernetics. This article draws on the latter, which adds a reflexive level to the concept of steering by stressing the system's cognitive qualities and its self-referentiality as opposed to its effect on the object of steering. As such, the article's concept of steering provides insight into the way in which the guiding difference *in* the system constitutes the possibility of steering *for* the system. This represents, in Luhmann's words, the system's basic self-referentiality. Cybernetics has moved on to develop into many different directions, from mathematical models to the study of mechanical, biological, and social systems. With respect to the latter, Luhmann draws in particular on Wiener, Von Foerster, and Bateson.

provides a good illustration of the principle underlying steering, but defining the organization accordingly as a trivial machine that can effortlessly be calculated and adjusted would show a lack of understanding for any management practice. In almost every municipality, the economic debate becomes exceedingly heated and sometimes results in overheating (economic steering). Steering cannot simply be perceived, therefore, as calculations without friction, but is rather the registration of the deviations that keep the management busy. This leads us to the observation of a specific form of reproduction in management. Implied are techniques such as implementation, control, and evaluation. In organizing expectations about the fulfillment of causality, they in fact produce a reason for the process of steering because they make it possible to observe deviations, which can then be brought up for correction. As Luhmann points out, "the steering of the system is thus always self-starting" (1997a, p. 46). Or in the context of management: the registered output functions as input for the continuation of management. Thus, based on Luhmann's concept of steering, the argument of management theory is reversed. Steering of others becomes self-steering, that is, a self-sustaining business. This becomes apparent when accounts deviate from the budget, which often results in overheating and consequently as the cause of more management (economic steering/accountancy). This means that the steering aspect of technologies makes it possible to observe management as a system that is initiated by calculation as ideal and reproduced through the feedback of deviation.

Summing up, the steering aspect of technology allows us to observe the reproduction of management as system. And this reproduction is formed across the difference between certainty and uncertainty. Steering has to strive for certainty in the form of calculations in order to be able to recognize deviations. In practice, the relation between certainty and uncertainty is often expressed in the fact that the management function's steering of the whole depends precisely on its ability to observe phenomena as uncertain. Otherwise there would be no reason for steering. Management, in turn, has to subscribe to anticipated and certain causality, otherwise it would lose confidence in itself. These two central features taken into account, management depends on the self-creation of uncertainty (steering) that contributes to the justification of its existence by drawing up calculations in order to ensure certainty. Thus, by placing itself between certainty and uncertainty, steering opens up for the observation of the reproduction of management, that is, the fact that the basis of its existence is self-created.

The perspective on management
This account of the way in which the concepts of technology and steering form the observation of the phenomenon management suggests a program that observes management's observation of the whole, made possible as the establishment of causality (technology) and the registration and minimization of deviation from the anticipated causality (steering). The combined perspective is illustrated in the following table:

Table 3: The Perspective on Management

Concept	*Management*	*Technology*	*Steering*
Function	The part that is responsible for the whole	Calculation	Reduction of difference
Distinction	Part/whole	Cause/effect	Calculation/deviation

The table is described on the basis of the three outlined dimensions in the left-hand column: concept, function, and distinction.

Together with management, the concepts of technology and steering represent the three fundamental concepts in a program for observation whose objective is to be able to analyze how technology outlines new possibilities and conditions for management. The concepts' status in the program for observation is defined with reference to Luhmann. Based on this epistemological approach, the observed phenomenon, that is, management, presents itself as the specific characteristics that are rendered observable through technology and steering as categories of observation.

Function comprises the definition of these three concepts. The first concept is the management function as the part that takes responsibility for the whole. I argue that management is observed as a phenomenon when we observe the way in which technology makes it possible for the part to ascribe wholeness to the organization. The next two concepts are technology and steering. Extended to the study of management, it is not possible for the part to observe the organization in its totality because the level of complexity is too high. That is why it becomes important to observe steering technology as a complexity-reducing function, that is, as a contingent possibility for management to obtain a special relation to the whole. As suggested above, this means that management's observation of the whole is observed as the establishment of causality (technology) and registration and minimization of deviations (steering).

Distinction represents a condensation of the concept as category of observation, expressed through a particular difference. The observation of management is defined through the difference part/whole. The observation of management's possibility of having a creative relation to the whole is defined through the difference cause/effect. And the observation of the reproductive mechanism consists of the difference calculation/deviation.

From the perspective of this program for observation, the organization is not presumed to be a natural condition, which calls for a specific form of steering. Instead, the organization emerges relative to the horizon provided by specific steering technologies. And when steering produces a specific basis for feedback, we may speak of management as a meaningful function that is closed around itself in its steering function.

This brings us to the way in which a general management program opens up for the specific observation of it. Quite a few Danish empirical studies have been carried out with reference to Luhmann and with an eye for the constituting and causality-creating functions of technology (Amhoj, 2004; Andersen & Thygesen, 2004a, 2004b; Andersen, 2003; Hojlund & Knudsen, 2003; Rennison, 2003; Thygesen, 2003). In an international context, Andersen (2003) and Thygesen and Andersen (2007) have illustrated the potential inherent in a systems-theoretical approach to the study of technologies. Below, I will pursue one technology, goal management, as it is employed in the Danish welfare and decentralization model (Greve, 2003; Thygesen, 2002; Andersen & Born, 2001; Hansen, Ejersbo & Rieper, 2000).

Goal Management in the Danish Public Sector

Goal management represents one of today's popular mantras among public managers all over the world, and Denmark is no exception. It is here considered a tenable alternative to the regulatory control of bureaucracy. It was introduced into the Danish public sector as a means to restructure the governance of municipalities in the early 1980s, and much of the communication analyzed in the present article stems from the public debates that this restructuring occasioned.

Like many other approaches, goal management is a steering technology that focuses on time, but it does so, not in the form of sequences as in the case of scientific management, and not in the form of character and motivation as in the case of HRM, but through the observation of the organization as a future desired state. Structured across the fundamental concept of the program for observation – management, technology and steering - the analysis' epistemic interest can be illustrated like this:

Table 4: Epistemic Interest

Epistemic interest	Distinction	In what way does technology have a constituent effect on management in the municipality?
Management	[Part/whole]	With what authority does the manager as part become capable of controlling the whole?
Technology	[Cause/effect]	Which causal effect-based relation develops?
Steering	[Calculation/deviation]	In what way is the manager able to manage on the basis of the calculated causality by registering deviations from it?

The interesting thing about goal management is that steering in a growing number of technologies ultimately refers to goals. This pertains, for example, to quality management, which defines goals for quality; learning, which defines goals for personal development; new forms of economic steering in which the budget has to not only be balanced but also defined in terms of goals; personal development reviews, where it is up to the individual to define his contribution to the organization; and, not least, evaluation tools, which occasion the definition of new goals. The list could go on, and does go on in the sense that municipalities in particular select, renew, and refine their own steering technologies. Thus, goal management refers to one and to many technologies at once. It is present as the base constituent in other technologies, which gives it the character of meta-technology. Therefore, it becomes important to scrutinize goal management's constituent effect on management. As mentioned above, this is achieved by splitting up the analysis on the basis of the three fundamental concepts: technology, steering, and management.

Technology: the construction of cause/effect
Many people defend the prevalence of goal management in municipalities as a way to counteract centralized sector planning. However, what is different in the planning is not planning itself; it is the establishment of causality, which is no longer linear but instead circular. That means that the municipal organization no longer relates to the central administration in a linear way, where the sectorial target was supplied from the top and the municipality possessed the means at the bottom. The initiation of municipal self-governance by virtue of the modernization program of 1982 forced the municipality to bend the line of reference so that it originates from the organization and refers back to the organization itself, a maneuver by which the municipality governs itself as goals and means and emerges as both the originator and final destination of the decision. We see an increasing number of managers enter this goal rationality. A number of local politicians have become involved in large political vision workshops where they are asked to define the goals for the municipality in terms of a future desired state while also being asked to identify the municipality as a means to achieve this vision. Moreover, almost every municipality has business plans, which makes it possible to repeat this process for each individual institution. Even the employee is defined as a governing entity to the extent that each employee is required in the personal development review to define own goals and seek out the means to reach these goals. Normally, management is associated with the process of defining limitations and responsibilities. But the goal-oriented technological turn seemingly brings on an unprecedented level of freedom in its swift transformation of exterior responsibility into inner freedom and other people's orders into individual decisions. The consequence is that freedom no longer appears on the opposite side of power. Freedom becomes a precondition of a new power by which the individual is defined as a powerful cause of himself as effect.

Steering: Minimizing the difference between calculation/deviation
If we observe the use of goal management from the perspective of the concept of steering, it seems at first as if goal technologies in fact represent unmanageability as steering ends up in the hands of institutions or employees. However, it does not in any way mean that management is surrendered or abolished. In fact, it increases in scope. Steering does not disappear but is about something else, that is, it is about premises for decision. Goal management primarily constructs two such premises.

The first decision premise is time. The fact that management is a discipline obsessed with the future is not news. However, it is in fact the technology of goal management that causes management to be obsessed with the future. For example, management often seeks to solve a problem by activating the mantra of a new vision. And many types of sanctions and discouragements are used against those who wish to carry on tomorrow with what they are doing today. In that sense, goal management installs time as an entirely new premise for steering. That becomes apparent in the challenge that steering poses to management, which is to minimize the difference between the future and the present. In fact, when managers convince themselves and others of the benefits of being proactive, it is an expression of the ideal of creating a present that coincides with the future. It is a complete minimization, and yet on second thought also an inconceivable situation, since the notion of the present hardly makes any sense if conceived as being ahead of the future. However, this logical impossibility does not impede the municipal practice. On the contrary, it means that everyone's workload increases and that management on all levels takes on the added work of accelerating their own and everyone else's workload. Management has become change management, and its acceleration continues to increase with the ambition of making the present overtake the future. And this is ensured by goal management's reference to the future. Consider, for example, this job posting from Fuglebjerg Municipality:

> The conditions in the municipalities are ever-changing. Demands for development and prioritization are continually on the agenda. The Municipality of Fuglebjerg has developed a new administrative management structure, which is to enable the municipality to act proactively in relation to responsibilities concerning citizens. The municipal director will be responsible for managing the work with the municipality's continued development.[5]

The disciplining of continual change results in an extreme organizational overload despite the fact that management and management decisions are usually meant to produce simplification and relief. The efficiency that goes along with the space of routines and tradition is rendered useless when the future is presumed to dictate new routines and new traditions triggered by new visions. The compulsion of self-inflicted continuation inherent in this perception of management does not allow for peace of mind or peace in the organization.

In addition to time as a premise, goal management manages on the premise of the self. Fundamentally, the goal-oriented technological turn represents a transition from external reference to self-reference. In this lies the possibility of decision. In a regulatory regime, the decision could only refer to that which was outside the decision; to what had already been decided. Hence external reference. The technology of goal management reverses this relation. It is now up to municipal leaders to define goals and means, and this freedom cannot be decided about. Thus, goal management organizes self-referentiality. This tendency was significantly reinforced during the government's modernization program when the conservative government came into power in 1983 and represents the essence of municipal self-governance. In particular,

---

5.   Nyhedsmagasinet Danske Kommuner (News Magazine Danish Municipalities). (2003) nr 9.

this led to the combination of economic decentralization and independent goal management, which constitutes a technology that is now known as goal and framework-based management. What is interesting about the goal technology is that not only managers are responsible for managing but that municipal institutions, project groups, administrations, departments, and even employees are expected to contribute their own self-governance. The introduction of goal technologies has abolished the automatic relation between person and function. Management has become a decision function, which all players are expected to engage in and be able to perform. Accordingly, to manage means to take on goals, means, and self-control; to appoint oneself as the final destination of responsibility, obligation, and effects. Despite such differentiation of the management discipline, the central characteristic of all its forms is the relation between steering and steered as an integrated and merged relation inherent in each self-governing party. The goal management technology requires the ability to double oneself in the effort to define oneself on all levels in the capacity of both steering entity as well as the object of steering. The change provided as a measure for steering when the future is established as premise becomes supplemented with the capacity for individualized self-change. And today self-governance appears to be of the super-semantic variety, which refers to the ability to govern oneself on premises of goal rationality. Consequently, management has multiplied despite the fact that there are in fact fewer managers. The function transcends the person, so to speak. Moreover, due to this self-referentiality, management has become a discipline with a self-starter. Management is not a question of making decisions at the top for those at the bottom. This conceptualization simply does not hold. Management means to be a self-starter and to be one's own most distinguished authority.

Management: the part whose object is the whole
Reviewing these two premises for steering – time and self – the productivity of management consists in the fact that management operates by means of a notion of the future (time), which means that it is condemned, like Sisyphos, to carry on, and that all management becomes a self-relation (self), which means that it continues to increase in scope.

This leads to the urgency of the question of management's authoritative function vis-á-vis the organization as a whole. How is it possible to act with authority when central management is rendered impossible due to the self-governance of others? Initially, self-governance is associated with a loss of power since it is difficult to make decisions for others who make their own decisions. Therefore, many managers perceive having to combine a *yes* to goal technology with what appears to be a *no* to power as a management encumbrance. However, this perception is linked to our association of authority with a specific organizational position; the higher this position, the more power is associated with it. Goal management, however, significantly upsets this distribution of power. Power no longer makes sense as positional power as in the case of the bailiff and the hierarchy. As conceptualization, top positions (over-)ruling bottom positions are not sufficiently nuanced to identify the self-starting and self-referential steering mechanisms which goal technology brings on in all levels of organizations. Power becomes omnipresent because it is located in strategic islands of increased productivity. This creates a decision and transformation productivity much greater than the one occasioned by regulations, control, and planning. Management is no longer a singular function whose task is to represent the whole. Management has been transformed into manifold functions, that is, many parts, each with their ability and right to conceive of the whole and of the future. We may say that the organization becomes many wholes and many futures. In a formalized definition, this management function is given by a particular dynamics, that is, the relation between decision maker and justification. The breath of management consists, therefore, in deciding its own justifications and justifying its own decisions. It achieves this by acting as the part that establishes itself as the whole and by appointing the whole of which it makes sense to be a part. And the purpose of this is to ensure continuation and goal fulfillment.

I conclude my example of a steering technology here. It is far from exhaustive, which an abundance of research in the field indicates. But it seeks to illustrate the constitutive effect of goal management on management. These management characteristics have been summed up in the following table, and again in relation to the three fundamental concepts: technology, steering, and management.

Table 5: Management Characteristics

Epistemic interest	Observation-based guiding difference	In what way does technology have a constituent effect on management in the municipality?
Technology	[Cause/effect]	Circular causality
Steering	[Calculation/deviation]	Time: Reduction of distance between future - present Self: Reduction of distance between self and imagined self
Ledelse	[Part/whole]	Decision maker/justification

From a general perspective, the widespread use of goal management in Denmark has had an unusual implication with respect to steering. Normally, we associate steering with clarity, breadth of view, and a certain degree of calculation and prediction. The proposed program for observation opens up to a different management dynamic as defined by goal management: steering leads to increased complexity, complexity has to be managed, and this obviously requires additional steering. This increase in complexity is due to two circumstances. First, the fact that goal management, with its orientation towards the future, abolishes the familiar structures of routines and tradition and leads management into unknown territory. That results not only in the vast complexity of progress but also leaves an equally vast demand for relating to existing conditions as they are phased out. Second, complexity is further increased when the definition of goals is no longer reserved for the top of the organization but functions as a demand on all players to manage themselves. The number of decisions that have to be made increases to the extent that the need for additional steering becomes apparent. As the Danish example shows, new futures are fixed and multiplied, and this poses new demands on all actors on all municipal levels. This conclusion leaves us with the same pertinent question, which ultimately constitutes Luhmann's own reservation about management, that is, whether management in fact controls the growth of itself and of the organization. Is it not the other way around, we may ask, so that steering and its technologies control what management can be and that management has become a function that merely creates the need for more of itself. With Luhmann's sense of paradoxes we might say that it is a tendency in which management outgrows its own condition of impossibility.

Positioning

Having discussed the fundamental concepts of the program for observation – management, technology, and steering – and illustrated its power of enunciation, I will now discuss the general contribution of this program. The aim is to position the epistemological gain inherent in the program's proposal to observe steering technology as observation.

On a general level, the program writes itself into a post structuralist tradition by constructing a perspective for the way in which technology appears as a constitutive and reproductive feature of management. Goal management provided an example of this and illustrated the way that technology not only conditioned the possible way in which management is able to relate to the environment, but also functioned as catalyst for a reproduction in which management creates the need for more of itself. Thus, the reason that the program can be said to subscribe to a post structuralist tradition is that structures are not seen as determining or unchangeable but precisely as the emergent (constitution) and dynamic (reproduction) element of a system.[6] This insight into management differs from three alternative proposed positions of technology: subjectivism, structuralism, and structuration theory. As suggested, I will not present the three positions in their entire paradigmatic scope but only discuss the status they assign technology in the analysis of management.

Subjectivism, structuralism, and structuration
Subjectivism asks: In what way do managers produce the organization through technologies? Thus, it assigns technology the status of a neutral tool in the hands of strong managers.[7] *Structuralism* asks: How does the environment produce

---

6.   It is in part due to Luhmann that structures are considered the dynamic aspect of social phenomena and his critique of Parson's structural functionalism (1951), (Luhmann, 1995); Kneer & Nassehi, 1997). Following the communications-theoretical turn, Luhmann installs autopoiesis as a structural dynamic and subsequently he introduces paradox as the mechanism of this dynamic.

technological pressure on organizations and managers? It thus defines technology as institutional standards resulting in a presumed organizational and management isomorphism.[8] *Structuration theory* represents a constructive complementarity between the conflicting perspectives of the other two traditions. It asks: What constitutes the reciprocal production of technology? And it installs the exchange between actor and structure as the creative mechanism.[9] As three different starting points for an analysis of technology, they each possess their point of observation: the manager as subject, the structure, or the reciprocal relationship between them. These three epistemic strategies are outlined below:

Table 6: Subjectivism, Structuralism, and Structuration

Subjectivism

[Manager-Technology] $\rightarrow$ Environment

Structuralism

Manager $\leftarrow$ [Technology-Environment]

Structuration

Manager $\leftrightarrow$ [Technology] $\leftrightarrow$ Environment

---

7. Subjectivism refers to the definition in economy and business economy of the subject's self-optimization and rational choice as the cause of sociality. Adam Smith was a philosopher and despite the fact that *Wealth of Nations* was written as a diagnosis with concern for and critique of morality (Smith, 1982), it formed the basis for modern (economic) virtue, with self-optimization as the central point of departure. That fraction of classical management theory, which we can refer to as 'strategic choice' (Clegg, Hardy & North, 1996, p. 412) maintains in different ways this individualized conception of sovereignty but defines the manager as the person whose function consists in the optimization of his own goals for his own organization through his choice of the right technology. The most comprehensive account of this view is known from Marxism whose analyses focused on how technology was selected and implemented in order to secure and carry out capitalist interests. The philosophical branch of this political view is comprised by Ferré's definition of technology as "*practical implementation of intelligence*"(Ferré, 1995). Of similar significance in management theory and among countless (modern) management theorists, we may point out P. Drucker, who argues that technology is about how the organization works and that it is management's function to optimize this *how* (Drucker, 1970).

8. Structuralism refers to Scott's fundamental disinction between regulative, normative, and cognitive structures, with reference to Durkheim, Weber, and Parsons respectively (Scott, 1995). Based on this theoretical construction, structuralism assumes many forms among which the neo-institutional approach is the most productive in the study of management and technology (Røvik, 1998; Scott, 1995; Powel & DiMaggio, 1991; Meyer & Rowan 1977). Here, technologies are seen as institutional standards, which provide an institutional pressure and results in organizational isomorphism. However, Neo-institutionalism has evolved since then and we can mention in particular studies of *decoupling* in which technologies are embedded in symbolic ceremonies, and studies of *translation* in which the subject of the analysis are the organization's/management's structured and structuring patterns of interpretation (Czarniawska & Sévon, 1996).

9. Structuration theory refers to the modern interpretation of the reciprocal relationship between actor and structure (Giddens, 1984). The dialectic relations also represent the point of departure for Bijker's, Callon's, and Law's sociological analyses, which illustrate how we produce through technologies and simultaneously are produced through technologies (see e.g., Law, 1991; Bijker, Highes & Pinch, 1989; Latour, 1983).

Post Structuralism
As the table shows, we still have to define technology as the point of observation for an analysis which answers the question: how does technology constitute the possibility of management? In its answer to this question, the present article has specified the way in which steering technologies can be observed as observations and the different ways in which they condition management's possible relation to the environment. This approach is in line with a *post structuralist* tradition and is proposed as an alternative to the subjectivist ideal of the governing manager, the structuralist assumption about intrusive technologies, and structuration theory's emphasis on reciprocal constitution. This epistemic strategy is outlined below:

Table 7: Post Structuralism

Manager ← [Technology] → Environment

The chosen perspective does not presuppose a sovereign manager who resides above any form of technology, nor does it presuppose an environment of intrusive technologies. Instead, it inquires into the technology's constitution of these two entities – management and its systems-created environment – and to the relation between them. Thus, the proposed program for observation does not suggest that management, environmental intrusion, or the relation between them are abolished but that the relation emerges relative to the observation provided by the technologies. The analysis of goal management showed that management is assigned the character of self-management (role), the way that this function is responsible for conceiving of itself and the organization as a future desirable state (environment), and how this results in self-inflicted compulsory change and steering (the relation).

Across this discussion of three alternative analyses of technology, we are able to specify the insight provided by the program: first of all, technology is installed as *point of observation* in preference to either the manager's will (subject), a surrounding and determining pressure (structure), or reciprocal constitution between subject and structure (structuration). Again, this does not imply the abolition of notions of management, environmental pressure, or the relation between these; but it does mean that the program reintroduces their significance with a variety of novel results. Secondly, technology is observed as *observation*, as a fundamental characteristic that is either played down or completely disregarded by the three alternative analyses. Instead, these alternatives point in different ways to questions of influence in the relation between manager and technology: The manager is presumed to be the master of the technology and uses it as a neutral tool for translating his own will into effect (subjectivism); the opposite relation is at stake when institutional structures appear as technological pressure on managers and almost seem to deprive the manager of free will (structuralism); and, finally, the question of influence is evident in the reciprocal relation between manager and technology (structuration). Technology influences or is influenced, the message seems to be, which is why technology in these analyses appears as a variable outside of management rather than management's possibility for observation. This insight is elaborated in relation to the three fundamental categories inherent in the proposed program. The first question is how technology establishes the possibility for management to relate to its object with authority, given the outlined observation. The second question is how steering delineates the possibility for management to reproduce itself. And the third question is how the management function, rather than influencing or becoming influenced, reproduces itself across the possibility of self-influence provided by the technology.

Conclusion

As I mentioned at the beginning, the ambition of this article has been one of observation. I have tried to present a program of observation for the sociology of management, guided by systems theory. By way of introduction, the article installed three fundamental concepts based on Niklas Luhmann's definition of technology, steering, and management. Next, the article illustrated the potential for enunciation in the proposed program through an analysis of goal management. In conclusion, the article discussed the epistemic potential inherent in the program in the light of three alternative analyses of technology. As a whole, the article contributes a program that suggests new and significant insights in the study of the constitution of and dynamic in new forms of management that become closed around themselves as system.

This contribution is also empirically pertinent. Steering technologies have been placed on the agenda as never before in the public domain and are increasingly referred to as the solution to all sorts of organizational problems. The same pertains to management, which is expected to be able to solve these problems when equipped with the appropriate tools. However, the limitation of this steering fetishism is that it is unable to reflect upon new management functions brought on by new steering technologies. As Scheytt notes: "technologies are seen as neutral tools in the hands of strong managers which neither distort an organization's reality nor intervene in the context in which they are applied" (2005, p. 388). As such, the present article builds on emergent research, which seeks to employ systems theory as the point of departure for analyses of management and organizational questions (Seidl & Becker, 2005).

This program is far from complete since its focus has only been on three fundamental categories – technology, steering, and management. The organization of the further epistemic potential might very well base itself on four additional systems-theoretical concepts, which have been given a general introduction by Andersen (2003). The semantic approach, which describes the constitution of technology as a question of the semantic forms that are historically made available to further communication; a differentiation analysis, which describes technology's different effects as a response to the system's complexity increase; a form analysis, which examines the possibility of studying reproduction as deparadoxification; and finally, the analysis of structural couplings, which examines the way in which a steering technology shapes the observation of other technologies. As such, the stage is set for further construction of the proposed systems-theoretical contribution and productive analyses of technology and management as a topical research field.

References

Amhøj, C. B. (2004). Medarbejderens synliggørelse i den transparente organisation – om styring af frihed og usynliggørelse af ledelse. In D. Pedersen (Ed.), *Offentlig Ledelse i Managementstaten* (pp. 268 - 286). Copenhagen: Samfundslitteratur.

Andersen, N. Å. (2003). *Discursive analytical strategies: Understanding Foucault, Koselleck, Laclau, Luhmann*. Bristol: The Policy Press.

Andersen, N. Å., & Born, A. (2001). *Kærlighe og omstilling*. Copenhagen: Nyt fra Samfundsvidenskaberne.

Andersen, N. Å., & Thygesen, N. (2004a). Styring af styringsteknologier. *Nordisk Administrativt Tidsskrift, 85* (juli), 28-38.

Andersen, N. Å., & Thygesen, N. (2004b). Den selvudsatte organisation. *GRUS, 73*(25), 8-29.

Bakken, T. & Hernes, T (2003). *Autopoietic organization theory: Drawing on Niklas Luhmann's social systems perspective*. Oslo: Abstrakt

Bijker, W. E., Hughes, T. P. & Pinch, T. J. (Eds.). (1989). *The social construction of technological systems*. Cambridge, MA: The MIT Press.

Brown, G. S. (1979). *Laws of form*. London: George Allen & Unwin Ltd.

Clegg, S. R., Hardy, C. & Nord, W. R. (1996). *Handbook of organization studies*. London: SAGE

Czarniawska, B. & Sévon, G. (1996). *Translating organizational change*. Berlin: De Gruyter.

Drucker, P. (1970). *Technology, management and society*. New York: Harper and Row.

Ferré, F. (1995). *Philosophy of technology*. Athens, GA: The University of Georgia Press.

Giddens, A. (1984). *Constitution of society: Outline of the theory of structuration*. Cambridge: Polity Press.

Greve, C. (2003). *Offentlig ledelse: teorier og temaer i et politologisk perspektiv*. Copenhagen: Samfundslitteratur.

Hansen, P., Ejersbo, N., & Rieper, O. (2000). *Målstyring i kommuner. To casestudier*. Copenhagen: AFK Forlaget.

Højlund, H. & Knudsen, M. (2003). Kontraktparadokser i den kommunale organisation. In H. Højlund & M. Knudsen (Eds.),*Organiseret kommunikation* (pp. 92 - 108). Copenhagen: Samfundslitteratur.

Latour, B. (1983). Give me a laboratory and I will raise the world. In K. D. Knorr-Certina & M. Mulkay (Eds.), *Science observed: Perspectives on the social study of science* (pp. 141-170). London: Sage.

Law, J. (Ed.). (1991). *A sociology of monsters - essays on power, technology and domination*. London: Routledge.

Luhmann, N. (1989). Politische Steuerung: ein Diskussionsbeitrag. *Politische Vierteljahres-schrift, 30*, 4-9.

Luhmann, N. (1990a). *Soziologische Aufklärung 5*. Opladen: Westdeutscher Verlag GmbH.

Luhmann, N. (1990b). Technology, environment and social risk: A system perspective. *Industrial Crisis Quarterly, 4* (3), 223-231.

Luhmann, N (1992). *Beobachtungen der moderne*. Opladen: Westdeutscher Verlag GmbH.

Luhmann, N. (1993). *Risk: A sociology theory*. New York: Walter de Gruyter.

Luhmann, N. (1995). *Social systems*, Stanford: Stanford University Press.

Luhmann, N. (1997a). Limits of Steering. *Theory, Culture & Society, 14* (1), 41-57.

Luhmann, N. (1997b). *Die Gesellschaft der Gesellschaft*. Frankfurt am Main: Suhrkamp.

Luhmann, N. (2000). *Organisation und Entscheidung*. Wiesbaden: Westdeutche Verlag.

Mckinlay, A. & Starkey, K. (2000). *Foucault, management and organization theory*. London: Sage.

Meyer, J. W. & Rowan, B. (1977). Institutionalized organizations – formal structure as myth and ceremony. *American Journal of Sociology, 83* (2), 340-363.

Moe, S. (2003). *Den moderne hjelpens sosiologi – velfærd i systemteoretisk perspektiv*. Norway: Apeiros Forlag.

Munro, R. & Mouritsen, J. (1996). *Power, ethos, and the technologies of managing*. London: Thomson Business Press.

Parsons, T. (1951). *The social system*. London: Routledge

Powell, W. W. & DiMaggio, P. J. (1991). *The new institutionalism in organizational analysis*. Chicago: Chicago Press.

Rennison, B. W. (2003). Polyfonisk lønkommunikation. In H. Højlund & M. Knudsen (Eds.), *Organiseret kommunikation*(pp. 206 - 230). Copenhagen: Samfundslitteratur.

Røvik, A. K. (1998). *Moderne organisasjoner: trender i organisasjonstenkningen ved tusenårsskiftet*, Bergen-Sandviken: Fagboklaget.

Scheytt, T. (2005). Management accounting from a systems-theoretical perspective. In D. Seidl (Ed.), *Organizational identity and selftransformation* (pp. 386-401). Aldershot, UK: Ashgate Publishing Limited.

Scott, R. W. (1995). *Institutions and organizations*. London: Sage.

Seidl, D. (2005). *Organizational identity and selftransformation*, Aldershot, UK: Ashgate Publishing Limited.

Slack, N., Chambers, S., & Johnston, R. (2004). *Operations management*. London: FT Prentice Hall.

Spencer Brown, G. (1979). *The Laws of form*. New York: E. P. Dutton

Smith, A. (1982). *The theory of moral sentiments*. (D. D Raphael & A. L. Macfie, Eds.), Indianapolis, IN: Liberty Fund.

Thygesen, N. (2002). *Målstyret Ledelse*. Ph.D., Department of Management, Politics and Philosophy, CBS. Copenhagen: Samfundslitteratur.

Thygesen, N. (2003). Hvordan iagttages ledelse som styringsteknologi. In H. Højlund & M. Knudsen (Eds.), *Organiseret kommunikation* (pp. 287 - 307). Copenhagen: Samfundslitteratur.

Thygesen, N., & Andersen, N. (2007). The polyphonic effects of technological changes in public sector organizations: A system theoretical approach. *Ephemera, 7* (2).

Thyssen, O. (2003). Luhmann and management: A critique of the management theory in Organisation und Entscheidung. In T. Bakken & T. Hernes (Eds.), *Autopoietic organization theory: Drawing on Niklas Luhmann's social systems perspective* (pp. 213 - 234). Copenhagen: CBS Press.

Von Foerster, H. (1981). *Observing systems*. Seaside, CA: Intersystems.

Beer, S. (n.d.). *Computer Volovox* (detail).

Cybernetics And Human Knowing. Vol. 14, nos. 2-3, pp. 173-187

Applying Luhmann
to Conceptualize Public Governance of Autopoietic Organizations

Eva Buchinger[1]

The conceptualization of society and actors as an interrelated ensemble of autopoietic systems—as it is done in Luhmann's theory of social systemsĺ—raises above all the question: How is it possible to govern operationally closed entities? Luhmann himself was a steering-pessimist. He devoted considerable effort to the explanation of the constraints of governance. But closer examination of the theory of social systems shows that it could be used as well to develop ideas about "how to govern." The present text attempts to interpret the autopoietic self-steering approach against its original steering-pessimism-intention. Contrary to the argument that the autopoiesis approach contributes to the steering discussion in only a marginal way, it will be shown how the conceptualization of the governance of autopoietic systems is possible. This will be done by using the concepts of *resonance*, *openess to the environment* (Umweltoffenheit) and *media of steering* (Steuerungsmedien). The empirical relevance of this approach will be demonstrated by the example of public governance of organizational systems.

1. Introduction

In terms of practical application, the conceptualization of society and actors as an interrelated ensemble of autopoietic systems, as in N. Luhmann's (1997a, 1995) theory of social systems, raises above all the question: How is it possible to govern operationally closed entities? Before this question can be answered, terminological clarification is necessary: (a) *governance*[2] means here embedded steering,[3] that is steering-subjects consider the embedded character of their actions (b) *operational closure* indicates that autopoietic systems "create everything that they use as an element and thereby use recursively the elements that are already constituted in the system" (Luhmann, 1995, p. 444).

---

1. Division Systems Research, Austrian Research Centers GmbH - ARC, Tech Gate Vienna, Donau-City-Strasse 1, 1220 Vienna, Austria. Email: Eva.Buchinger@arcs.ac.at
2. There exist at least six separate uses of governance (Rhodes, 1997, p. 47): (i) as the minimal state, (ii) as corporate governance, (iii) as the new public management, (iv) as good governance, (v) as a socio-cybernetic system, and (vi) as self-organizing networks. Within the present text, the term aims at the public dimension and is used in its socio-cybernetic connotation, including interactive governance-learning (Kooiman, 2003). The focus is therefore on "governance with the government," and not "governance without the government" as Rosenau/Czempiel (1992) put it provocatively. Although a certain hollowing out of the state (Rhodes, 1994) can be observed, the governance-definition used in this text follows the idea that "the state in modern governance should be powerful and effective, but not dominant and overpowering" (Mayntz, 2003, p. 6).
3. Whereby the steering-discussion focuses on actors (steering subject, steering action, etc.) and state authority, the governance-discussion focuses on the rules of the game and on acceptance by the majority (Mayntz, 2004; Rosenau/Czempiel, 1992). I use the term *embedded steering* to indicate that both dimensions – the behavioral (actors/state) and the functional (rules/society) – are integrated (which will be elaborated in section 4).

The standard answer of the theory of social systems to the governance issue is that autopoietic systems are autonomous, and according to their self-reproducing operation mode they cannot be controlled or determined from outside (Luhmann, 1989b, p. 8). Consequently, the theory of social systems is associated with *steering pessimism* (Steuerungspessimismus) (Luhmann, 1997b) which questions the possibility of steering from outside and is therefore criticized by authors such as R. Mayntz, F. Scharpf and R. Münch.[4]

- First solution: Closer examination of the theory of social systems reveals not only steering pessimism, but offers also a steering-approach which is adjusted to the notion of autopoiesis: namely difference oriented steering. Therefore, the theoretical steering pessimism of the theory of social systems is solved within its own framework.

- Critique of the first solution: But this abstract overcoming of steering pessimism does not solve the concrete problem of how to influence self-steering social systems in a certain direction. Therefore, the challenge is to find aspects within the theory of social systems which can be used to develop a solution to this practical steering-pessimism, too, and serve as a basis for the explanation of governance processes.

Based on the first solution and its critique, the present text attempts to interpret the autopoietic self-steering approach against its original steering-pessimism intention. The sub-concepts of Luhmann's autopoiesis theory have been checked whether they can contribute to the explanation of governance processes or not. Contrary to the thinking that the autopoiesis approach contributes to the steering discussion only marginally, it will be shown how the conceptualization of the governance of autopoietic organizational systems is possible. This is done by using the concepts resonance, openness to the environment (Umweltoffenheit), and media of steering (Steuerungsmedien).

The elaboration starts with the explanation of autopoiesis, the related steering pessimism and its theoretical solution. Thereupon follows the discussion of practical steering pessimism and a first attempt to its solution within the framework of social system theory. Based on these considerations, in section 4, a general model of public governance of organizational systems is presented, which integrates the functional as well as the behavioral dimension.

2. Autopoiesis: Theoretical steering-pessimism and its solution

Autopoietic systems come into being (and maintain themselves) as a "network of processes of production (transformation and destruction) of components that produces

---

4. Mayntz (1987), Scharpf (1989), Mayntz/Scharpf (2005), Münch (1994).

the components" (Maturana & Varela 1980, p. 79);[5] in the case of social systems by meaning-based *re*-production of communication elements (Luhmann, 1997a, p. 97). The reproduction takes place in the form of self-referential processes, whereby self is represented on three levels (element level, process level, system level) and reference is rooted in the meaning system, an evolutionary universal (Luhmann, 1995, p. 62) which serves as a world-encompassing referential nexus[6] for all different kinds of references.

(a) Steering pessimism as a consequence of self-referential operational closure
Self-reference is defined as "indication according to a distinction" (Luhmann, 1995, p. 442). The following forms are described (fig. 1): (i) Basal self-reference, which indicates communicational elements and uses the element-relation distinction. (ii) Processual self-reference, which indicates communication sequences and uses the before-after-distinction. (iii) Reflexional self-reference, which indicates communication systems and uses the system-environment-distinction.

Figure 1: Three self-referential modes of autopoietic social systems

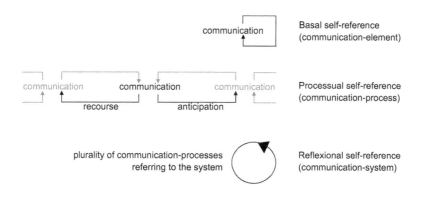

One of the consequences of these multiple self-referential operation modes of autopoietic systems is that they produce their own elements, processes and system identity (Luhmann, 1995, p. 9, 1990b, p. 3). This results in self-referential closure. Since autopoietic reproduction and closure takes place on the level of operations, the preeminent question of a theory of autopoietic systems is: How is one operation linked with the next? The answer is: Structure secures the connectivity of autopoietic reproduction whereby social systems use meaning-based "structures of expectations"

---

5. The neurophysiologists Humberto Maturana and Francisco Varela introduced the term *autopoiesis* to explain the realization of the living (Maturana, 1980, p. xvii).
6. This idea is derived from Husserl. For a discussion of the philosophical basics of Luhmanns autopoiesis concept, see Buchinger (2006).

(Luhmann, 1995, p. 292ff) which are primarily "expectations about expectation"[7] and not expectations about behavior.

The steering of a system is therefore always only self-steering (Luhmann, 1997b, p. 46), because there are no crossborder inputs/outputs as conditions determining the structure of autopoiesis. Even self steering – for example, in the form of hierarchy, asymmetries or differences in influence – is confronted with the fact that any control must be exercised in anticipation of counter-control (Luhmann, 1995, p. 36).

The requirement of operational closure in the course of reproduction excludes steering from outside or could/must result in destruction. Consequently, the autopoiesis approach leads to theoretical steering pessimism. Per definition, autopoietic social systems cannot be the steering object of an outside located steering subject (Luhmann, 1997b, 1991).

(b) Autopoiesis of organizational systems
Following the theory of social systems, organizational systems consist of decision communications – they come into being and reproduce themselves whenever communication of decisions takes place and the system is operationally closed exactly on the basis of this process (Luhmann, 2000a, p. 63). In modern societies, organizational decision communications are condensed in forms such as enterprises, public-administration units, universities, schools and hospitals which do have the form of a public or private legal entity.

Referring to decisions to explain organizational dynamics is not new, but based on mainstream organizational theory. One can start with Max Weber (1978, p. 956ff), who introduced the concept of bureaucratic rationality as institutional form, relying on decision rules in the form of competences, office hierarchy and written documents (Akten). Individuals as such are not of interest, but only in their function of matching the pre-formulated competences. "Objective discharge of business primarily means a discharge of business according to calculable rules and without regard for persons" (1922, p. 975). Whereas Weber emphasized the hierarchical and binding aspect, Herbert A. Simon explained organizations as decision-making entities, dealing with "... the process of choice which leads to action ..." (1997, p. 1) within a hierarchy of decisions. Behavior is purposive in so far as it is guided by general goals or objectives and it is rational in so far as it selects alternatives which are conductive to the achievements of the previously selected goals. For both, individuals and organizations, it is true that knowledge is limited and they are operating with bounded rationality, which means that risk, uncertainty and incomplete information about alternatives must be considered (Simon, 1972). Reasoning, the product of bounded rationality, can be characterized as selective searching through "large spaces of possibilities" (Simon, 1992, p. 4). Beyond that Michael Cohen, James March and Johan Olsen explained decision making processes within organizations as a "garbage can model." A choice

---

7. The social aspect of meaning is not exhausted by referring to the fact that another person exists, but includes that indented meaning can be recognized and this recognizability has structural relevance. Someone forming expectations can also take into account the expectations directed at her/him. (Luhmann, 1990b, p. 45)

opportunity within an organization can therefore be viewed "as a garbage can into which various kinds of problems and solutions are dumped by participants as they are generated" (Simon, 1972, p. 2). In a garbage can model, a decision is an outcome or interpretation of several relatively independent streams within an organization. Participants come and go.

Obviously, social system theory's conceptualization of organizations as decision-machines combines well-debated aspects. Luhmann's (2000a, p. 132ff) definition of the term decision considers four aspects: (i) Decisions are observations which indicate a preference on the basis of prior existing alternatives and include therefore the concept of *choice*; (ii) Decisions are attributed to decision makers and are therefore linked with the concept of *subject*; (iii) Decisions are time-dependent – they are based on the resources of prior decisions (which could also have been used in a different way) and include at least some future projections. According to the last criterion, the main foci of decisions are not subjects, but possible alternatives; (iv) Decisions are *communicative events* (they do not take place in the head of a subject) which includes the meta-information that the decision communicator is either hierarchically allowed to do so, or has good reasons.

New to the conceptualization of organizations as autopoietic systems is the uncompromising application of the notion of operational closure. This has far reaching consequences since it poses the system-environment question in a different way and gives, therefore, the issues of self-steering and steering from outside a new analytical framework.

(c) Overcoming the theoretical steering pessimism
Despite the described constraints, one can use the term steering within the framework of the theory of social systems. This is possible because of the re-conceptualization of what is meant by steering object. Luhmann proposes that it is not the addressees (organizations in our case) who should serve as steering objects, but differences (Luhmann, 1989b, 1991, 1997b). This idea is derived from classical cybernetics, in which system-related changes are dismantled in measurable unities (Ashby, 1957, p. 9ff): That which is acted on will be called the operand; the acting factor will be called the operator. What the operand is changed to will be called the transform, the change that occurs is the transition which is specified by two states and the indication of which changed to which: $A \rightarrow B$.

Exactly this difference approach is used by Luhmann in the course of re-conceptualizing the steering object. An example which he liked to use is that of a law, which prescribes a certain threshold-value for environmental pollution, and which—if effective—minimizes the difference between the actual and the desired ecological state (Luhmann, 1991, p. 143) Therefore, steering within the framework of social system theory is *difference-oriented steering*.

Concerning organizational systems, difference-oriented steering means that a steering subject thinks about observable differences related to steering-addressees and comes to a decision about a desired difference minimization. This approach does not necessarily require that the steering subject and the steering addressee use the same differences. They are still isolated entities with individual self-reference in each case.

3. Autopoiesis: Practical steering pessimism and a first step to its solution

As soon as the theoretical steering-pessimism is solved, the practical steering-pessimism comes in the focus. Even if organizational systems are disentangled from being steering objects – they remain central elements within steering processes. And they remain unpredictable elements, because their actions/reactions are not, or only partly, calculable.

> All discussions about political 'steering' focus on causal relations. If one uses social action-concepts, all hopes for the control of the results are smashed into pieces in practical terms (and consequently also in theoretical terms) because of the problem of unintended consequences and the 'perverse,' the original intensions disavowing effects. (Luhmann, 2000b, p. 109[8])

The freeing of the addressees of their object character does not solve the problem of achieving an appropriate steering effect.

Although Luhmann, during his work over decades, increasingly emphasized his steering skepticism, one can find sub-concepts in his theory architecture which support *moderate steering optimism*. These sub-concepts are *resonance*, *openess to the environment* (Umweltoffenheit) and *media of steering* (Steuerungsmedien). They can be used to explain the accessibility (Erreichbarkeit) of addressees and have been implicitly and/or explicitly discussed (partly by Luhmann himself and partly by his scholars) in the context of steering issues.

(a) Resonance
Resonance is the mode in which autopoietic systems respond to their environment. Because of the high complexity of these systems it is impossible to describe them as a kind of factory which transforms inputs to outputs (Luhmann, 1989a, p. 40). If the black box of social systems is opened, it can be said that resonance is achieved whenever signals in the environment affect the system's self-referential operation mode. As a consequence, autopoietic systems can be set in motion by placing appropriate signals in their environment. Accordingly, the accessibility of steering addressees means the target-oriented placement of signals in their environment. Every autopoietic social system responds to different kinds of signals.

Organizational systems can be addressed if a signal is connectable to their flow of decisions, or to their decision programs. For example, organizational systems of the type firm can be addressed via their economic rationality by money (subsidy, tax, etc.) or other signals (knowledge, skilled employees, and physical infrastructure) that are connectable to their decision programs.

---

8. Translation by the author.

Summarizing, it can be said that the main issue of steering is not addressability, but the achievement of the desired resonance within the addressed systems.

(b) Openness to the environment

Openness to the environment is a basic concept of the theory of social systems, because systems are not only occasionally, but structurally oriented towards their environment and are not able to survive without their environment (Luhmann, 1995, p. 35). Autopoietic social systems "constantly scour their environment for impulses" and are "endogenously restless and very sensitive" (Luhmann, 1989a, p. 119).

The difference between system and environment is constituted via self-reference (Selbstreferenz) and reference to something other than the self, that is, hetero-reference (Fremdreferenz) (fig. 2). In contrast to living systems, meaning-based systems are able to include system boundaries and environments in their operations, and can therefore operate internally by using the difference between system and environment (Luhmann, 1995, p. 37). To distinguish the self from the environment, organizational systems use self-descriptions (Luhmann, 2000a, p. 417ff). This guarantees that the self remains identical and substitutes a body, which serves as a referential nexus for psychical systems.

Figure 2: Referential categories of meaning processing autopoietic systems

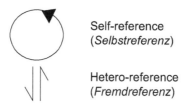

Self-reference
(*Selbstreferenz*)

Hetero-reference
(*Fremdreferenz*)

Source: Symbol adopted from Maturana and Varela (1992, p.74).

(c) Self- and hetero-references of organizational systems

Since organizational systems are decision based, *processual self-reference* means that the organization's decisions refer to earlier decisions and should enable future decisions (Luhmann, 2000a, p. 63). Everything else – goals, hierarchies, membership and so forth – must be seen as a result of decision-operations. Organizational systems dispose not only of processes, but also of structures in the form of decision premises combined with a binding to binary codes of functional systems[9] (e.g., firms' binding to the code pay/not pay of the functional system economy). Premises and code orientations do not determine decisions but build a framework for them (structures are focusing decisions). Therefore one can speak about the "organization of the organization." Examples of decision premises are:

- Job descriptions (roles)
- Communication channels (who reports to whom)
- Decision programs (if-then decision programs based on strict coupling, purposive decision programs based on loose coupling)
- Other structures regulating modes which form together specific organizational cultures. (Luhmann, 2000a, p. 316ff)

Reflexional self-reference is based on organizational self-description, which contains typically the organizational purpose (e.g., public administration, hospital, which expresses also the self-binding to functional systems/binary codes), name/ address, legal form, functional characteristics (e.g., which products or services are offered), number and composition of members (e.g., employees, white/blue collar), budget, organization-chart and so forth. The main features of an organizational self-description can usually be found in the annual report.

Hetero-reference can potentially be everything connectable to the organizational flow of decisions. Inspired by Dirk Baecker (2003, p. 233ff), one can distinguish generic areas of organizational hetero-reference such as (i) reference to symbolically generalized communication media, (ii) reference to the society, and (iii) reference to the individual.

Beyond that, there exist decision premises which emerge in the oscillation-process between self- and hetero-reference. They are called *cognitive routines* (Luhmann, 2000a, p. 250ff, 1997a, p. 120ff). Although they are internal constructions, organizational systems assume that cognitive routines represent *environment reality* sufficiently. They trust their routines about purchase orders, interactions with clients/ customers and so forth.

Decision premises, decision programs and cognitive routines enhance the repertoire of causal options of organizational systems. They develop *eigen causality* (Eigenkausalität) which allows them to vary their hetero-references and decide which signals from the environment will gain causality within the system and which not (Luhmann, 2000a, p. 278). This secures that environment-signals trigger not only resonance in the form of blind irritation but also in the form of causal connections within the system.

(d) Media of steering

The most powerful means by which politics can influence actors are the symbolically generalized communication media *law* and *money*, and they are therefore referred to

---

9. Decision premises are the functional equivalents at the level of organizational systems to codes at the level of functional systems (Luhmann, 2000a, p. 238). According to the theory of social systems (Luhmann, 1989a, p. 44ff), at least two levels of system structures can be distinguished: the level of coding and the level on which the suitability of operations is fixed and, if necessary, varied. Criteria refer to binary coding, but they are not a term of the code itself and therefore one can distinguish between coding and programming. Whereas codes (e.g., the code pay/not pay referring to the symbolically generalized communication media money) offer only closed contrast sets, programs offer conditions for the suitability of the selection of operations. That means programs represent variable concretization or operationalization of the requirements that a system has to satisfy and allow for structural change, whereas codes represent unchanging identity. Through differentiation between coding and programming a system acquires the possibility of operating closed and open simultaneously.

as media of steering (Steuerungsmedien) (Luhmann, 1981, p. 94). In nations characterized by constitutional law and market economy, both media will be effective in making individual and organizational actors resonate. There is no doubt that legislation and government subsidies can have a tremendous effect and the autopoietic approach does not question that effects are possible.

In knowledge-based economies the symbolically generalized communication media *truth* gains importance. Truth is proofed knowledge (Luhmann, 1990a, p. 167) and can be used as media of steering in the form of expert knowledge (Willke 1994, p. 227ff). In a "lighter" version compared with the symbolically generalized communication media truth, knowledge can serve as media of steering in the form of information. It may be information produced by steering-subjects and directly offered (signaled) to a selected target group or information produced by mass media and offered to the general public.

Beyond that it is possible to speak in a very general sense about artifacts as media of steering (Buchinger, 2005). They result in built infrastructure such as transport-infrastructure, municipal utility infrastructure, information-infrastructure and building-infrastructure (social-centers, art-centers, research-centers etc.).

(e) Moderate steering optimism
On the basis of resonance, openness to the environment and symbolically generalized communication media, the governance of autopoietic systems is possible in the following way:

*   First, systems are intrinsically motivated to search for useable signals in their environment.
*   Second, on the basis of pre-existing references to the environment, autopoietic systems are sensible to media of steering.
*   Third, if some/sufficient knowledge about the individual operation-modes of addressees exists (decision premises, decision programs, cognitive routines) not only non-oriented resonance is possible, but also the convergence to desired reso-nance.

What is questioned, however, is the possibility of forecasting the effects, and hence the targeted precision of governance.

4. Towards a model of public governance of organizational systems

(a) Embeddedness
Since governance means embedded steering, steering-subjects have to consider the framework of their actions. Their and their addressees' behavior relies on legitimate order which provides the steering conditions. Socioeconomic literature discusses this usually on the basis of concepts such as trust (personal relations/networks), convention (formal & informal institutionalised constraints to individual behaviour)

and law (North, 1993; Granovetter, 1985; Weber, 1978, p. 33ff). Within the theory of social systems, the term legitimate order does not appear,[10] but functional systems together with their media, rationalities and couplings represent societal order which is used (one can say trusted[11]) by the majority and therefore legitimized.

(b) Components of the model
The model is constituted by structural and processual components and the respective steering conditions.

Structural components of the model of public governance presented here are defined as more "persistent" than processual components (distinguished by their temporality). They are stabilized either in the form of organizational systems or in the form of symbolically generalized communication media. Organizations represent the focus of the action dimension of the model. As collective actors they are equipped with intentions and social roles and capable to produce activities according to a specific intention-role-mix. Types of involved organizational actors are for example:

- Enterprises (production, services)
- Universities
- Schools
- Hospitals
- NGOs
- Policy maker on national, supranational (e.g., European Union), regional and global (e.g., UN) levels
- Intermediaries such as funds and agencies
- Sector-specific experts such as scientific/research or consulting organizations

According to the action dimension, organizational systems are clustered on the basis of their respective roles (whereby an actor can play different roles within the cycle). Roles identified within the model are:

- Steering subject
- Steering addressee
- Steering administrator
- Steering observer

The second form of structural components – symbolically generalized communication media – represents the functional dimension, because they serve as media of steering which rely on the structural background of functional systems. Media of steering in policy making are above all money and law, which are directly linked to functional systems, namely the economic system and the legal-system. The

---

10. Instead, the term social order is used in connotation with meaning, system-building, interpenetration, references, and evolution (Luhmann, 1993).

11. This time trust in communication media (and not in personal relations) (Luhmann, 1997a, p. 383ff).

third media of steering used in the model is knowledge, which is more indirectly linked to the science system and its respective media truth. The fourth media of steering is artifact, which is linked to the state, since it results in a specific kind of built public infrastructure.

Contrary to structural components, processual components are characterized by their event-nature and have, therefore, a significant higher change rate. An idealized steering cycle consists of two processes which follow the same direction. The inner process is of constitutive nature, derived from the logic of difference oriented steering (as described above) and consists of four cornerstones. The outer process is of escorting nature and indicates activities related to these cornerstones which are:

- Steering difference (whereby difference minimization is the steering goal)
- Steering signal
- Steering effect
- Steering learning

Processes as well as actors rely on societal infrastructure which is represented by functional systems. They provide the steering conditions (opportunities, constraints) which appear in several forms. First, media of steering rely on the structural support of function systems in the form of codes, criteria and programs[12]. Second, rationalities on the functional-system level provide orientation standards for steering actors and allow successful expectation-building. Third, structural couplings (e.g., the tax system between the functional systems economy and politics which emerged in the course of their co-evolution), strict couplings (e.g., formal contracts), and loose couplings (e.g., informal network-interactions) provide the institutional background which integrates functional and organizational system rationalities.

(c) Dynamics of the idealized steering cycle of public governance
Since the feedback-dynamic is constitutive, the model is built around the processual components (fig. 3). It starts with the most important activity of governance – difference-construction – which requires knowledge about desired changes (e.g., in the form of a mission), knowledge about relevant differences (what is possible, what is impossible) and appropriate indicators to mark the initial and desired state. Difference-construction never starts at zero but always on the basis of prior knowledge and experiences and (1) steering learning is therefore the ending and the beginning of every cycle. The importance of steering-learning cannot be overestimated, because difference construction has consequences for every other component of the cycle.

---

12. See footnote 8, chapter 3.

Figure 3: Public governance: A model based on an idealized steering-cycle

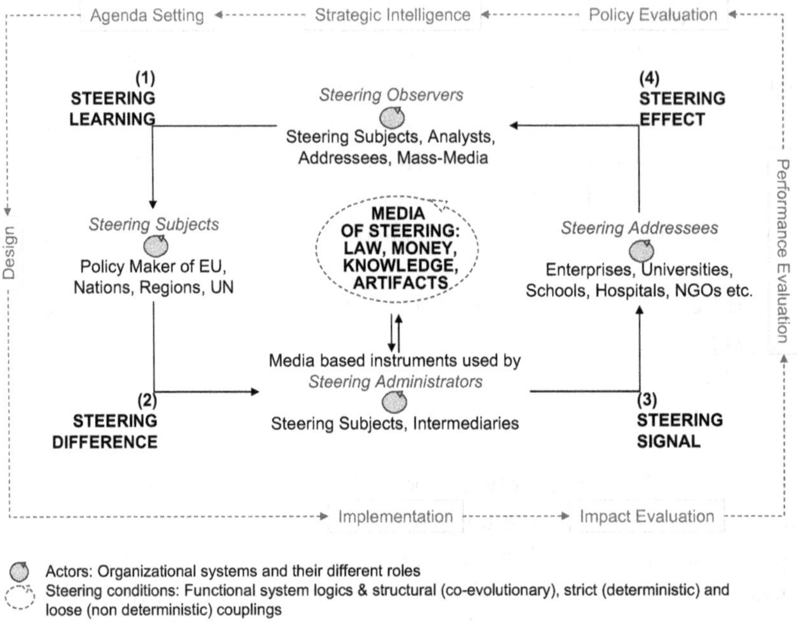

Actors: Organizational systems and their different roles
Steering conditions: Functional system logics & structural (co-evolutionary), strict (deterministic) and loose (non deterministic) couplings

Only if sufficient evidence about relevant differences is given, is it possible to formulate the (2) steering difference. In this process-step it will be decided which specific difference must be minimized to zero and in which time span this should happen. The formulation of the steering difference goes together with an implicit or even explicit pre-selection of steering addressees and steering instruments. Consequently, steering learning as well as the formulation of the steering difference requires at least some knowledge about the possibilities and constraints of the reciprocal effects of steering instruments, steering addressees and expected steering effect. Whereas steering learning is preferably participative (including analysts, addresses, intermediaries etc.), the decision about the steering difference is exclusively reserved for policy makers (which are the steering subjects in the case of public governance). Therefore, the model construction requires the placement of the *structural component steering subject* between learning and difference formulation.

The next processual component is the (3) steering signal. It is produced by the use of media-based steering instruments by steering administrators. Normally, a mix of steering instruments is implemented to achieve a certain goal (policy mix) and therefore a steering cycle is characterized by a signal mix which requires the proof whether the different signals are reinforcing (and not hindering) each other. Policy instruments are often based on several media (e.g., some amount of money is involved in every instrument) – therefore, the term *predominantly based* is appropriate. Predominantly law-based instruments are for example intellectual property rights and market regulations. Predominantly money-based instruments are either[13] indirect fiscal instruments (e.g., tax relief), or direct financial instruments (e.g., subsidies), or catalytic financial instruments (e.g., public investments in private financing-institutes to guarantee the provision of venture capital). Predominantly knowledge-based instruments are either operative knowledge instruments (e.g., consulting), or strategic knowledge instruments (e.g., councils). And last but not least, predominantly artifact-based instruments result in built infrastructure (e.g., broadband infrastructure).

The last processual component of the steering cycle is the (4) steering effect. Even if steering addressees are no longer conceptualized as steering objects, they are crucial within the cycle because they and nothing else do (or do not) produce the steering effect. All efforts remain useless if the addressees' resonance fail to appear or result in unintended (or even perverse) effects. Therefore, steering subjects as well as steering administrators must dispose certain (significant) knowledge about addressees' decision processes and/or decision premises. Here the role of steering observer gets effective. Every actor of the steering-cycle is a potential *steering observer*, but professional observers (e.g., analysts) gain importance because evaluation is increasingly used as background to argue the legitimacy of policy intervention.

The two processes of the idealized steering cycle are related, but more loosely than strictly coupled. That means, the outer process consists of activities which are related to the inner process, but do not necessarily have the same speed. One can distinguish between the following activities:[14] Agenda setting takes place on the societal as well as on the sectoral level. This part of the cycle is strongly influenced by interest groups and provides the background for the understanding of why certain issues are on the political agenda and how they got there. Design covers the part of the cycle in which the issues on the policy agenda are translated into steering goals in the form of relevant differences. This involves an assessment of the situation and of the needs of the addressees and the planning of concrete actions. Implementation comprises activities necessary for the execution of planned actions and can be summarized as instrument set up. Practical trade offs are often not foreseeable within the design phase and steering-administrators must be able to cope with unexpected difficulties in this phase. Evaluation is executed in the form of impact, performance, and policy evaluation (other common terms are ex-ante, interim and ex-post evaluation) whereby the first two of these allow timely correction of the instrument set-up if necessary. Strategic intelligence should be an integral part of policy learning. It comprises international comparison and benchmarking, the use of evaluation-results, user studies (addressees' needs, constraints, and eigen logic which determine resonance and resulting actions), policy studies (quality of policy processes), monitoring, and foresight.

Whereas the inner process of the cycle represents predominantly the steering logic, the outer process stands mainly for the activity logic. In the middle and long

---

13. This distinction is derived from European Commission policy approaches (EC, 2003, p. 10).
14. This distinction is adopted from OECD (2005, p. 91).

range it is necessary that steering logic and activity logic are at least to some extent consistent, because otherwise it is not possible to argue policy legitimacy in a convincing way.

5. Summary

The question, how is it possible to govern operationally closed entities, is neglected within the theory of social systems in favor of the explanation of autopoiesis and self-reference. Nevertheless, closer examination of Luhmann's social system theory reveals that he gives quite interesting clues how to conceptualize governance, even if they are often implicit and scattered across the voluminous work.

Within the text, first governance-relevant sub-concepts of the theory of social systems – resonance, openness to the environment, and media of steering – were discussed. Based on that, the conceptualization of public governance was explored and the conditions of moderate steering optimism described. This primarily functional approach was complemented by the social action dimension – actors, roles, activities – and both were integrated in a model of public governance which follows the logic of an idealized steering cycle.

"Luhmann Applied" is the title of this special issue and consequently it is the main aim of it: to demonstrate the practical relevance of social system theory. Although the presented model of public governance considers already several of the central issues of contemporary policy-making discussion (e.g., evaluation, use of strategic intelligence), it must be further developed to provide evidence for the deduction of concrete actions.

References

Ashby, W. R. (1957). *An introduction to cybernetics*. London: Chapman & Hall.

Baecker, D. (2003). *Organisation und management*. Frankfurt: Suhrkamp.

Buchinger, E. (2005). *Innovationspolitik aus systemtheoretischer Sicht: Ein zyklisches Modell der politischen Steuerung technologischer Innovation*. ITA manu:script 05-03 (http://www.oeaw.ac.at/ita/ita-manus.htm).

Buchinger, E. (2006). The sociological concept of autopoiesis: Biological and philosophical basics and governance relevance. *Kybernetes: The International Journal of Systems & Cybernetics, 35* (3-4), 360-374.

Cohen, M. D., March, J. G., & Olsen, J. P. (1972). A garbage can model of organizational choice. *Adminstrative Science Quarterly 17* (1), 1-25.

EC (2003). Raising EU R&D intensitiy: Improving the effectiveness of the mix of public support and mechanisms for private sector research and development. Expert Group Report to the European Commission EUR 20713.

Granovetter, M. (1985). Economic action and social structures: The problem of embeddeness. *American Journal of Sociology 91* (3), 481-510.

Kooiman, J. (2003). *Governing as governance*. London: Sage Publications.

Luhmann, N. (1981). *Politische Theorie im Wohlfahrtsstaat*. München-Wien: Olzog.

Luhmann, N. (1989a). *Ecological communication* (J. Bednarz, Trans.). Chicago: The University of Chicago Press.(originally published in 1986)

Luhmann, N. (1989b). Politische Steuerung: Ein Diskussionsbeitrag. *Politische Vierteljahresschrift, 30* (1), 4-9?

Luhmann, N. (1990a). *Die Wissenschaft der Gesellschaft*. Frankfurt: Suhrkamp.

Luhmann, N. (1990b). *Essays on self-reference*. New York: Columbia University Press.

Luhmann, N. (1991). Steuerung durch Recht? Einige klarstellende Bemerkungen. *Zeitschrift für Rechtssoziologie, 11,* 137-160.

Luhmann, N. (1993). Wie ist soziale Ordnung möglich? In N. Luhmann (Ed.), Gesellschaftsstruktur und Semantik 2 (pp. 195-285). Frankfurt: Suhrkamp. Is Luhmann the editor or the author of this book?

Luhmann, N. (1995). *Social systems* (J. Bednarz & D. Baecker, Trans.). Stanford: Stanford University Press. (Originally published in 1984 as *Soziale Systeme—Grundriss einer allgemeinen Theorie by* Suhrkamp Verlag of Frankfurt.)

Luhmann, N. (1997a). *Gesellschaft der Gesellschaft.* Frankfurt: Suhrkamp.

Luhmann, N. (1997b). Limits of steering. *Theory, Culture & Society, 14* (1), 41-57. (English translation of Chapter 10 of *Die Wirtschaft der Gesellschaft.* Frankfurt: Suhrkamp, 1988).

Luhmann, N. (2000a). *Organisation und Entscheidung.* Wiesbaden: Westdeutscher Verlag.

Luhmann, N. (2000b). *Die Politik der Gesellschaft.* Frankfurt: Suhrkamp.

Maturana, H. R. (1980). Introduction to autopoiesis and cognition. In H. R. Maturana, & F. J. Varela (Eds.), *Autopoiesis and cognition: The realization of the living*(pp. xi-xxx). Dordrecht: D. Reidel Publishing Company.

Maturana, H. R. and Varela, F. (1980). "Autopoiesis: The organization of the living," In H. R. Maturana, & F. J. Varela (Eds.), *Autopoiesis and cognition: The realization of the living*(pp. 63-135). Dordrecht: D. Reidel Publishing Company.

Maturana, H. R. and Varela, F. J. (1992). *The tree of knowledge* (rev. ed.). Boston: Shambala.

Mayntz, R. (1987). Politische Steuerung und gesellschaftliche Steuerungsprobleme. In: Mayntz, R. (Hg.), *Soziale Dynamik und politische Steuerung: Theoretische und methodologische Überlegungen* (pp. 186-208). Frankfurt: Campus Verlag.

Mayntz, R. (2003). From government to governance: political steering in modern societies. Paper presented at the Summer Academy on IPP (Integrated Product Policy, Würzburg, Germany, September 7-11.

Mayntz, R. (2004). Governance als fortentwickelte Steuerungstheorie? MPIfG Working Papers 04/1, Köln: Max-Planck-Institut für Gesellschaftsforschung.

Mayntz, R., & Scharpf, F. (2005). Politische Steuerung – Heute? MPIfG Working Papers 05/1, Köln: Max-Planck-Institut für Gesellschaftsforschung.

Münch, R. (1994). Politik und Nichtpolitik: Politische Steuerung als schöpferischer Prozess. *Kölner Zeitschrift für Soziologie und Sozialpsychologie, 46* (3), 381-405.

North, D. C. (1993). Economic performance through time. Nobel prize lecture, December 19, 1993. Retrieved December 15, 2006 from http://nobelprize.org/nobel_prizes/economics/laureates/1993/north-lecture.html

OECD. (2005). *Governance of innovation systems.* Paris: Organisation for Economic Co-Operation and Development.

Rhodes, R. A. W. (1997). *Understanding governance: Policy networks, governance, reflexivity and accountability.* Maidenhead: Open University Press.

Rhodes, R. A. W. (1994). The hollowing out of the state: the changing nature of the public service in Britain. *Political Quarterly , 65*, 138-151.

Rosenau, J. & Czempiel, E.-O. (1992). *Governance without government: Order and change in world politics,* Cambridge: Cambridge Universitiy Press.

Scharpf, F. (1989). Politische Steuerung und politische Institutionen. *Politische Vierteljahresschrift, 30* (1), 10-21.

Simon, H. A. (1972). Theories of bounded rationality. In C. B. Radner & R. Radner (Eds.), *Decision and organization* (pp. 129-148). Amsterdam: North-Holland Publishing Company.

Simon, H. A. (1992). Economics, bounded rationality and the cognitive revolution: Introductory comments. In H. A. Simon, M. Egidi, R. Marris, & R. Viale (Eds.), *Economics, bounded rationality and the cognitive revolution* (pp. 3-7). Aldershot, UK: Edward Elgar Publishing.

Simon, H. A. (1997). *Adminstrative behavior.* New York: The Free Press. (originally published in 1945)

Weber , Max (1978). *Economy and society.* Berkeley: University of California Press. (orignally published in 1922)

Willke, H. (1994). *Systemtheorie III: Steuerungstheorie.* Stuttgart: Lucius & Lucius

Beer, S. (n.d.). *Moose*(detail).

Beer, S. (n.d.). *Tiresias at the Violet Hour.*

Cybernetics And Human Knowing. Vol. 14, nos. 2-3, pp. 189-196

A (Cybernetic) Musing: Ashby and the Black Box

Ranulph Glanville[1]

Introduction

Over the years that I have written this column, I have often referred to the *Black Box*. I believe the Black Box is such a powerful device, that it is time to explore it seriously, in its own right; for it allows us that most magical of tricks, a way of acting confidently with/from the unknown/unknowable. From this position and with this device, we can build an understanding of a world regardless of whether we can honestly regard it as "real" or existing knowably independent of our knowledge of it. We can also build descriptions of the world that, ultimately, are based not in presumed knowledge but in ignorance.

I shall do this by means of an argument based, in the first instance, on the work of Ross Ashby, as far as I know one of the few scholars to write extensively and seriously about what the Black Box is. Before that, I will provide some context. In a later paper I will explore the consequences and use of the Black Box, and some of the extensions to and critical sequitors of the arguments presented here. This paper is intended to explain what the (classic) Black Box is. The interested reader will understand from this argument how radically misused the notion has often been, even before this is argued and explained in the follow up paper.

At the end of this paper, I shall show how, in developing his understanding of the Black Box, Ashby joins that band of early cyberneticians whose cybernetics was already, in effect what became called second-order cybernetics.

Which Black Box?

The term *Black Box* is used confusingly. Before I begin, I need to clarify what I intend to write about.

The use of the term I will explore is associated with the great Scottish mathematician and theoretical physicist, James Clerk Maxwell.[2] Apparently, Maxwell first used the term, in this sense, in 1871 in his *Theory of Heat*.[3]

---

1. CybernEthics Research, Southsea, UK; Email: ranulph@glanville.co.uk
2. Interestingly, a google search on the terms Black Box Maxwell scarcely mentions this (earliest) use of the Black Box, in the first 200 returns.
3. I owe this information to Dr Albert Mueller of the Institute for Contemporary History at the University of Vienna. Although Maxwell is regularly credited with the invention of this use of the term *Black Box* finding a reference is difficult indeed, and so I am specially indebted to Dr Mueller for this information.

Amongst the uses we will not consider but which I mention in passing, is that of the Black Box as an alternate/synonym for a radiant Black Body in thermodynamics, and the recent development of the Black Box flight recorder. This device – properly known in the first instance as a *Flight Memory Unit* – was created in response to the Comet jet crashes of the early 1950's by Dr Dave Warren of the (Australian) Aeronautical Research Laboratories in Melbourne, in 1957 and has since become universally adopted not only in aeroplanes, but in many other vehicles. Although this is the best known use of the term Black Box, it is, in fact, usually bright orange!

Dr Warren's original "Flight Memory Unit" prototype (source *The Black Box Flight Recorder* (2000, downloaded from: www.kidcyber.com.au, April 22, 2007)

The American psychologist B. F. Skinner also used the Black Box concept in a manner that has lead to major misunderstandings—as I shall explain in the next section.

A short historical prelude: The Black Box and behaviour

While it is difficult to access Maxwell's origination of the concept, we are not left without guides. Both Wiener and Ashby mention the Black Box and its significance. In fact, Ashby does more than mention it: he devotes his paper "General Systems Theory as a New Discipline" (Ashby, 1958/1991; a paper without a single reference in it)[4] almost entirely to a discussion of the Black Box; and there are 17 acknowledged entries dated between 1951 and 1956 in the notebooks that make up his journal.[5]

---

4. Ashby studies the Black Box extensively in his *Introduction to Cybernetics* (Ashby 1956). However, those studies are more technical and less philosophical. I have not found the account in Introduction so compelling as the account in the paper I quote from so extensively in this column.

5. Ashby's journal was given by his family to the British Museum. A web site is currently being finalised. I am fortunate enough to have been given access to this site, but cannot reference it, since it is not yet in the public domain. This is one reason I do not quote from or reference the journal.

In fact, it was a remark at the beginning of the Black Box section of the paper that first really excited my interest. Here is Ashby introducing the Black Box notion:

> there is …no finer approach than that given by the so-called Problem of the Black Box. It arises in electrical engineering, but its range is really far greater—perhaps as great as the range of science itself. (Ashby in Klir, 1991, p. 252)

If anything, I have come to believe that Ashby under-, rather than overstates the range of application of the Black Box, for here he talks of it as an existing machine that cannot be opened, whereas I believe we are all familiar with a Black Box approach as part of the conceptual development we go through. I believe it is interesting and valuable to look at the way we learn about the world as a Black Box type of exploration.[6] If I want to argue this, I need do no more than refer to the amazing way I can understand (at least, present an understanding of) how you think, and even how I do, without recourse at all to any form of mechanical examination of what goes on in the brain. As we shall see, Ashby also understood this.[7]

This may seem a bizarre, if familiar position: and perhaps particularly odd coming from a second-order cybernetician. It's the position of B. F. Skinner and his school of behaviourist psychology; and, indeed, Skinner did write of the Black Box (e.g., Skinner, 1984). But is this really so strange? Cybernetics is, after all, a subject deeply tied in to the concept of behaviour, and of explaining (accounting for) behaviour through mechanism.

What makes the difference between a cybernetic position and Skinner's is not the behavioural interest, not the use of the Black Box, but how we interpret the nature of what the Black Box approach can tell us. Skinner may have chosen to present the behaviour associated with a Black Box as mind-less and mechanical (automatic), but for the cybernetician who takes into account the observer there is a big difference. The behaviour is not of the Box alone, but is shared between Box and Investigator (observer). As Ashby writes:

> for what *we* are considering can be viewed as a compound system, composed of Box and Investigator. He acts on the Box when he stimulates it, and the Box acts on him when it gives him a dial-reading as observation. Thus each acts on the other. (Ashby in Klir, 1991, pp. 252–253, emphasis in original)

Furthermore, the Black Box, as we shall see, is an unknown. The behaviour that results from the "interaction" (Ashby's word) between Box and Investigator is

---

6. However, see later Ashby quote from *Introduction to Cybernetics*.
7. Luhmann also came to describe the experience of communication between 2 entities through the image of the Black Box. Soeren Brier, our editor, provides this quote: "Two Black Boxes, by whatever accident, come to have dealings with one another. Each determines its own behaviour by complex self-referential operations within its own boundaries. Each assumes the same about the other. Therefore, however many efforts they exert and however much time they spend, the black boxes remain opaque to one another" (Luhmann, 1995, p. 109.). Luhmann's views were developed from Ashby's (see next Ashby quote, pp. 252–253), and my own work which I will introduce in a later paper.

described (generally) by the Investigator: We do not know what happens in the Box. Furthermore, we cannot know what is "going on in the head" of anyone—but we are getting ahead of ourselves.

Finally, for Skinner it seems the explanation of the behaviour should be taken as a precise 1:1 mapping of the mechanism – the map was the territory. In cybernetics, we try not to confuse these two, but to recognise that an explanation is precisely an explanation and not what is explained.

Introducing the Black Box

Ashby:

> We imagine that the Investigator has before him a Black Box that, for any reason, cannot be opened ... In its original, specifically electrical, form, the problem was to deduce the contents in terms of known elementary components. Our problem however is somewhat wider. The questions we are interested in ... are such matters as:
>   What *general* rules of strategy should guide the exploration, when the Box is not limited to the electrical but may be of any nature whatever?
>   When the raw data have been obtained from the outputs, what operations should *in general* be applied to the data if the deductions made are to be logically permissible?
>   What can in principle be deduced from the Box's behaviour and what is fundamentally not deducible? (Ashby in Klir, 1991, p. 252)

And then:

> Whether the Box is behaving in a machine-like way does not require study of its internal details ... to find something of the connections does not demand the opening of the Box. (Ashby in Klir, 1991, p. 253)

Later:

> Thus, Black Box theory leads us naturally into the theory—most important for those who study the brain—of the mechanism that, for whatever reason, is not wholly accessible.(Ashby in Klir, 1991, p. 256)

And:

> You will have noticed that a good deal of what I have had to say has not been concerned directly with the Black Box but rather with what the Investigator can or cannot achieve when faced with one. *We*, the systems theorists, have in fact been studying, not a Black Box, but a larger system composed of two parts, the Black Box and the Investigator, each acting on the other. ... Thus, if the Investigator is a scientist studying the Box, *we* are metascientists, for we are studying both; we are working at an essentially different level. (Ashby in Klir, 1991, p. 257)

Ashby's Black Box

What does Ashby tell us about the Black Box?

First, he makes a claim for the generality of the Black Box. He tells us that the Black Box need not remain in the realm of Electrical Engineering or deal with the behaviour of discrete components we are already familiar with. And he tells us that it may be applied in a wide range of situations. For reasons I will explore in the follow up paper, I specially like this notion, and would extend it towards the universal. If this generality is not clear in the quotes above, consider this further quote (from Ashby's *Introduction to Cybernetics*):

> Back Box theory is, however, even wider in application than these professional [engineering, RG] studies. The child who tries to open a door has to manipulate the handle (the input) so as to produce the desired movement at the latch (the output); and he has to learn how to control the one by the other without being able to see the internal mechanism that links them. In our daily lives we are confronted at every turn with systems whose internal mechanisms are not fully open to inspection, and which must be treated by the methods appropriate to the Black Box. (Ashby, 1956, p. 86)

Second, he tells us the Black Box can remain unopened: there is no need to open the Box to determine (model) the behaviour that the observer observes and, to some extent at least, instigates. Ashby is quite specific about this. It is interesting, in this light, to note he never mentions, in the paper, journal or "Introduction," whitening the Black Box. Whitening is the term used when explaining what "really" is in the Black Box: the term White Box implies that the Box is somehow fully known, and, in that sense, is opened, stripped back and revealed. Leaving aside epistemological questions of whether we can ever "really know," that is, whether there is not always another question that may be asked, another recursion that may be applied, it is often held that the point of examining a Black Box is to know what goes on in it. I maintain that to attempt to open the Box is both improper and, in principle, impossible. Ashby's approach is a proper precursor to this position: He insists we do not need to open the Black Box, and (many would say fortunately) that it is not always possible to think we could—as for instance is the case with the head of another human. Two more quotes are appropriate, even if coming in a little from the periphery:

> That homo has a brain, no more entitles him to assume he knows how he thinks than possession of a liver entitles him to assume that he knows how he metabolises. (Ashby, 2004)

And:

> A man no more knows how he thinks, just because he has a brain in his skull, than he knows how he makes blood, because he has marrow in his bones. (Ashby, 2004)

Third, the Black Box is a device for changing input (value) into output (value). This means that there is an input and an output; and that there is, also, a before and after (the input becomes the output). Associated with this is the notion of behaviour, which is recognised by the observer whose job it is to try to relate (find an apparently causal connection between) them. Thus, central to the notion of the Black Box are the notions of behaviour and of regularity/pattern. The importance of behaviour makes the

Black Box a seemingly ideal device for Skinnerian psychologists (I will argue more fully than above, in a follow up, that their interpretation is completely inappropriate). The importance of pattern, of finding the general, brings us into other Ashby realms, such as variety: but it also places Ashby in the same camp as Piaget.

Fourth, not everything is deductible. Ashby argues that there are situations in which Black Boxes are not determinable through observation. It is, I will argue, but a small step to say that none are. Ashby intimates this when he talks of the history and unopenability of the Black Box. If we take these points seriously, then we will also want to move beyond Ashby to the point where we deny that using the Black Box to develop explanations ever leads to certainty—though it may lead to a high degree of likelihood. That is essentially what Popper (1963) insisted, a mere decade after Ashby's paper was published.

Ashby and second-order cybernetics

What should we learn about Ashby's thinking in general, from his view of the Black Box?

Consider perhaps the most startling statement in the paper, the quote given above from p. 257 of the paper. This tells us that already in 1958,[8] Ashby had understood what later came to be called second-order cybernetics. In his description of the Black Box and its Investigator, he describes the recursion of observation that is at the heart of both von Foerster's and Maturana's work, and which (as it occurred in Pask's extension of Loefgren [1968] in his classes in 1971–2) was also central to Pask's arguments towards second order cybernetics. Ashby is, here, explicitly talking not only of the observer, but the observer of the observer. Ashby is observing observing, (von Foerster, 2003)

There is, I think, an irony that Ashby, perhaps the most classically mechanistic of all early cyberneticians, and the one who created the most thorough mathematical description of the subject and its working, is also already in 1958 an embryo second-order cybernetician. I have made a similar argument concerning Pask (Glanville, 2005): His *An Approach to Cybernetics* (Pask, 1961) is full of statements, coming out of his experience designing truly interactive machines, that are precursors to both his own later development and the general development of second order cybernetics. In my view, Pask was always at least on the edge of second-order cybernetics. This view can be extended to Bateson and Mead (the official mother of second-order cybernetics), whose understanding was, I maintain, always of a second-order cybernetics. This is why, with the exception of the briefing paper von Foerster commissioned (Mead, 1968) they didn't mention it. What other sort of cybernetics was there?

If I am correct in my assertions, it is clear that, from the earliest days, at least several of those involved in cybernetics were taking what when fully articulated

---

8.   In fact, this point is made in Ashby (1956). So 1958 (when this paper was first published) is not the dawning of this understanding in Ashby's work.

became called a second-order cybernetic position as their position.[9] That is to say that, for many (specially those whose roots were in the arts, humanities and social sciences), second-order cybernetics was implicit in first order cybernetics, but for some it was explicit. Or, perhaps, there was little difference. Maybe we should no longer maintain the distinction.

Is there confirmation of the claim about Ashby's cybernetics? Yes, in the first quote I gave. Here, Ashby insists that whatever is found out about any Black Box is not from the Black Box alone, but from the observer's (Investigator's, using his term) interaction with the Black Box. Thus, in regard to the Black Box, Ashby's position is exactly that of second order cybernetics: that we cannot ignore the observer. As Maturana famously says:

Everything said is said by an observer.

To which von Foerster retorts:

Everything said is said to an observer.

Summary: Introducing the Black Box

In Ashby's usage, the Black Box is, then, a unopened device, observed by an observer (or Investigated by an Investigator) that exists between behaviours observed at an input and (assumed-to-be consequent) behaviour observed at an output, that is taken to cause the change of input into output. By changing the behaviours we input and observing the corresponding output behaviours, we test the understanding we have of the connection between input and output, taken to be the mechanism assumed to be inside the closed Box. The Box does not need to be opened—indeed some would suggest that it cannot be—that it is essentially a conceptual device, a *gedenken* experiment, though the argument to support this position has to await the follow up paper. The power of the Black Box is that we do not need to know what is in it. Nor do we need to understand the nature of the observed change: through using the Black Box we are enabled to work with the unknown and, some would argue, the unknowable. It is a truly extraordinary invention.

References

Ashby, W. R. (1956). *Introduction to cybernetics*. London: Chapman and Hall
Ashby, W. R. (1991). General systems theory as a new discipline. reprinted in G. J. Klir (Ed.), *Facets of Systems Science* (pp 249–257). New York: Plenum Press. (Originally published in 1958 in *General Systems, 3,* 1-6)
Ashby, W. R. (2004). *Aphorisms* (collected by John Ashby). Retrieved from http://www.cybsoc.org/ross.htm April 22, 2007.
Foerster, H. von. (2003). *Understanding understanding*. New York: Springer.
Glanville, R (2007). An approach to cyberntics. In R. Glanville & K. H. Mueller (Eds.), *Gordon Pask: Philosopher Mechanic*. Vienna: edition echoraum. (Originally published as Lerner ist Interaktion: "Gordon Pask's An Approach to Cybernetics." In D. Baecker [Ed.], Schlüsselwerke der Systemtheorie [pp.75-94] published by Verlag für Sozialwissenschaften of Wiesbaden in 2005)

_____

9. I once asked Gordon Pask, the only person I knew well who knew Wiener, if Wiener would have considered it impertinent to modify his cybernetics. Pask's response was that Wiener knew there was another, crucial step to take, but that he did not know how to take it himself.

Loefgren, L. (1968) An axiomatic explanation of complete self-reproduction. *Bul Math Biophys, 38* (3).

Luhmann, N. (1995). *Social systems* (J. Bednarz & D. Baecker, Trans.). Stanford, CA: Stanford University Press.

Mead, M (1968) The cybernetics of cybernetics, in H. von Foerster, J. D.White, L. J. Peterson, & J. K. Russell. (Eds.), *Purposive systems* (pp. 1-11). New York: Spartan Books.

Pask, G. (1961.) *An approach to cybernetics*. London: Methuen.

Popper, K. (1963). *Conjectures and refutations*. London: Routledge and Kegan Paul

Skinner, B. F. (1984). Selection by consequences. *Behavioral and Brain Sciences, 7*, 477-510.

Beer, S. (n.d.). *Fabeltier Spirale Blätter*

Cybernetics And Human Knowing. Vol. 11, nos. 2-3, pp. 197-200

ASC
American Society for Cybernetics
a society for the art and
science of human understanding

Epistemological Awareness
A Systemic Inquiry

Ray Ison[1]

Having accepted an invitation to contribute this column I decided that I in turn would extend an invitation to readers. My invitation is to contribute to a systemic inquiry (Box 1) into epistemological awareness through the auspices of this journal, and when it becomes available, the new CHK website.

Box 1. Systemic inquiry

Systemic inquiry is a particular means of facilitating movement towards social learning (understood as concerted action by multiple stakeholders in situations of complexity and uncertainty). It can be seen as a meta-platform or process for *project or programme managing* in that it has a focus on (i) understanding situations in context and especially the history of the situation; (ii) addressing questions of purpose; (iii) clarifying and distinguishing *what* from *how* as well as addressing *why*; (iv) facilitating action that is purposeful and which is systemically desirable and culturally feasible and (v) developing a means to orchestrate practices across space and time which continue to address a phenomenon or phenomena of social concern when it is unclear at the start as to what would constitute an improvement (see Ison, in press).

The motivation for my invitation arises from my experience—I would contend that epistemology has been a major concern of ASC members for many years, yet it is rarely up-front in the meetings and conversations I have experienced other than in an abstract conceptual sense, as for example when discussing a paper at a conference. I recently described the trap that arises whenever we remain silent about our epistemological assumptions (Ison & Schlindwein, 2006). For me the trap is not that one epistemological position or the other is right or wrong, better or worse, but that so many people act without awareness of the position that they hold or uphold. They appear unaware of the historicity of their thinking and acting. The product of this lack of awareness is conflict, rejection, talking across each other, lack of valuing of difference, bifurcation into smaller and smaller communities of practice, unethical

---

1. Visiting Professor, Uniwater, University of Melbourne, 3010. Professor of Systems, Director Open Systems Research Group (OSRG), Systems Department, Centre for Complexity and Change, The Open University, Walton Hall, Milton Keynes MK7 6AA, UK. Email: R.L.Ison@open.ac.uk
Blog: http://rayison.blogspot.com/; Homepage: http://systems.open.ac.uk/page.cfm?pageid=RayIhome

practice, and struggles to build institutional capital or brand around particular groupings or discourse or unexpressed epistemological commitments. Situations where epistemological awareness particularly matters include the design and evaluation of research projects, refereeing research papers, conference and workshop designs, the devising of policies and implementing particular practices (e.g., knowledge transfer).

Let me offer a recent example of what I mean by epistemological awareness by quoting from a paper my colleagues and I have prepared for the Australian and New Zealand Systems Society (ANZSYS) Conference in Auckland in December 2007 (Ison et al., 2007). An adapted extract from this paper is given in Box 2.

Box 2. A situation in need of epistemological awareness?

In 1968, in a lecture at the École Normale Supérieure in Paris, Alain Badiou (see http://en.wikipedia.org/wiki/Alain_Badiou) delivered a stinging critique of positivist epistemology in cybernetics and structuralism, but despite this and other critiques, the issue of epistemological awareness is like the elephant in the room in most systems and cybernetic journals and events. … The significance of this issue arose whilst writing this paper. The example was in an email distributed by ISSS (International Society for the Systems Sciences) seeking inputs to an article being prepared by Tom Mandel to provide a summary overview of systems theory (see http://en.citizendium.org/wiki/Systems_theory/Notes).[2]

From our perspective, in what is written thus far, Mandel puts the primary focus on "science" rather than holism. His perspective is that systems is a transdisciplinary and multiperspective scientific inquiry. This to us is a cultural predisposition entrenched within, particularly, the USA and is a claim often made with little appreciation of what scientists do when they do what they do (Latour, 1988; Maturana & Varela, 1987; Meynell, 2003). In our arguments for systemic inquiry as part of an overall process of systemic development, the seeking and providing of scientific explanations [sensu Maturana] is a legitimate and often important form of inquiry – but it is not the only form of inquiry needed to engage with and understand and manage complexity and change. An exclusive focus on scientific inquiry avoids any connection with other ways of knowing, such as intuition, spirituality and so forth.

As expressed thus far Mandel is concerned with the dynamics of "the system," ignoring the **context**, the environment within which the system sits (i.e. from our perspective a system is always distinguished by someone and through the distinction that is realised, a system-boundary-environment relationship is produced). Mandel's perspective seems to be, implicitly at least, that the system is known, agreed upon etcetera, rather than being contestable depending on the purpose—it is a "real" thing inferred by Mandel not a construct (i.e., something brought forth by an observer). In our view, systemic development is concerned with dealing with these boundary critiques, and how that effects an exploration, a description and an understanding of issues of concern, and above all how one learns participatively to move forward, while reflecting back to check if an "improvement" has occurred, as the definition of the improvement is contextual and changeable, yet grounded and definable at a particular point in time.

Many cyberneticians have contributions to make to this inquiry. Heinz von Foerster addressed it when he asked, following Wittgenstein:

> Am I apart from the universe? That is, whenever I look am I looking through a peephole upon an unfolding universe [the first-order tradition]? Or: Am I part of the universe? That is, whenever I act,

---

2. This is a worthy project and in Ison et al, 2007 we do not seek to criticise the purpose for which it has been pursued.

I am changing myself and the universe as well [the second-order tradition]? (von Foerster, 1992, p. 15)

He goes on to say

Whenever I reflect upon these two alternatives, I am surprised again and again by the depth of the abyss that separates the two fundamentally different worlds that can be created by such a choice: Either to see myself as a citizen of an independent universe, whose regularities, rules and customs I may eventually discover, or to see myself as the participant in a conspiracy whose customs, rules and regulations we are now inventing. (von Foerster, 1992, p. 15)

It seems to me that we limit our ability to respond to human induced climate change (the conditions that conserve *Homo sapiens'* structural coupling with the biosphere) when we are unable to encounter each other in ways that transcend our unacknowledged epistemological commitments.

How might we break out of this trap? Suggestions are welcome. One way might be to accept Maturana's explanation of explanations? He invites us to consider when an explanation is an explanation. For example how many of you would accept Tony Blair's explanation of the reasons for going to war with Iraq? What about Einstein's equation $E=mc^2$ as an explanation of the quantum world? Or the account in Genesis of the origins of human beings? Of course we are living through this process at the moment in relation to explanations about human-induced climate change!

Drawing on Maturana I have argued that all explanations arise in social relations (see Ison & Schlindwein, 2006; Schlindwein & Ison, 2005); following Vickers (1965) they give rise to our standards of fact and value and our relationship maintaining or breaking. Moreover all explanations arise this way but some are conserved over longer time frames than others. Explanations also "enter our bloodstream" as we live our lives – throughout our biological and social development. Maynard Keynes' oft quoted remark that in his experience those who claimed to be practical men (sic) were usually victims of some theory 30 years out of date exemplifies my point. Maturana also draws attention to the role that explanations play in the lives of human beings – as young people we seek explanations, inquisitiveness is a feature of children raised in supportive contexts, and explanations are something we find satisfying, or not; they thus trigger emotional reactions (see Maturana & Poerkson, 2004). This is an important qualitative feature that rises from the explainer-listener- explanation relationship. My question is, can the quality of this relationship be improved through micro and macro practices that pay attention to, and draw into conversation, our epistemological commitments?

References

Ison, R. L. (in press). Systems thinking and practice for action research. In P. Reason & H. Bradbury (Eds.), *Handbook of Action Research* (2nd ed.). London: Sage Publications.

Ison, R. L. & Schlindwein, S. (2006) History repeats itself: current traps in complexity practice from a systems perspective. Proc. 12th Australia New Zealand Systems Society (ANZSYS) Conference, "Sustaining our Social and Natural Capital," December 3 – 6, 2006.

Ison, R. L., Bawden, R. D., Mackenzie, B., Packham, R. G., Sriskandarajah, N., & Armson, R. (2007). From sustainable to systemic development: an inquiry into transformations in discourse and praxis. Invited Keynote Paper, Australia New Zealand Systems Conference, 2007: "Systemic development: local solutions in a global environment." December 2 – 5, 2007. Auckland, New Zealand.

Latour, B. (1987). *Science in Action: How to follow scientists and engineers through society.* Milton Keynes: Open University Press.

Maturana, H.& Varela F. (1987). *The tree of knowledge: The biological roots of human understanding.* Boston: New Science Library, Shambala Publications.

Maturana, H. & Poerkson, B. (2004). *From being to doing: The origins of the biology of cognition.* Heidelberg: Carl-Auer-Systeme.

Meynell, F. (2003). *Awakening giants: An inquiry into the Natural Step UK's facilitation of sustainable development with sector leading companies.* Unpublished Ph.D. Thesis, Systems Department, The Open University, Milton Keynes.

Schlindwein, S. L. & Ison, R. L. (2005). Human knowing and perceived complexity: Implications for systems practice. *Emergence: Complexity & Organization (E:CO), 6* (3), 19-24.

von Foerster, H. (1992). Ethics and second-order cybernetics. *Cybernetics and Human Knowing, 1,* 9–19.

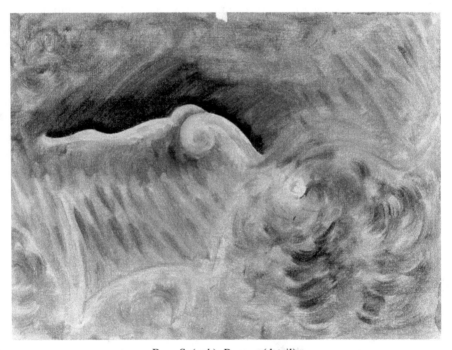

Beer. S. (n.d.). *Descent* (detail).

www.ingramcontent.com/pod-product-compliance
Lightning Source LLC
Chambersburg PA
CBHW060601060326
40690CB00017B/3785